LET IN THE SUN

LET IN THE SUN

WOODY KLEIN

THE MACMILLAN COMPANY, NEW YORK

The author wishes to thank the
*New York World-Telegram and
Sun* for permission to use in
somewhat different form excerpts
from his series on a drug
addict in East Harlem which
appeared in that newspaper on
June 17 and 18, 1963; copy-
right © 1963 by the *New York
World-Telegram and Sun.*

First Printing
The Macmillan Company, New York
Collier-Macmillan Canada Ltd., Toronto, Ontario
Library of Congress catalog card number: 64-23890
Printed in the United States of America

To
Audrey

To
Audrey

FOREWORD

I represent the 17th Congressional District on Manhattan's East Side in New York City. Some people call it the "Silk Stocking" District. This is a misnomer because the District contains the most varied mixture of people and incomes and living conditions of any Congressional district in the United States.

My District is made up of the great central part of Manhattan Island; ranging from Yorkville to Cooper Union, from Greenwich Village to Columbus Circle, from the garment and theatre areas on the West Side to the United Nations on the East River. The Bureau of the Census marks it as having the largest number of nationalities living within its borders of any Congressional district in the country.

From block to block, the contrasts are sudden and striking. Around the edges of Central Park and down the avenues on the East Side are big luxury residential buildings. In this part of the city, many of the buildings have large rooms, penthouses, every modern-day comfort, and doorman protection. The apartment houses on Fifth Avenue have breathtaking views of the park and the entire skyline of Manhattan. Along the side streets there is good living, too. But there are also the refuse-strewn blocks where the sun never enters. It is always gray and one can sense fear and tension.

At night you want the day and in the day you want the night to hide you from it and it from you.

I have spent endless hours cruising the avenues and streets of Manhattan—examining the construction wave that has demolished a sizeable portion of the city, talking with families who are being displaced, and with distraught parents looking for a place to live that is both within their means and large enough.

Weekend after weekend I have come up to my district from Washington and listened to the frightening, oft-repeated tale of people who bear the burden and hardship of inadequate housing.

Four years ago, I set up a housing team, young men and women volunteers from my district who contribute their time and energy to assist constituents of mine who need a place to live, who are being choked by the rent squeeze, who are caught up in the tangle of landlords, lawyers, and local rent administrators, who are being forcibly relocated in the name of urban renewal and who have no one to turn to for help.

This housing team handles every kind of housing hardship imaginable. The volunteers spend many hours tramping up darkened stairways. Every day we receive a succession of requests for help to get into public housing. These are often sad and desperate cases and deserving of help, but there is never enough room.

A few blocks north of my district is the neighborhood known as East Harlem. In this community is a tenement, 311 East 100th Street, which is the subject of the pages that follow. *Let in the Sun* is the story of the life and death of this building. Erected to help solve the housing problems of New York shortly after the turn of the century, this house stands in 1964 as a tragic symbol of the failure of New York's housing reforms in the last 60 years.

Woody Klein, who has himself lived in New York's slums on assignment as a newspaper reporter, wrote a remarkable series of articles in 1959 in the *New York World-Telegram and Sun*. His graphic reports awakened the conscience of many New Yorkers, among them my own constituents in the district next door to East Harlem.

In this book, Mr. Klein takes us inside the tenement at 311 East 100th Street in the "worst block" in New York City. He introduces us to the people within, the landlords who owned the property and the government officials and social workers who tried in vain to save the building from total collapse.

The author says that the making of a single slum is a crime against society. He reenacts this crime, presents the testimony of each suspect, and draws a dramatic verdict which leaves no doubt where the guilt lies.

For the first time in recent history, the blame for our slums is fixed where it belongs. In a vigorous style reminiscent of Jacob Riis—the famous newspaper reporter who crusaded in New York against poverty in the 1890s—Mr. Klein gives us a firsthand account of what the people involved in the making of a slum feel and think.

His story of the building on East 100th Street is enough to alarm even the most complacent. He shows us how slums are malignant and how they spread. He shows us that no matter where we live in a city, it is a short walk to the tenements.

In the City of New York in 1964, housing is a problem of vast proportions. But the shortages we suffer are not confined to this city. Other great urban centers throughout the nation are faced with comparable needs. In 1900, there were 24 million people living in American cities. Today there are more than 100 million.

I have been interested in housing ever since I became a member of Congress. I have also been in favor of public housing because I know what it means to my district and to the City of New York and to all of the great urban centers of this country.

Adequate housing goes to the root of most urban problems. Education, safety, delinquency, narcotics, and health are directly affected by the housing conditions of the neighborhoods in our cities and towns.

The problems of adequate shelter in our great cities cannot be neglected, and no public officer can pretend they do not exist. Those of us who hold public trust are elected because we are expected to be leaders. If Government has any function at all it is to take action when needs arise which cannot be met by the individual acting on his own.

Let in the Sun is an important book. It should inspire a crusade for better housing in the 1960's. Mr. Klein skillfully demonstrates that none of us can afford to forget the slums—that bad housing and the injury it inflicts on our communities are my problems and yours.

This book clearly shows that national wars on poverty will never be won unless they embrace within their strategy massive assaults on all of the elements that make up the slums. *Let in the Sun* is an eloquent appeal for a slumless America.

John V. Lindsay
Member of Congress

PREFACE

*That is the offense of the slum which kills
the home, that it will not let either the one
who is in it or the one who built it see God.*

—*Jacob A. Riis*

This book is an attempt to give a new perspective to a very old problem. "The slum," as Jacob Riis wrote more than half a century ago, "is as old as civilization itself." Although many Americans seem indifferent to the poverty around them, the slum and all its evil side effects have stirred me deeply throughout my adult life. As a result, I feel compelled to challenge public apathy and let those who neither know nor care about the slum learn how it is born, nurtured, and supported by a society that has turned its back on it.

Ever since I first set foot inside a rotting tenement I have felt a sense of alarm, almost fear. I have wondered how we can truly call ourselves a civilized people when so many of our neighbors are without the barest minimum shelter, food, and clothing. I am shocked and hurt by the neglect and callousness with which most people in New York react to the ugly fact that one million of their fellow citizens live in the slums. At first, I thought myself naïve and idealistic. But is it too much to expect that somebody should become alarmed by the presence of thousands upon thousands of rotting tenements which stand out like eyesores in this city? Is it too much to expect that some of us will view these tenements and the people trapped in them as bitter examples of what public indifference can produce? Does this not point up the paradox of wealth and poverty side by side in the same city—even in the same block?

What disturbs me more than anything else is not that the slum exists—almost every schoolchild knows it is there— but that most of us have developed such a tough skin that we don't even feel it any more. So long as we are secure in our own existence, we don't even know that the "other New York" is alive. And what's worse, we don't want to know.

My first memory of seeing a slum—and being inside one—was when I was twelve years old. I remember the crowded fire escapes and the noise and the heat.

The first real contact I had with the slum was not until twelve years later, however, when I went to work in Washington, D.C., as a police reporter. I sat at a battered old desk from midnight to dawn and listened carefully to every call the police dispatcher relayed to prowl cars cruising the streets. Sometimes I went to the scene of the crime—often a slum—to get a story.

In 1956, I went to work for the *New York World-Telegram and Sun.* One of my first assignments was to investigate a complaint of bad housing conditions in an old building in the Williamsburg section of Brooklyn. Since that time, I have seen thousands of equally uninhabitable dwellings in this city and in others in the United States, in Europe, and in Israel.

The cruelty of the slum oppresses all races and nationalities. It is the same ruthless weapon of destruction wherever it is found—in New York's East Harlem or San Juan's El Fanguito. All slums, no matter where they are, exemplify man's depravity in the twentieth century.

In 1959, as an undercover newspaper reporter, I lived as a tenant in some of New York's worst slum tenements. I saw animal-like overcrowding, prostitution, gambling, drunkenness, fire and building violations, petty thievery, lack of water, air, heat, and light. In the filthy buildings where I lived, I also saw unscrupulous rent-gouging and exploitation.

More than anything else, the thing that depressed me and made me want to quit my assignment at the end of each day during those hot summer months five years ago was the overpowering stench of the slums. It comes from decades of overpopulating a building, from the nauseating mishmash of uncollected garbage, decayed food, stale urine and excrement, rotten wood, rat dirt, and the sweat of human flesh steaming through the airless hallways. It creeps out of the walls and poisons the air you breathe; it seeps into your skin and crawls into bed with you at night; it infests the streets and sidewalks of the neighborhood. After a month of enduring this misery, I began to understand what the word *slum* meant.

I tried to tell the story in a series of newspaper articles. I reported my disgust and dismay. I believed then—and I still do—that the slum is as great a threat to America's well-being as the challenge of communism or the hydrogen bomb or the Russians landing a man on the moon before we do. And, because it is man-made, the slum is a human tragedy greater even than a natural disaster such as earthquake or flood. Out of the slum come the racketeers, dope addicts and degenerates, disease, and death. The slum breeds segregation, lack of education and employment, welfare and real estate profiteering, fear, ignorance, violence and hatred, loss of human dignity.

In the United States, the richest country in the world, we are losing the battle against the slum.

One fifth of our nation—some 38 million Americans—live in slums today. Millions of others live in the path of blight and face the prospect of seeing their homes become slums unless corrective steps are taken immediately. They live in the tenements of New York, Washington, Chicago, and Los Angeles, the brownstones of Baltimore, the wooden shanties of Oklahoma City, Atlanta, New Orleans, Baton Rouge, and Birmingham. They are of all races and religions and nationalities.

Each year in this country the number of slums increases. The slum population is expected to swell to more than 45 million persons by 1975. Slums cost our municipalities seven to ten times the tax revenues which are collected from them. The slums are spreading so fast that city planners can't provide enough decent housing to keep up with the present rate of deterioration.

Decent housing is one of the prime goals of the national civil rights movement. It is one answer to the widespread poverty which engulfs a large segment of the American people, white as well as Negro. The promise of good housing is good politics. It is therefore a plank in every politician's platform. It is a key issue in every Presidential campaign.

Still, we think of the people in the slums only as statistics, numbers in official reports, anonymous shadows. As we view them from a distance—if we bother to look at them at all—the buildings and the people make up a depressing, sunless scene which seems to play no part in our lives.

We have taken our slums and the people in them for granted much too long. As a symbol of this big, colorless, almost formless picture which most of us refuse to look at closely, I have chosen one building in Manhattan. It contains thirty-three of the millions of families scarred by blight across the nation. The building I have selected in the East Harlem section of New York stands on what has come to be known as the "worst block" in New York City. It is a symbol of all slums everywhere.

Why does it exist? How did it become a slum? Who is to blame for this crime against civilized society? This book is an attempt to find out where the guilt lies.

WOODY KLEIN

New York City
June 1964

ACKNOWLEDGMENTS

This book was written with the cooperation of many individuals who have shown concern for the social conditions of the poor people of New York and other parts of the United States. I am especially grateful to Raymond Rubio, a native New Yorker, whose insight and skill as an interpreter and member of the staff of the Commonwealth of Puerto Rico helped me to interview Puerto Rican families in the slums of East Harlem.

A great many government officials opened their files to me during the course of my investigation and gave generously of their time. In this connection, I would like to thank the following city officials: Harold Birns, Commissioner, Department of Buildings; Judah Gribetz, Deputy Commissioner, Department of Buildings; Hugh F. Riley, Assistant to the Commissioner of Buildings; Mrs. Hortense W. Gabel, Administrator, Rent and Rehabilitation Administration; Samuel Estis, Acting District Director, Manhattan, Rent and Rehabilitation Administration; Milton Mollen, Chairman, Housing and Redevelopment Board; Jerome Trichter, Assistant Commissioner, Department of Health; Samuel Gartner, Inspector, Department of Health; Leon Schneider, attorney and housing consultant to the Housing and Redevelopment Board; Martin Scott, Chief Fire Marshal, Bureau of Fire

Investigation, Fire Department; and Sidney J. Frigand, Director of Public Affairs, City Planning Commission; two New York State officials: Louis J. Lefkowitz, Attorney General, Robert E. Herman, Administrator, Temporary State Housing Rent Commission; and other helpful officials in city, state, and federal housing agencies.

To Eugene J. Bockman, Librarian, Municipal Reference Library, and to his staff, I would like to express my gratitude for making available vital records and reports dealing with the housing history of New York. The New York Public Library, the Columbia University Oral History Project, and the New-York Historical Society were also very helpful. My appreciation also to Roger Starr, Executive Director, and Mrs. Marian Sameth, Associate Director, Citizens' Housing and Planning Council, for their assistance in providing documents and books pertaining to the history of slums in New York City; and to Dr. Leonard Covello, Educational Consultant to the Commonwealth of Puerto Rico, for background knowledge and material about East Harlem.

For other invaluable assistance, I give thanks to Wayne Phillips, a former newspaper associate, who as administrative assistant to federal housing chief Dr. Robert C. Weaver, supplied background information about the nation's housing; to Doris Nathan, an architect who provided the drawing of a typical floor plan of the new-law tenement; to Albert C. Lasher, a businessman, free-lance writer, and friend, whose suggestions helped to shape the form and content of this book; and to Howard M. Sonn, of the real estate and insurance firm Sonn-Saalberg Co., for his expert estimates.

To Robert Markel, my friend and editor at Macmillan, I extend my deepest appreciation for his guidance in making this book a reality.

I am also indebted to my editors and associates at the *New York World-Telegram and Sun* for their understanding, advice, and direction during the years I have been covering housing in New York City. These people include Wesley First, former Managing Editor; Norman Herington, City Editor; Herbert Kamm, Managing Editor; Frank Kappler, former Assistant City Editor; Norton Mockridge, columnist and former City Editor; Richard D. Peters, Editor; Lee B. Wood, President; Lester Carson, John Ferris; William Longgood, and Robert H. Prall, staff writers.

World-Telegram and Sun photographers Walter Albertin and Phil Stanziola contributed all the photographs reproduced in this book.

To the National Broadcasting Company I extend my thanks for making available tape recordings of interviews conducted in the filming of a documentary about the house at 311 East 100th Street which was aired on the *David Brinkley's Journal* program in 1961. And to producer Ted Yates and director Leo Seltzer, whom I assisted in the preparation of the NBC film, I express my appreciation for their help in gathering background information used in this book.

Finally, to J. Anthony Panuch, a noted attorney and expert in government reorganization, I would like to pay special tribute for reading and criticizing the complete manuscript. His own personal views are not necessarily reflected in these chapters, but his experience and knowledge are.

CONTENTS

Tear down the old. Build up the new. Down with rotten, antiquated rat holes. Down with hovels. Down with disease. Down with crime. Down with firecraft. Let in the sun. Let in the sky. A new day is dawning. A new life. A new America!
—*Fiorello H. La Guardia, 1944*

PART ONE

THE
CRIME

THE
CRIME

CHAPTER 1

"IT CALLS ME BACK, MAN"

The most pitiful victim of modern city life
is not the slum child who dies, but the slum
child who lives.

—Dr. Charles Gilbert Davis
(PSYCHOLOGIST), *1919*

EDDIE WAS BORN in the tenement at 311 East 100th Street twenty-two years ago. He is one of the many people permanently anchored to East Harlem and to this one block. He is virtually lost anywhere else. Ask him why he doesn't try to find a home elsewhere and he says quietly:

"It calls me back, man. It calls me back. There is no other block for me except 100th Street."

Why does he stay on East 100th Street?

"I try to stay away from here," he replies, "but I can't. I been walking around this neighborhood all of my life. When I go away I miss it. I went over to the West Side for a while, but I couldn't make it. While I was there I came around here every night. Like I got to stay here on this block . . . the fellas . . . I feel it . . . I lived here so long—all my friends are here, the kids I grew up with—everything is here."[1]*

Eddie lives in the dark, dank basement. He sleeps on a

---

* Notes begin on p. 281.

3

dirty mattress on a stone floor. He is unshaven and needs a haircut and his clothes are tattered. His long and hollow face is drawn and sad and his eyes are bloodshot and tired. His shoes are worn through. Next to his mattress stands a ragged armchair. A dim light bulb hangs from the ceiling by an exposed wire and on the stone walls of his basement room are a few pictures of Christ and two water-color scenes of New York buildings which he painted himself.

Descend into his cellar room and look closely at this desperate young man. His deep-set brown eyes are glazed, fixed in a blank stare, and he is breathing heavily. Listen to his muffled voice as he talks about his life on East 100th Street:

"I started using the stuff when I was thirteen. I grew up with junkies," he mumbles. "After hanging around with them, they says, 'Come on, you can get high if you want to.' I wanted to see what it was, you know. I wanted to get a kick. When I got my first skin pop, I shouted, 'Man, this ain't doing nothing for me.' But then it hit me fast. When you first use drugs, the first shot, you get real sick. I got sick . . . threw up . . . I was high . . . I went home and went to sleep. I stayed away from them for about two months, but I liked it.

"I tried to get with them again . . . tried to get some money . . . it costs three dollars a pop. I need an eighth of an ounce every day . . . costs me twenty-two dollars a day . . . you got to steal for it. You got to rob, man, you got to rob. The first time I got caught I was sixteen . . . for burglary. They sent me to Elmira. After a while I was on parole and I started using drugs again. They arrested me again and gave me a year . . . then I got arrested four times after that. I been in jail more than I been out since I was sixteen. I tried to shake it in prison, but they don't give me no help. They don't pay no attention to me . . . when I got out last year I met my friend and he says, 'Come on, let's get high.' We went up to the roof and he put out the set of works, you know, the needle, the eyedropper, two bags, the works. I told him, 'Man, I just came home, I'm clean. I don't want to mess around.' He says, 'Don't worry, just take a little pop.' I just took a little but I kept on using it. Once I shot it, I kept liking it, and I got the habit . . . now I don't really like it no more. It's no fun. I use it because I need it.

"I'm tired of it. I'm tired, man. I just sit down here and I'm disgusted. When I started using drugs I stopped going out with girls. I look at girls all the time, but when they see I'm a junkie they don't want to bother with me. I feel bad. I'm tired of living around here . . . the same thing every day . . . nothing changes. People don't show me no respect no more. They talk about me. They say I steal from them but it's a lie. I steal but I don't steal around here. Sometimes I wish I could take an overdose and just die because I'm tired of it all.

"I got the habit, that's all. I use heroin. I could kick the habit, but I can't do it by myself. I want to kick it. It don't do nothing for me any more. I feel nothing. If I could just take the pains out my stomach and my back and stop sweating. I just use it for my cure. It helps me feel straight. I don't take it because I like it . . . I'm tired of living. I'm tired of my life. I wish I could get married and have some kids. That's what I really want. Some day I want to have a family. I love kids. I wish I had my own. I could have a girl now and have sex with her and have kids but I don't want that . . . I can't give the kid nothing and I can't give a girl nothing. I don't want to put myself in that position, see? I would just make them suffer . . . all I live for is my next fix. That's all I ever think about. . . .

"My family left for the Bronx two months ago. They just picked up and left. My father was always drunk, always cursing at me, telling me I'm a bum, a junkie, a no-good. He says, 'Get out of the house.' I don't blame him. I rob him all the time for drugs. I sell the covers off the furniture to get money . . . he hit me, he cursed me. . . . I tell him, 'Don't hit me, I'm no baby no more,' and he just says, 'Get out of the house, you don't pay no rent here, you just come here to rob.'

"He's right, but I hauled off and slugged him . . . I didn't mean to . . . he's my father . . . he's Irish . . . my mother is Puerto Rican. . . . I just argue with her, I don't hit her . . . she understands me. She knows I don't really want to do it . . . I'm a different person when I don't use drugs. But my family don't show me no love the way they brought me up . . . I was a shoe-shine . . . I bought my own clothes and all that . . . they never gave me nothing. They never shown me that they loved me and I really didn't love them because they didn't show me no love.

"When I was a kid this block was better. You needed a key to come in through the front door. It was private-like. The neighborhood was clean. The yards were very clean. We used to play in the back yards. You can't play there now. They're filthy. People throwing garbage out the windows. The yards used to be clean, the whole street, everything. Soon the people started moving out, the old people who lived here a long time, then others started coming in . . . the Negroes, they mess up the whole block. It's filthy. The block is filthy. People throwing garbage. Always cursing in the streets. They don't care. Girls. People always fighting out there. I never seen this when I was younger. When I was thirteen I first seen the addicts. That's when it began. Now the block is like Korea. Everybody always fighting. Junkies. A whole lot of them, hanging around the halls, the roofs . . . bums around here . . . drunks right in the streets.

"Now they want to get the junkies off the block. I tell them I'm not moving out nowhere. I was born here. I was raised here and I'm going to stay here. Nobody's going to chase me off this block. I was born right in this apartment house. My father was out . . . he was in the yard and he didn't hear when my mother was giving birth of me . . . she couldn't do nothing . . . she was lying in bed and she had me right there . . . I came out. That was it. The ambulance came. It was too late. My mother told me they took her over and she was all right. We lived in this house on the second floor . . . there were eleven in the family . . .

"My brother, Joey, and my sister, Mary . . . I think of all of them these two have made out the best . . . Mary lives in the Bronx married to a cab driver who works in a garage and makes good money and has a nice house. I been up to the house. Very nice. She got everything, she got three little kids, three little boys. She's one of five sisters. Then there's Joey. He's the oldest. His daughter is eighteen years old now. He's a cop in Washington. He got a nice house, too. I got other brothers who didn't do so good, too. One's in jail now. But everybody's gone from here. I'm the only one left.

"Now I live here by myself. I got to hide from the cops. They come looking for dope addicts. They call us all kinds of names. They hate addicts. They know who we are. Like I been here all my life. They know me. Every time they see me they want to pick me up. They always bother me. You know, I wanted to be a cop once, a narco cop. I had that in mind when I left school in the ninth grade . . . but I never went back to school.

"I didn't have no habit at the time, but I wanted the habit so I could brag about it to my friends . . . but now I hate to get arrested. When I first got arrested, they hit me a while. I'd be crying and they'd throw cold water at me and they kick me and smack the shit out of me. They didn't care. They say, 'Shut up, you junkie!' You know what it is to try and kick the habit when they be hitting you? . . . Before they catch me I rob all over, mostly 67th Street in the East Side, around York. I go into the new buildings to score. I go through the fire escapes at night and open the windows. The people down there, they keep their windows open. I been spotted, though, and I been shot at, too. The cops chased me. Sure, I'm frightened when I rob, but I know I'm sick and I got to get money . . . people don't help me so I got to take a chance. . . .

"A few times I almost fell off the roofs. In the nighttime I'd be running and I don't know . . . I think there's another roof there . . . I had to jump and I've been lucky that I landed on the other roof. It's far away and I had to jump it.

"When I go out, I go for jewelry. When I see a hi-fi or a portable radio and a TV, I don't touch it. I'm only good for jewelry and money. I carry a stiletto. I use it to jimmy open windows. I use it on the junkies, too. I tried to get some stuff off them once. I went to a pusher and got stuff without paying. I just pulled out the knife and told him I ain't got no money. He give it to me. I make it.

"There was another time I was gang-busting. I stabbed this guy. They called it attempted homicide. We stabbed these guys—Dragons. We were using drugs in the street. I stabbed him in the stomach with a stiletto. I stabbed him twice . . . me and my friends. I joined when I was fifteen. I was bopping with the Viceroys against the Dragons. I'm an old Viceroy. I get a lot of respect from the kids around here because I belonged. They don't try and mess with me.

"I take the jewelry and stuff to this guy, a racketeer. I know him when I see him. He give me the right money for it. I know jewelry. I'm good at jewelry. He gives me up to six hundred dollars for one ring. He comes around every day. He goes to the bar. He drives up in a big Cadillac. You gotta do business with him because you can't count on your friends for a fix, you know. They got their own habit. My kid brother doesn't steal, though. He counts on me. He's fourteen years old and I get the stuff for him.

"But I don't offer no other youngsters a fix. I can get into trouble for being a pusher. I ain't no pusher. There are about eight pushers around here. Some of them are girls. They hustle and try and beat the men for their money. They get ten to fifty dollars as a regular charge. But most of the time they charge five dollars or three dollars . . . whatever they can get. I used to go to one of those girls. She got no lower than three dollars.

"There's a lot of gambling on this block, too. Cards . . . shooting dice in the houses . . . in this building right here. Everybody's trying to cut each other's throat around here. Always trying to make money. Everybody wants money in this block. They're robbing each other and everything . . . these pushers, they make the dough . . . they get half a loads from uptown, and they bring it down here—right in this building—and sell it for three dollars a bag. I cop three bags. It lasts about twenty minutes. It don't last too long. When I use it I got to be thinking about another fix every time. I use my money and I'm thinking about the next time. . . .

"I don't have time to do anything else . . . I used to do a little art. I learned to paint in prison . . . but I haven't got no paint left . . . I'd like to paint again but I don't think about it much . . . I think about my next fix . . . don't even eat much . . . I'm not hungry. Maybe soda—I drink soda . . . do I feel sorry for myself? Yeah, I feel sorry for myself but I don't want nobody else feeling sorry for me because I know what I'm doing. I'm not a baby no more. I'm using drugs because I want to, that's all. Nobody ain't putting that dope in my arm or that needle . . . I blame myself and I feel sorry for myself. But I don't want nobody else feeling sorry for me.

"I walk back and forth all day trying to figure out how to get three dollars, trying to get two bags, always trying to steal something, always trying to get some money . . . I don't even know what day it is sometimes . . . Friday, Thursday, or Sunday. We drug addicts don't worry about what's going on in New York or anywhere else. We just worry about dope.

"Some day I'll stop. It could be a year from now . . . three years from now . . . it could be tomorrow . . . next week . . . but I'll stop. I know I will. I'm just waiting. I got to kick this habit. I got to get away from it. The stuff don't do nothing for me . . . it's killing me. . . .

"I don't know what I'm going to do. Sometimes I pray. I'm a Catholic. I been to church a few times, St. Cecilia's at 105th Street. I don't know the Father. I just went on Sundays. I don't go no more. I went there when I wasn't using the drugs a few times. I was going because I believed in God. I pray to God to help me, but seeing as I can't get no help, I think maybe I should try and help myself. I think that maybe God don't want to help me, that's how I feel."

C H A P T E R 2

THE NESTING PLACE

The battle with the slum began the day
civilization recognized in it her enemy.
When common sense and the golden rule
obtain among men as a rule of practice, it
will be over.

—Jacob A. Riis

ON THE GROUND FLOOR of Eddie's tenement at 311 East 100th Street is a dilapidated apartment in the rear which appears no different than thousands of others in East Harlem.

Its plaster-broken walls are faded and the rooms are dirty. Not a trace remains of an unusual experiment which began on these premises in 1950, when Dr. Beatrice Bishop Berle, physician and wife of former U. S. Undersecretary of State A. A. Berle, opened an air-conditioned neighborhood medical clinic on this spot.

Doctors and nurses volunteered their time to help Dr. Berle take on the gigantic task of running the clinic weekday afternoons. More than 3000 individual patients came through its doors. But the clinic was forced to close down in 1962 owing to lack of funds. The dismal flat which it occupied was rented by a neighborhood family. The clinic was a noble effort to raise the health standards of the people in this slum, but—like many other social reforms—it could provide no permanent solution.

11

Many thousands of people like Eddie are buried alive in the house at 311 East 100th Street and in other tenements on the block. This street in Manhattan between First and Second avenues has become known as the "worst block" in New York City.

The twenty-seven six-story tenements which stretch like a stone canyon down both sides of this "worst block" are filled with a mass of humanity, captives of the buildings in which they live.

More than 5000 people (see Table 1, Appendix, p. 270) are jammed into the two sides of this block, which has been compared to the slums of Calcutta. Nearly two thirds of the people are Puerto Ricans and about one third are Negroes. The average household numbers 3.56 persons, much larger than the city-wide average of 2.88. More than 15 per cent of the people are on welfare.

The average monthly rental on this block is $36, less than half of the city-wide average of $76 or the Manhattan average of $85. The buildings are a generation older than most of the people in them. More than 70 per cent of the dwelling units in these tenements are classified as "deteriorating" or "dilapidated."[1]

One major reason the street is called the "worst block" is its high crime rate. Local 23rd Precinct police officials list the block as a "high hazard" area. Foot patrolmen are stationed at both ends and in the center of the block twenty-four hours a day.

Youths frequently set off fires in the yards and alleys. In the cellars and dark hallways young boys get their heroin "fixes." On the crowded street throngs of men, jobless and hopeless, play cards and gamble openly on overturned garbage cans. Drunks lie in doorways, sometimes for days.

A visitor first touring the upper East Side of Manhattan cannot fail to note the striking contrast between the peace and quiet of the stately old apartment houses of upper Park Avenue and the turmoil of East Harlem nearby.

Ninety-sixth Street, where the railroad track emerges from underneath Park Avenue, is the dividing line. It is the invisible boundary segregating wealth from poverty.

To the south lies the so-called Silk Stocking 17th Congressional District, the greatest single concentration of residential and commercial real estate wealth in the world, where land sells for as high as $200 a square foot.

To the north lies a loosely joined neighborhood of Old-World slums mingled with synthetic new public housing projects, where land can be bought for as little as $5 a square foot.

Here, only a few short blocks away from the luxury of Manhattan's most famous promenades—Park, Madison, and Fifth avenues—lies a community of people who are unknown and unwanted by their neighbors to the south. It is hard to imagine two sections of a great city so different: the elegance of a harmonious tree-lined boulevard where people live safely and securely away from the noise, smell, and dirt of the street, next to the drabness of a dissonant, depressed neighborhood of small shopkeepers, light industry, and colorless housing.

Yet there they are, side by side, the invisible line between them as real as the Berlin Wall.

The boundaries of East Harlem's 905 acres are generally defined as Fifth Avenue on the west, the East River and Harlem River on the east and north, and 96th Street on the south.[2] To many of its inhabitants East Harlem is a new, emerging part of Manhattan's upper East Side. Many of its newcomers, social workers and settlement leaders, emphasize the new construction of middle-income cooperative housing in the 1960s, and the generations-old community spirit.

To these community people, East Harlem is no longer

part of Harlem, the biggest Negro ghetto in the world. It is an area grown up on its own which has left the past behind and which has developed a distinct character and personality. Local leaders are concerned that East Harlem's residents work out their own destiny. They want self-determination and will fight the compassionless outside city government down to the last street corner. These new East Harlemites have brought with them a genuine desire to uplift their home.

But to the untrained visitor looking at this section of New York for the first time, there are few outward signs of a cleaner and better life. The general impression is still that East Harlem is not much different from the rest of Harlem—a segregated, second-class portion of Manhattan.

New low-cost public housing projects have replaced many East Harlem slums, but they have also perpetuated East Harlem's reputation as a poor community for minority groups. As the big projects went up, more and more white families left for middle-income neighborhoods in other parts of the city.

The westernmost corner of East Harlem, known as *El Barrio* or Spanish Harlem, is almost exclusively Puerto Rican. To the east of this bleak section lies East 100th Street. The block between First and Second avenues occupies only a tiny segment of East Harlem. It is just 650 feet long, but its reputation stretches far beyond its boundaries.

It is perhaps at once ironic and pathetic that more money and manpower have been spent trying to save the poor people and old buildings in this one block during the past two decades than any other single piece of real estate in New York City.

The effort to clean it up began in 1948 when four Protestant denominations, sensitive to the church's failure to respond to people's problems in the East Harlem area, joined together and opened an experimental store-front ministry.

In 1951, the year after Dr. Berle's clinic opened in the house at 311 East 100th Street, the New York City Housing Authority designated East 100th Street and four surrounding streets as one of twenty blighted sites in the city which were to be cleared and replaced with low-rent housing projects. After many delays, however, this renewal plan never materialized.

In 1959, a new political club—the East Harlem Reform Democrats—won community support campaigning from building to building. In 1960, this club elected their candidate, Mark Lane, a thirty-three-year-old attorney, to the State Assembly. Once in power, Lane complained bitterly to City Hall about housing conditions in East Harlem and he demanded reforms on East 100th Street.

Oregon's youthful Republican governor, Mark O. Hatfield, was one of the first national political leaders to observe what poverty and neglect has done to the "worst block." His visit during the summer of 1959 was well protected and well publicized. A police plainclothesman walked beside him as he strode down the block.

During the summer of 1960, fifty-three East Harlem community groups co-sponsored a Town Meeting at which Mayor Robert F. Wagner and commissioners from thirteen city departments heard pleas from community leaders for improved city services. They asked the city fathers to renew the large slum pockets which had not been cleared for public housing projects. They complained that the area containing East 100th Street was filled with deteriorated tenements.

East Harlem's tainted reputation was soiled even more when *The New York Times* carried a page-one story reporting that local social workers and police called East 100th Street the "worst block" in the city during this same summer of 1960. The newspaper account, appearing under the head-line NIGHT CLOAKS CRIME IN CITY'S TOUGHEST BLOCK, stirred up resentment in the community. A few local leaders called a rally to defend East Harlem's reputation. The rally was held on East 100th Street in front of a store-front church of the East Harlem Protestant Parish. Clergy and civic and political leaders led the stormy outdoor meeting. They attacked *The New York Times* for characterizing the block as "the toughest" in the city.

Despite the community's protest, however, the following year—the early spring of 1961—the vigorous new U. S. Attorney General, Robert F. Kennedy, came to New York and took a firsthand look at the slums of East Harlem. On an unannounced walking tour he passed East 100th Street and he spoke with the members of two local gangs in a nearby park. He said his mission was to find out more about juvenile delinquency. Although the visit was not immediately publi-cized, news of it got into the press four days later. Once again East 100th Street found itself, unwittingly, in the national spotlight.

By the summer of 1961, East 100th Street had become so well known that Mayor Robert F. Wagner decided he should see the street, too, at a time when he was seeking a third term in office. The Mayor had already countered public criticism of his housing programs by creating a new housing agency in 1960. But his best weapon in a political campaign was himself. A warm and friendly person, Wagner's person-ality came through to the man on the street. Short, modest, and unassuming, Wagner was a leader whom the people could understand and with whom they could identify.

His forty-minute inspection of the block was widely

reported in the daily newspapers. Two days after his visit, the mayor issued an order for the block to be converted into a play street for the summer under the supervision of the Police Athletic League. The presence of youth workers and recreation activities, the Mayor apparently felt, would help relieve East 100th Street of its problems.

It did not, of course. And toward the close of the event-packed summer of 1961 an incident occurred only two blocks away from this street which once again pointed up the latent hostility of the slum. Assemblyman Lane was struck on the head by a beer can as his open car drove on East 102nd Street between First and Second avenues to a political rally one night after dark. The can was tossed from one of the five-story tenements and landed with such a violent impact that Lane had to have four stitches taken in his head in a nearby hospital. Mrs. Franklin Delano Roosevelt, seated in the same car, escaped injury.

One year later—in September 1962—Mayor Wagner announced that virtually all of East Harlem, including what by then had become celebrated as the "worst block" in the city, was to be incorporated into the expanding municipal neighborhood conservation program. The program's goal was to stop further housing and social deterioration in blighted areas. His announcement designated East 100th Street between First and Second avenues as a "pilot block" in the rehabilitation project.

Less than a week after the Mayor's "pilot block" announcement, the federal government once again stepped into 100th Street. This time it was Senator Thomas J. Dodd, a Connecticut Democrat, whose subcommittee investigating juvenile delinquency throughout the country heard testimony from local community spokesmen during two days of New York hearings. The Senator walked through East 100th

Street the night before the hearings opened at the U. S. Courthouse in Foley Square.

Following all the local and national publicity, appropriate steps were taken by every administrator whose agency had even the most remote connection with the block. Nobody was going to be accused of not joining in the crusade to clean it up. The city's Youth Board, blaming the trouble on racial discrimination and the "ghettoization" of Negroes and Puerto Ricans, sent teams of youth workers into the block. The city's complicated network of code enforcement agencies increased inspections and sent more and more men to the street. Local churches, settlement houses, and community groups called meetings, appointed committees, made surveys, issued reports. Political clubs came alive with renewed vigor and began voter-registration drives. Social workers from all parts of the city, newspaper reporters, magazine and book writers, radio and television producers and crews all flocked to the scene in the hope of getting in on the city's most sensational slum story.

The National Broadcasting Company depicted the "worst block" as an American disgrace in 1962. A documentary film showing life in the house at 311 East 100th Street was televised to 40 million people who watched *David Brinkley's Journal*.[3] The film vividly brought into the homes of viewers everywhere in the United States the upsetting spectacle of cockroaches swarming all over a kitchen ceiling and stove, garbage strewn in hallways, and barefoot children playing in the filth and mire of the tenement yard.

The house at 311 East 100th Street is no better off in 1964 than it was two decades ago. It has stubbornly resisted all attempts at change. It is still with us even though it seems too old and crowded and dirty to be part of the 1960s. In the winter when the weather is cold, it stands alongside others like it in a graveyard of junked buildings, their dull exteriors monotonous to the eye, broken only by the pattern of jagged fire escapes clinging to their sides.

In the spring and summer, the street below comes alive with people yelling and singing and swearing, black and brown-skinned bodies sweating on the hot pavement, hydrants gushing water in the gutter, radios blaring, bottles crashing, children screaming. The people come out of the hovel at number 311, down its dark, battered stairways, and burst into the street like a pack of restless animals who have been caged too long.

But few have the ability or the will to escape permanently from the confining walls of this tenement. They are afraid to move elsewhere. For them, the house at 311 East 100th Street is the only home they know. It is their nesting place and they cannot leave it.

A HOUSE OF HORROR

The slum is a cancer that has long roots
reaching the avenue as well as the alley.

— *Jacob A. Riis*

IN A DIMLY LIGHTED CORRIDOR of the tenement at 311 East 100th Street, at 1:25 P.M. on May 28, 1961, Anthony Bonner, a thirty-year-old ex-convict and dope addict pulled out a knife in the heat of an argument with a dope pusher. As the two men fought, the addict lunged at the pusher and drove the blade deep into his chest.

Police records show that the victim, Floyd Reel, died at 10:10 that night at nearby Metropolitan Hospital. Bonner, meanwhile, was arrested and taken to the 23rd Precinct station house, where he was charged with homicide.[1]

The fatal struggle between these two men, although it took the life of one and sent the other to prison, went almost unnoticed in this tenement where knife battles occur frequently. The police handled the case in a routine manner.

Bonner later pleaded guilty to the lesser charge of manslaughter in the second degree. He was sentenced on January 11, 1962, by General Sessions Judge Harold P. Culkin to serve from five to ten years in state prison.

The brutality of this crime would have shaken the inhabitants of an ordinary residential community elsewhere in the country. But this was East 100th Street in New York. One more fatal stabbing did not create much of a stir among the tenants of number 311. The death of Floyd Reel was just another passing incident in their lives.

Thirty-three families occupy the house at 311 East 100th Street. A total of 139 people live in seventy-two rooms, excluding kitchens and bathrooms. Family sizes range from single people to two adults and eight children. The average adult age is forty-two. The average length of stay in the house is 6.3 years. The oldest tenant has been in the house for twenty years.

The adults and teen-age children have had an average of six years of schooling. Family incomes average $60 per week, or about $3100 per year. The highest income is $110 per week in one family where the husband and wife are both working. The lowest is $10 per week, a death benefit for a woman from the British West Indies.

The working men and women hold jobs which include delivery man, porter, dressmaker, housecleaner, laborer, mechanic, desk installer, power press operator, laundry worker, hospital worker, machinist, food-store helper, garment worker, construction worker, and superintendent.

To understand the tragedy of the house at number 311—the human suffering which goes far deeper than the physical neglect of the building—we must look at more than statistics and the vague shadows of people packed layer over layer in this tenement. We must study their faces and listen to their hopes, fears, and ordinary thoughts.

Marcellino Rodriguez, a forty-nine-year-old native of Río Piedras, Puerto Rico, came to the United States in 1957 and worked as superintendent of the house at number 311. On his sad, cinnamon-colored face is an expression of bewilderment and weariness.

"In Río Piedras I work as a cabinetmaker, a carpenter,"

he tells you in broken English. "But I need more money for my family. Salary no good there. Carpenter make about twenty-five to thirty dollars a week there. So I come here. But here I no gotta union carpenter so I take other jobs. When I first came here I lived in Cherry Street downtown. I like it better there."

Rodriguez is the father of twelve children, including four adopted from his wife's first marriage. His oldest child is his twenty-four-year-old son, Marcellino, Jr., who quit high school after his junior year to take a job as a grocery clerk, moved next door to his parents and family in number 311. Rodriguez' other children range in age from two to twenty-two. It is a handsome family with five robust boys and seven pretty girls.

Unable to acquire a membership card in the carpenter's union, Rodriguez finally found an apartment and a job in 311 East 100th Street. He took on the task of superintendent of the building in 1960 and relinquished it in 1963 when, disgusted and depressed by his financial problems, he gave up everything and fled to a nearby New Jersey town one day to get away from his home. Before he left his family and his job, however, he had learned enough about the maintenance operations of the building to complain:

"Too much work. I have three rooms and twelve in the family. My family has no room. The money is no good. I was on welfare but they close my case because when an investigator came to my house he argued too much with my wife. Too much trouble with my family. I had to take my big children out of school because I got no money to buy them clothes. I got no money for one dollar fifty a day for lunch. My one son doesn't go to work or to school because he has no clothes, carfare or money. Once I make hundred dollars a week in New Jersey as a carpenter when I first come here, but now they got no more work for me. I need more money for my family. The money I win now is no good money for my family."

Does he like where he is living?

Rodriguez pauses, his blue eyes forlornly expressing his feeling of hopelessness.

"No, I no like it here," he says slowly. "I don't like this area because too much drunk, too many, I see people too much drunk . . . I want to have a house for my family . . . when my family gets sick we have no room here . . . I send them to hospital. I have no refrigerator. Day by day good food in my house spoil because I got no money to buy refrigerator. I asked the landlord for one. He says he can no give me one. I said to him about the electric light. He says same. He says I must fix it myself. He no want to take care of it. He says it is my business. The whole building is no good. The halls no good. The door out front no good. No glass in the door. The mailboxes no good. The boiler no good. I work all day there. I live in the boiler. I put coal in the boiler, too much. He no fix nothing. He pays me hundred twelve dollars a month, that's all."

How are the other tenants in the house?

"Regular, regular," he replies with a faint smile. "Some are good. Some are no good. Bad people. Poor. I get off my bed at four o'clock in the morning. I don't go to bed at night until eleven o'clock. I work all the hours. I get up and go to hallway. I take broom and sweep the stairs in the house. I take the garbage out of the building. I go to the boiler and check the boiler."

He points to his small apartment. "Here I got leak in the stove, the mirror is no good, my television is damaged, the light no work . . . it is DC. My radio is bad. I got no telephone. The light is no good. The sink leaks. The window no good. No glass in the window. Nobody comes to make nothing about the insects . . . to this day, nobody . . . many *cucaracha,* nobody to come clean up this place. I put plaster behind the sink because of a rat hole. There's a rat in there. At night, all the night the people no sleep. Too many noise all the night, too many. The street is full of people all the night. This place is too hot in the summer. It is ninety degrees. The people don't sleep. Sometimes this street is cleaned, but when I came here it was too bad. Garbage in all places."

Ask him how often he gets out of the house and if his wife has any complaints and Rodriguez will tell you:

"My wife is good woman, domestic woman. She make all work in my house. She can no go out. She get up at six o'clock in the morning. She work to ten or eleven o'clock at night cooking, washing, cleaning."

Petra Rodriguez is a strong-looking, forty-five-year-old woman whose chiseled features give her an almost classical appearance. She is thin and her slender hands move gently even though they are scraped and worn from the hard household chores she performs. Like her husband's, her face is sad, almost fixed in an expression of enduring pain. She rarely smiles. She ties together her thick long black hair in a pony tail with a single rubber band. She wears no lipstick or powder and her face is pale from lack of sunlight. She speaks from inside her kitchen:

"My father was a farmer and I worked on the farm," she begins in answer to a question about her background. She grew up near Río Piedras, the town in Puerto Rico from which her husband came. "We all worked, my seventeen brothers and sisters. We grew sweet potatoes, bananas, yams, tomatoes. I worked on the farm until I was twenty-five years old. I was raised in the country and I never went to school. I never learned to read or write. I met my husband when I was twenty-five."

Why did she come to New York?

"We had a bad house in Puerto Rico," she says. "My husband, Marcello, used to drink a lot. We fought all the time. So I came over with some of the children. Later he came with the others. When we first came we lived downtown. Our super had a brother who lived in this building. He told us about the job of super in this building so we came here. Marcello left the factory in New Jersey to become a super here. He didn't like it because this building is bad to be super."

Why don't she and her family move out?

"I live here," she replies, shrugging her shoulders, "because I can't move. If I were able to move, I would have already. I always liked it downtown, near Delancey Street. I don't like it here because for people like me with a lot of children there are so many people with bad habits and there are a lot of drugs. Once in a while I go out. I have a lot of relatives here but I don't visit them. I have only once visit a brother who lives on 104th Street. I also leave the house when they send for me from school. From here I don't go anyplace. In this building I have lived for two years and I don't know anybody."

Rodriguez deserted his family early in 1963 to live in Paterson, N. J., but he returns to number 311 to visit his children once every two months. Ask his wife why he left and she says matter-of-factly:

"He packed up and left because the children are all big and he has a bad temper. He fights with them and throws them out of the house. He fought with the children all the time. And he doesn't get along with me because I am in favor of the children. They are not bad children. He got mad because one of the girls is one of those crazy kids who fell in love and had a baby and then separated from the boy. She never got married. Marcellino wouldn't let her come home with the baby because he said she already put her foot into it and would keep on having children. I say she doesn't bother anybody here. After he left she came home with the baby."

Does Petra Rodriguez feel that she needs her husband?

"No," she answers flatly. "The ones that are necessary are the ones who are here. Not the ones who leave. He didn't speak to any of us. He ignored the children, except when he fight with them. He used to come home, come upstairs from his work and lock himself into one of the rooms."

Now Petra Rodriguez and her family live on the earnings of two of her teen-age children who between them make $105 a week. Marcellino left his family an unpaid back rent bill of $120.54 covering two months' rent for their third-floor apartment. They made one apartment out of two apartments by knocking down a few walls on the third floor. The first thing Mrs. Rodriguez did after her husband left was to pay the rent.

"My daughter had to borrow some money and my son used up all he had saved to pay the landlord," Mrs. Rodriguez recalled. "We sent it to him in three money orders to the address on the yellow slip of paper." She pointed to a small 6-by-3-inch piece of paper on which was written:

FINAL REMINDER. This is to remind you that we have not as yet received your remittance for rent. Your prompt attention in this matter will be greatly appreciated. Amount due: $120.54. Unless payment is received in 3 days, dispossess will issue. HYMAN LEHON, Trustee, Second Equity Corp., 170 Broadway, N.Y. 38.

The notice had been sent to Rodriguez but he had forgotten to tell his family about it. It was from a man who, during the long period when the building's former owners had gone into bankruptcy, had taken over management of the house as a court-appointed receiver.

How does Petra Rodriguez feel about her life in 311 East 100th Street?

"I like it better in Puerto Rico," she confesses shyly, "because there are more people I know there. That's my country and I know it well. I can go out and walk around. Here I don't do much. I smoke cigarettes in my spare time. My daughter works in a factory and she bring home some material. I am working on a dress. I really don't know how to sew. That machine (pointing to a sewing machine in the kitchen) has been with us for years but I don't know how to use it yet. My daughter will teach me."

The Rodriguez family received money from the Welfare Department when they first arrived in the United States in 1957. But after Marcellino began to work, the department withdrew its support. Now Mrs. Rodriguez could turn to the city again for assistance, if she felt she needed it.

"No, I no go to welfare," she says. "I need money but I know what they say. They tell me to get it from husband for leaving us. The welfare no help us now."

Why doesn't she sue her husband for nonsupport?

"I don't bother him," she says. "I don't make trouble for him."

While Mrs. Rodriguez may be too proud or too stubborn a woman to seek funds from the city, her son, Marcellino, Jr., who lives next door to her with his girl friend and her baby, is benefiting from a Welfare Department check. He hasn't paid his rent either, but his Irish girl friend Pat explains why:

"The landlord sent us a 'final reminder' but we paid no attention to it. Why? Because we're on welfare and no welfare pays rent in this block. The worst buildings are in court so the welfare don't pay rent. They don't have to as long as the building is beat up. Last year they took the landlord to court but all he did was to put a little paint like water on the walls."

Under a New York state law introduced in 1962 by former Assemblyman Samuel A. Spiegel, the Welfare Department was given the power to withhold rents in buildings with "hazardous" violations until the landlords made the repairs. The landlord, who normally has the right to evict a tenant for nonpayment of rent, was prohibited by the terms of the new law to take such action in welfare cases.

Pat is twenty-two years old and the mother of two children, ages two and three, by a former husband. She completed eighth grade at a parochial school. How does she like living in 311 East 100th Street?

"This building is corroded," she answers sharply. "It's all full of rats. We have rats as big as cats. We use rat traps and put rat poison all around. But it don't make much difference. We're getting out of here. We got a new apartment in Brooklyn and we'll live there before Marcellino goes into the Army. It cost sixty-nine dollars a month. Welfare will pay for it. I'll feel happy. This hole is bad. The people—the dope addicts come in here."

Marcellino, a lean, handsome boy with black hair, complains that the addicts make life miserable in the house, and he tells how innocent people become involved:

"One day the cops came in and thought I was a junkie because I was standing in the hallway in the dark. The cops pointed their guns at me. I ran. But I stopped because I was scared they might shoot. They searched me and roughed me up. Then they let me go. They finally got their man. He lived upstairs in this house."

Three flights above the Rodriguez family, in the rear of the house, sixty-year-old Francisco Matos, a tired-looking, heavy-set construction worker, lives with his docile wife Candida, forty-six, and their three children. Since 1946 Matos and his wife have climbed the five filthy stairways from the main hallway to their squalid three-room flat on the top floor. The physical world in which they live has revolted them, but they could do nothing about it.

"I been trying to get into the housing project for eight years," Matos tells you when you ask him about his eighteen years in number 311. "I make two times application for Housing Authority, but they don't care for application. The last one two years ago. Nobody answers me. They send me one card, but when I go to office with the card they say they let me know but I hear nothing. We got to live so tight here. One room for me and my wife and my oldest girl and another for my son and my other girl."

The cramped and lightless 6-by-10-foot bedroom in which Matos and his wife and daughter sleep had a huge hole in the ceiling for many months before it was repaired. "You could see the sky," Matos recalls. "I fixed it myself at the beginning of the winter when the rain came in. The landlord don't pay for it. Four years he no paint apartment. Broken window I got to put glass in myself. Kitchen sink leak and bathroom no work."

The Matos' apartment is filled with old stuffed furniture. The blue walls are faded in the living room and bedroom and the pale yellow kitchen walls are dirty and peeling. Several pictures of Christ hang from these walls. Two black

Bibles on a table in the 6-by-10-foot living room are the only books visible.

"Our apartment has many troubles," Matos continues. "The landlord no care. Three year no steam heat. All the time we got a rat, sink broken, pipe broken. We here for eighteen years. I would like to move from here. It's so small for my family. The neighborhood is so bad, too bad. Noise and fight, talking bad—swearing."

A laborer, Matos has a big, broad-shouldered body. His 175-pound, 5-foot 6-inch frame, though stooped, is solid despite his age. His large, strong hands show the wear of years of physical toil. He has not worked for some time, however, because of an accident on his last job. He was standing on the ground when a brick fell from a height of twenty stories and hit him on the shoulder. Since then he has been unable to raise his arm without great pain. As a result, he has been out of work and without an income for many months.

"I owe grocery bill. I owe grocer five hundred dollars. All I have is debts," Matos says sadly. "To pay the house and everything I have to look elsewhere. I have other debts, including a fifty dollar bill here and a ninety dollar bill there . . . if I can't work the government has to do something with me. I can't go on like this because I can't live from the air."

When Matos was working, he earned as much as $4.30 an hour and when "times were good" he made more than $125 a week. "That was a lot of money," he says. "That's why I'm angry. I got in high school two children. I must find money. My hands are tied. I want to work but I can't. My family needs me to work."

Born in Morovis, Puerto Rico, Matos was the son of a farmer and worked on the farm until he was twenty. He completed four years of schooling. "When I was twenty," he recalls, "I went to San Juan and I had my own little business selling fruits as a vendor in Santurce. Then I worked on construction in a sugar boiler factory in a sugar mill. After that I worked for the government for ten years as a skilled laborer in the Parks Department, helping in the warehouse and in the government print shop and transportation shop. I got married in 1944 but in 1946 I left government work and couldn't find another job there. I was making thirty-six to forty dollars a week but I could find nothing better than eighteen dollars a week in Puerto Rico so I came to the United States.

"I went first to Philadelphia. I came under contract as a farm laborer. The job wasn't what I was expecting so I came to New York thinking of going back to Puerto Rico and a cousin of mine told me to stay here. He said he would get work for me. I started work as a dishwasher for thirty dollars a week. There I worked for a year and left to start a job in construction. I worked all over, until now. In construction I lose the job because I can't speak English. Nobody want to give me a job. Then I went on relief for fourteen months. The government unemployment office look for a job for me. I go back to work and don't go back to home relief. After that I started working in the union and got up to four-thirty an hour and worked all over, until I got hurt. Last year, working on and off, I make twenty-eight hundred dollars."

Why doesn't he reapply for welfare?

"I don't like to go to the welfare," he replies in utter sincerity. "I got the social security. I don't like the welfare. I don't like to take money without working for it."

Hidden away in the back of a rat-ridden tenement in East Harlem without a job and deep in debt, Matos will still turn down a welfare check. Why?

He is injured, out of work, and has only a fourth-grade education. But he is also a Pentecostal minister. He has a store-front church in the neighborhood where he holds services every night from eight to ten o'clock. "Sometimes I am talking," he says modestly. "I am the helper there. All my brothers come." Matos got his diploma from the Spanish-American Bible Institute in the late 1950s and ever since he has devoted all of his spare time to religion.

"My only religion," he tells you in his hoarse voice, "is for us to try and live life and do things the way of the Lord. Certainly I hope God will be better to us. We follow his words when he says to try and save your spirit. The body is worth nothing. It's the spirit that counts. We have to look out to see that the spirit comes to the same place . . . in the glory of God . . . when the time comes."

To pay the $100 a month rent for the dingy quarters in which the church members meet, Matos and his friends collect contributions for the rent from their "brothers" in the neighborhood and from the people who come to the church. "When I worked," Matos explains, "I paid most of the rent because some of our people are on welfare and can't pay at all. Now it's very hard. We must even borrow from our friends to pay our eighteen dollars' rent for our apartment at home."

Despite their adversities, Matos and his understanding wife are friendly, polite people. Their three children are all ambitious: Juan, seventeen, in third year high school, says he wants to be a doctor; Lucy, fifteen, in first year high school, says she wants to be a nurse; Naomi, ten, is in fourth grade. Candida Matos, a plumpish, pleasant-looking woman whose sad brown eyes peer at the listener when she talks, is philosophical about her life:

"All the time there are rats here. The high stairs hurt my

health. The apartment is too small. The dust came down from the ceiling and the roof collapsed in the bedroom," she complains. "But we must be satisfied with the little we have because we haven't the means to do any better," she adds quietly.

"My husband suffers and we suffer because of his beliefs," she continues. "He has not worked steady since he got hurt. The last time he was out of work he go on welfare because I insisted. I said, 'Are you going to let the children die of hunger?' He said, 'I don't want assistance. I don't want to depend on anyone.' This time I don't know what he will do."

Even in despair, Francisco Matos thinks of his son's future. Juan wants to be a doctor so his father recently signed a contract with a visiting salesman to pay $12 a month for a set of encyclopedias and a new dictionary. The total cost amounts to $244. "I want my boy to learn," is all Matos says when asked if he could afford the books and how he intends to pay for them.

Mrs. Matos' life in number 311 grows worse with the passing of each day. "When we first moved in," she remembers, "there were more Americans . . . colored Americans. People come and go. A lot of young Puerto Ricans without any sense use the needle and have the habit. To my way of thinking they are not to blame because they learn that in the war and bring it back. They still need it. They go crazy. The only change on 100th Street is that there are many more addicts.

"I think that every place in this section of the city is the same. They always kill and do this and that. I've visited my relatives in Brooklyn. I've visited parts of the Bronx—good parts. I've been to Central Park West. To be truthful, this is the worst part of the city where we live. But we Christians have to live, even in the worst places because we have to.

We have to bring peace to people even if they are bad. We must bring peace within people.

"Today in our block it is much worse than it ever was before. Now it's falling apart. It is very bad. It is tremendous. When we first came there was no addicts, no noise. Now there are twenty-five to fifty addicts at any time. They take handbags from the women on the stairways. People are found dead in the halls. The truth is that in this city no matter where you live you will find evil ways. If I could I would like to live in the country . . . Mount Vernon, Tucka-hoe, New Rochelle. My husband has worked in all of those places on construction and I like it, but it costs money. It is beautiful to live there."

The Matos have no illusions about their fate in number 311. "We're in this house," Mrs. Matos says flatly, "because we can't move and we can't pay more. If we could pay seventy or eighty dollars a month we would move today." Her husband is even more blunt. "We're living here," he says angrily, "like a cat tied by the tail. It's a bad place to bring up the family but anyplace else with three rooms would cost much more. I can't pay more."

Sam and Mary Williams, a Negro couple, live on the fifth floor in the three-room apartment directly below the Matos' flat. Seven people are jammed into the Williams home, including four of their children and one daughter-in-law. The rent is $28.15 per month. The Williamses can easily afford this because they both work. He has a job as a porter in a City Housing Authority project and she works as an office cleaning woman. Between them they bring home over $90 a week, enough to enable them to buy an automobile on time. Yet they have remained in number 311 for fourteen years. Why?

"We could afford to live someplace else," says Mrs. Williams, "but one thing, we likes to eat and I don't like the idea of paying all of our money in rent and not eating. If we move someplace else we know we'll have to pay much more rent than we pay here. We don't want to pay too much. I suppose you can live anywhere if you can afford it."

Mary Williams was born in West Virginia. She came to New York at the age of sixteen to live with her brother's family in Brooklyn. "I liked it in West Virginia," she says. "Once in a while I go back to visit my family."

When the Williamses first moved into number 311 in 1949 with one child the whole house lacked hot water. "It was a cold-water flat. My rent was sixteen dollars. The rent increases started after they put the hot water in. The worst time in this place is in the summer. I don't think I can describe it to you. All I can say is that when it gets hot in this apartment, it's just plain hot. When my children were small and it got hot here usually what I would do, we had a fan, so I'd bring them in the kitchen at night and turn on the fan. During the day I kept them in the tub. I kept them cool that way. But now that they are larger they just walk the floor and drink water."

Mrs. Williams's children, ranging in age from eleven to eighteen (the oldest is married but not working), all share the same broken-down facilities with their parents: one bathtub, which is located in the kitchen, and one small toilet adjacent to the kitchen. Most of the time the children are out of the house, thereby allowing the parents some privacy. But they don't really seem to mind.

"We don't have a shower here," says Mrs. Williams. "We just have a toilet and tub. This is the kitchen and the toilet is in the kitchen behind the door. When we get ready to take our bath, usually one be in here [in the kitchen] and the rest of us be in the other room. When the children were small all of us would be in here because I would bathe them one at a time. My bathtub is next to my kitchen sink. I use the tub for taking a bath and I wash my clothes in it, too. We don't take showers. My husband doesn't mind. We have cockroaches all over, but we don't have them bad because I spray.

"Usually, on the week end, we go out and get away from here for a while. Sometimes we're so tired that we just stay at home. Sometimes we go to the beach and sometimes we go visit our family. During the winter we don't do anything except stay at home. Sometimes we work on the apartment a little. My husband painted Christmas gone a year ago. The landlord gave us the paint but said he couldn't afford to paint. I put up that contact paper (pointing to a kitchen wall) behind the sink because the water flushes and the paint would peel off. I put it up to try and save the paint."

Mrs. Williams does not report to her office cleaning job until 5:30 P.M. every day. She says her daily routine runs something like this:

"I gets up about eight. Usually, if I have ironing to do I do my ironing and washing. I cook and clean up and that's about it. I watch TV, or sometimes I take a drive in our car. The neighborhood isn't as good as it used to be, though. It's very noisy here, especially when it's hot, but I've gotten used to it. It doesn't bother me. But if I could I would move to Long Island because there is less pavement there."

What is the worst thing she has seen since she came to East 100th Street in 1949?

"In the street, the worst thing that happened since I been here," she replies, "is when somebody threw a little girl off the roof of a house. I thought that was the worst thing in the world."

Down the hall from the Rodriguez family on the third floor, Anna Maria Vargas, a soft-spoken thirty-three-year-old native of Santurce, Puerto Rico, lives with her nine-year-old son, José, and her twenty-one-year-old common-law husband, Roberto Perez. She left Puerto Rico in 1956 for New Brunswick, N.J., where she lived with her former husband. One of five children from a poor family, she lived in poverty as a child. Today, she works as a sewing-machine operator and earns $60 a week. Her rent is $32.19 a month.

Sitting in her neat and clean three-room flat in the rear of the building, Mrs. Vargas tells you about her life in number 311. Her dark-brown hair is set in curlers over which she wears a purple handkerchief. Her heavy, bosomy body bulges beneath an orange blouse and brown skirt. Her round, pleasant face smiles as she talks:

"The building itself is no good," she begins. "It's always filthy and full of garbage. This building is the worst I've ever lived in. I found my apartment when I was visiting a friend next door and I was told there was an empty apartment. I don't have trouble here myself because I don't visit anybody, but I'd like to get away. I don't like the block. The building is dirty. The apartment is small. The street has a lot of drug addicts. The police come around. I've seen a lot of fights, but the police don't do anything. They are afraid of the people because there are so many of them. In the summer, they make noise and they drink and I can't sleep. It's worse than a slum here. I don't know what to call it."

Why does she remain?

"It's hard to get an apartment somewhere else," is her simple reply. "I have asked people who know. I look in the newspapers. But when I find something, the super always asks for a large tip—fifty or sixty dollars—and if you haven't got it, you don't get the apartment. You must also give the security and one month's rent to the agent or super. And they ask for money in the real estate offices, too. I stay here until I can get an apartment for rent and security only. I will pay no extra. I live here because I have no alternative. I have tried to get a four-room apartment but I can't find one. I have looked in the Bronx and I have looked through friends. I have lived in the Bronx and before that in a furnished rooming house with my son after my husband left me and went back to Puerto Rico. We are divorced now."

She came to New York in 1956, but she says she has never seen the United Nations, Rockefeller Plaza, the Empire State Building, or Greenwich Village. "I don't travel much," she says, not at all embarrassed, "only when I go to work." She does not vote ("I know nothing about politics") and she doesn't read ("I watch television and stay in my apartment at night"). She describes herself as "a very serious person. I just like to listen to Spanish music on my victrola. Out of life I expect that when I get to an age when I can't work I'll have saved something. I work now to save money."

What will she do with her money?

"Right now," she replies unhappily, "I'm working to save five hundred dollars for an operation." Turning her face fully toward the questioner for the first time since she has been talking, she points to an ugly four-inch scar on her right cheek. "I had my face marked up," she says slowly and self-consciously. "My husband was having a fight. I got in between and was cut by a razor. Maybe I can find a good plastic surgeon. The man from *El Diario* told me I could get my face fixed."

She also wants to plan for her son, who has been a source of heartache for her. "Ordinarily," she says with a wistful smile, "parents have hope for their children. But my son is hard to reach. He's the only child I have and I would like him to be something important. But when he was in Catholic school they told me he should be mentally examined. I have sent him to Puerto Rico to see if he would change. But he didn't. The teacher gives classes in school and he doesn't pay attention. He plays instead. He spent two years in the second grade. He doesn't get into trouble, but I kept receiving complaints he would wander. He doesn't pay attention. He doesn't remember what I tell him. He seems to forget everything. I don't know what to do with him."

Part of this problem is shared by her common-law husband, Roberto Perez, a slim, bashful boy with a tight, youthful body. He came from a family of seven brothers and sisters, went as far as seventh grade, and worked on a farm in Vegalta, Puerto Rico, before coming to New York a year ago. "I decided to come to New York for money," he says. "On the farm I earned only fifteen dollars a week. I would have liked to stay in Puerto Rico but for money I'll stay here."

Roberto works as a packer for a company at Farmingdale, L.I., where he goes every day. He earns $1.40 an hour. "Kind of a good job," he says. "I like this work better than farming. I have to travel two hours back and forth but it's worth it. I have had it with farming."

Ask this young Puerto Rican how long he worked on the farm in his home country and he replies, shaking his head:

"Mister, I think I was born with a handle of a hoe in my hand."

Does he like his new home?

"No. I don't like it here. This building is no good," he says quickly. "It's the worst you can imagine. There are a lot of people with bad habits. You can't go to bed in peace. A lot of them live in this block and some are in this house. They show up in the hallways, dancing in the hallways, putting on a show. At night, it's all alive with a bunch of drug addicts—the building and the street. The cops come around but they leave them as hopeless."

Does he think this building is a "slum"?

"Sí," Roberto replies. "It's El Fanguito here."

The worse physical shape a building is in, the more likely it will attract the pathetic people who are turned away from all other shelter—even low-rent public housing. Because many of them are social misfits, the people on welfare are shunted aside from the mainstream of American life.

Weneslau Torres, a thirty-one-year-old native of Ponce, Puerto Rico, lives with his common-law wife Enida and their four children on the fourth floor of number 311. He receives a check for $99.90 from the Welfare Department in the mail every two weeks. The money is supposed to be budgeted on a monthly basis, according to the department's basic allowance schedule,[2] as follows:

Food	$128.70
Clothing	34.60
Personal care	8.00
Shelter (rent)	21.92
Fuel for cooking	3.10
Electricity and refrigeration	4.80
Household supplies	4.20
Expenses incident to education	1.10
TOTAL	$206.42

"It's hard to live this way," Torres tells you when you ask him about this budget. "Sometimes the kids are hungry and you tell them you don't have no more. I don't have enough money to pay the rent and buy food. I'd rather live in a housing project but I have not applied. We're not married.

The children are ours—we have lived together for ten years—but the housing project doesn't accept you if you're not married. We can't get married because Enida is still married to another man."

Torres, a quiet-spoken, small man, has not worked for three years. For a while he did not even receive his welfare checks. The department suspended him when it found out he was involved in East Harlem's numbers rackets. Once he was arrested and spent twenty days in jail.

Ask New York City Welfare Commissioner James R. Dumpson about the welfare families in 311 East 100th Street and he dispassionately tells you:

"The house at 311 East 100th Street in East Harlem is rather typical of slums throughout the City of New York, Chicago, Washington, Denver, and other major cities of our country. Out of thirty-three apartments in this one house, six families are receiving relief. These are people who have lived in this house, some of them as long as eight years. They haven't all been on relief for that period of time, but three of the families are receiving what we call supplementary relief. That means that the man in that family is working full-time earning to the maximum capacity of his ability. His wages are inadequate and insufficient to care for the large family that he has. These three families represent many of the families who are consigned to the slums. These are people without skills that are marketable in the present employment market. As a result, these are the people who have no way of getting themselves out of the slums."

The Welfare Department sends more than $6000 a year to sustain the rent, food, clothing, and medical needs of the six families on relief at number 311. It pays the landlord approximately $2500 in rents each year, money which

actually subsidizes the squalor in which the welfare families
are trapped.

The ordinary gray brick building with the number 311
painted on the glass transom above the outside doorway is
similar in appearance to many other slum tenements. It
stands where it was erected in 1906, 180 feet east of Second
Avenue on the north side of 100th Street. It adjoins the tenement at 309 on the west, just as it did when it was one of
five contiguous buildings erected simultaneously. But on the
east its scarred walls today stand naked to the eye, over-
looking an empty lot. The buildings which once stood adjacent at numbers 313 and 315 were demolished in 1937 when
the city ruled them "unsafe and unfit for human habitation."
The city-owned empty lot that remains serves as a combination dumping ground for tenants' garbage and a playground
for the children who spill over from the overcrowded street.

The six-story building, 40 feet wide and 87 feet 11 inches
deep, rises 61 feet 10 inches; at its top is a stone cornice
which juts out over the street. The hallway entrance at street
level is barely distinguishable; it is located three short concrete steps above the level of the sidewalk and enclosed by
two stoops on either side which are topped by short black
railings. On either side of the doorway are two other doors,
leading into stores located on the ground floor. One has been
locked for years, its streaked glass windows dirtied by the
scrawl of neighborhood gangs; the other, with two basement
entrances from the street, is occupied by the Negro superintendent, William Davies, who uses it for a "candy store"
where he keeps old furniture and household wares which
he buys and sells to neighborhood people. Above the front
entrance, covering the building from top to bottom, are five
delicately designed wrought-iron fire escapes with four

slanted ladders connecting each balcony and casting shadows over ten of the thirty small windows which face the street. Above almost every window is a cast-stone lintel. In the summertime, the heat drives many of the building's 139 tenants out of their choked flats onto the fire escapes, which serve as terraces above the steaming concrete pavement below.

The inner core of the building is chopped up into 105 separate rooms, including bathrooms and kitchens, comprising thirty-three apartments. The average apartment size is about three rooms, in which as many as ten persons live. The basement does not contain any apartments, but it is used as a home for an occasional "squatter." The first floor has three apartments, two of which for years were used by a private medical clinic and a church parish office. The upper five floors contain six apartments each, three in front of the building and three in the rear. The apartment ceilings vary to some degree but average out to about nine feet in height. By modern standards the rooms are small, bedrooms measuring as little as 6 feet 8 inches by 10 feet 10 inches and living rooms 9 feet 1 inch by 11 feet 4 inches. (See Typical Floor Plan in the Appendix, pp. 268-269.)

The land and the tenement at 311 East 100th Street are assessed by the City Tax Department at $40,000, but private real estate men no longer value it at such a price because it is located in what is known as a "depressed" neighborhood. Nevertheless, during the past sixty years the house has been a source of income for some twenty-seven different corporations involving more than 150 individuals. Each owner has drawn out of this property whatever he could.

Collectively, the landlords have received nearly half a million dollars in gross rentals from this one building since it was built.

If a prospective buyer were interested in acquiring the property in 1964, he would want to know that it is rent-controlled, meaning that it is subject to a city rent law which limits the maximum rent on each apartment and therefore the building's total rents to $12,382.08 per year. Legal rents, which are low by New York standards, range from $18.62 to $38.34 per month per apartment.

He would also want to know that there are total fixed expenses of approximately $3300 per year. These include real estate taxes (based on the 1964–65 rate of approximately $4.50 per $100 of assessed valuation) of about $1800; water and sewage charges of about $500 per year; and fire insurance, liability, compensation, and disability costs of about $1000 per year.

In its present condition, the building would probably not make money. And, if an owner spent what is required to make repairs—a minimum of $4000 per year—he would almost certainly lose money on the property, according to the estimate of an expert New York real estate and insurance broker (see Table 2, in the Appendix, p. 273).

Although a potential buyer might be aware of the general facts concerning the building, chances are that few speculators in a hurry to make money would take the time to dig through voluminous inspection files from half a dozen city departments. However, if an inquisitive observer did spend the long hours necessary to study the city's records, here is the history of violations he would find:

The files of the Department of Water Supply, Gas and Electricity contain a long history of violations, including defective lighting fixtures, wire cords, and circuits; fuses too large and wires not protected from fire; unapproved switch outlets and illegal wiring in nearly every apartment; defective metal boxes and meter pans.

In 1962, this department threatened to disconnect the

electricity (it has the legal power to order Consolidated Edison, the New York utility, to turn off the current if the violations are hazardous) unless repairs were made. The violations were finally removed in this case, but not until five months after a warning had been sent to the landlord. Fortunately, no fires broke out during that period. Some of the apartments have still not been converted from DC to AC current.

New York City Fire Department records, which reflect inspections held periodically in the public areas of tenements, show that more than a dozen fires inside 311 East 100th Street took place during the past two decades, a few causing serious injury.

Numerous violations have been placed by the department against the building in recent years, including violations for blocked egresses, inflammable rubbish in public hallways, missing and broken steps on fire escapes, defective self-closing devices on doors opening to the public hallways, and rubbish and litter in the basement. However, since the inspections omitted the interior of the apartments, it can be assumed other fire violations existed but were not reported.

The tenement at number 311 has been in run-down condition for a number of years, but the city's Department of Buildings listed only thirteen infractions of the housing code against the house between 1951 and 1961. This was because little public attention had been centered on the block up to that time.

The "crackdown" on 311 East 100th Street by the Department of Buildings started quietly in the spring of 1961 when the East Harlem Reform Democratic political club encouraged local families to bring their housing complaints to a makeshift housing clinic in the club's store-front headquarters at 1673 Lexington Avenue.

On July 13, 1961, Richard L. Levenson, one of the club's

lawyers, went into the house at 311 East 100th Street and, after an apartment-by-apartment inspection, wrote down the tenants' complaints. He filed a "multiple complaint" with the State Rent Commission asking that the rents be reduced until the house was properly repaired.

"It was fantastic," Levenson recalls. "I have never seen such chaotic living conditions. The tenants were so uninformed the landlord could buffalo them. The landlord had them sign rent increases. We found instances of rent-gouging and we told the tenants they did not have to pay what the landlord wanted. They called him 'the boss,' and they were frightened of him even though they did not even know his name. Any outsider coming into East Harlem for the first time would have been appalled by what I saw. The tenants obviously didn't know what their rights were. That's why I went in—to help them understand what they could do to help themselves. Some of them could not write English, so I filled out the forms for them."

The tenants' complaints, recorded in their own words, included: "Steam and hot water many times is scarcely and it happened in colds day when one must need we have no steam at all. The landlord give me some paint of very low class, but it was no enough to paint the entire apartment."

Another tenant declared: "Bedroom window is broken. Bathroom leak from toilet bowl, living room radiator is leaking and kitchen ceiling needs repair." Still another said: "The wall in the kitchen is loose. The wall is in need of repair right away and also the bathroom ceiling . . ." ". . . holes in walls in living room and bedroom and bathroom, which are access to rodents . . ." and "Kitchen water pressure is very low—sometimes no water at all. Window frames rotten in all rooms. Large rat holes. Bedroom wall has crack from ceiling to floor from water from roof."

The complaints continued: ". . . I have no refrigerator. I am using my own ice box. The stove is the same one I met in my apartment when I moved in. Their [*sic*] is no improvement in the apartment since I moved in. That was ten years ago."

On July 25, 1961, less than two weeks after Levenson made his inspection of the house at 311 East 100th Street, a Rent Commission inspector's report on the house declared:

The premises appear to have been neglected for years. The halls, apartments and building in general need major repairs and better maintenance.

The report noted there were "dangerous conditions" in five apartments, including caved-in ceilings. Three days later, on July 28, 1961, the State Rent Commission issued an order reducing rents at 311 East 100th Street by 25 per cent. In exercising its legal power to cut rents, the Commission said in a report:

This reduction not only reflects the reasonable value of the services currently being withheld from the tenants, but it also represents the judgment of this office that the building is being maintained without regard for the safety of the tenants.

By coincidence, on this same day—July 28, 1961—Mayor Robert F. Wagner made a forty-minute tour of this turbulent block in East Harlem. While plainclothes policemen patrolled rooftops to guard against brick- and bottle-throwers, the Mayor and his staff walked along East 100th Street with newsmen.

The Mayor was smiling as he shook several hundred hands. When reporters questioned him, he lashed out at State Comptroller Arthur Levitt, who was opposing him in the forthcoming September primary. (Levitt had been publicly chiding the Mayor for his "newfound interest" in the slums.) On this tour of the "worst block"—his third slum tour in ten days—the Mayor declared:

"This is the time of the year when people make a lot of talk. I've been fighting this [slums] for seven and a half years now—even before that, when I was borough president."

The Mayor was led down the block by Assemblyman Mark Lane. They looked inside several apartments in the building across the street from number 311. One tenant showed the Mayor how rats had eaten away the stuffing from her sofa. Another pointed to a leaky sink and a toilet bowl which had overflowed. In another apartment, water leaks had loosened huge chunks of plaster.

The two men continued to walk through the tenements on East 100th Street. A sluggish, moisture-laden breeze which carried a foul stench from a broken sewer pipe beneath one of the tenements swept over the block.

The Mayor turned to his Commissioner of Buildings, Peter J. Reidy, and declared:

"You'd better get inspectors up here first thing Monday morning."

When the Mayor was informed that one landlord on the block had been fined only $85 for 149 building-code violations, he told the newsmen with him:

"Those fines weren't very heavy. Perhaps if the courts made the fines stronger, it might help."

As the Mayor prepared to leave "the worst block" and was about to climb into his car to return to Gracie Mansion, a man carrying a cigar box stopped to talk with some people lounging on the stoop in front of number 311 a few steps away from the Mayor's official car. The man asked the crowd for nickels and dimes. He said he wanted to help pay for funeral expenses for an eighteen-month-old baby, Angelo Luis Pachecho, Jr., who had toppled to his death the day before from the sixth-floor fire escape of the house at 311 East 100th Street.

"My husband was on the fire escape. My baby, too," Juanita Pachecho recalled after the tragedy. "My sister come and speak to my husband. My husband was putting laundry on the fire escape and my baby was next to my husband. My sister called my husband. My husband say, 'One minute, hold the baby.' My sister came over and say, 'I don't know, where's the baby?' My husband look outside and the baby's gone down the fire escape. He look outside on the street and my baby's dying downstairs. I went downstairs . . . I can't speak of it . . . I want to move because every time I remember my baby I can't sleep because my baby sleep. I can't live here. My husband outside now, he no eat, nothing, because he love my baby. I walk to the hospital with my baby and my baby die in the hospital. He got two operations and he die."

A neighbor below the Pachechos, Mary Williams, recalls what she saw happen that afternoon:

"I was washing clothes and I was looking down below. When I first saw this thing fall I thought it was a doll baby. When I look it was a baby. I heard the parents screaming and by the time they got downstairs, a man, he yelled them off, because he didn't want them to touch the child. So they waited for an ambulance to come but the ambulance never did. So the father took the child in his arms and went around to Metropolitan Hospital with it. That was all."

In the impersonal records of the 23rd Police Precinct a few blocks away from the scene of this tragic accident, all that one can find out is summarized by the precinct captain as follows:

"Our records disclose that the infant fell from the fire

escape. The father of the infant was out on the fire escape hanging clothes. A year-and-a-half-old baby was on the fire escape. The father went inside and while the father was inside the apartment the child fell to the street and was killed."

A private investigator's report several weeks later, based on a visit to the apartment and a talk with Mrs. Pachecho, revealed that one of the steps on the fire-escape ladder was broken. Asked about this step, Mrs. Pachecho replied:

"It has been broke a long time. Maybe my baby tripped on the broken step. I don't like to complain to the landlord. Nobody complains to the landlord. Maybe my baby fell. My baby speaks something. He says, 'Mama' and 'Papa' and sometimes he says, 'Mama, give me water.' Now I tell other women, 'Be careful for your children, it should not happen to you.' Now the police come no more. My baby was premature baby—eight months, four pounds. Nobody come to my apartment now. Nobody come to look at fire escape or the window to look at broken step after my baby fell."

The father, Angelo Luis Pachecho, who had been unemployed and on welfare for a year prior to the accident, blamed himself, even though he knew the broken step might have played a part in the accident.

During the days following the tragedy of the Pachecho child and the Mayor's celebrated visit to the block, state and city government agencies undertook separate and unrelated investigations of living conditions inside the tenements on East 100th Street, including the house at number 311.

On August 2, 1961, Robert E. Herman, state rent administrator, submitted a copy of the Rent Commission's July 28 report cutting rents 25 per cent at number 311 to Louis J. Lefkowitz, the state attorney general. In his letter, Herman described the squalid condition of the building and said it "warrants action under your authority." He recommended that Lefkowitz consider the possibility of dissolution of the corporate landlord and the appointment of a receiver who would operate the building.

This recommendation was part of a campaign against slum landlords which the attorney general's office had been waging since January 1960. As a result of Herman's recommendation, the attorney general subpoenaed the landlord of number 311 at the time, the Second Equity Corporation of 604 Fifth Avenue. The subpoena was answered by M. Monroe Fass, president of the corporation.

On August 18, Fass produced his records which included expense vouchers which he said totaled $3571.10 for plumbing, electrical fixtures, painting fire escapes, roofing, replacing a faulty fire escape, glass windows, and mailboxes. Apparently satisfied that the landlord had made a genuine attempt to repair the house, the attorney general's office closed its file on the case on September 13, 1961, and marked it "compliance obtained."

Meanwhile, the city's Department of Buildings had undertaken an investigation of its own. On August 3, a departmental inspector recorded seventy-six violations in the building. Throughout the house the inspector noted dirty painted surfaces and unsanitary conditions; broken glass windows and window frames; broken and defective plaster; defective electric-light fixtures; leaking and defective faucets; broken and defective door frames; broken wood floors; leaking water closets and waste pipes; iron gates illegally blocking some windows; drains obstructed; guard railings broken; brickwork worn and broken; all apartments missing self-closing doors; mortar eroded from joints of brickwork; broken wood treads on stairways, and illegal conversion of apartments from residential use for a medical clinic.

The presence of such serious violations led the Buildings

Department to certify on September 9, 1961—the same week that the state attorney general's office had closed its book on this case—that the house at number 311 was a "fire hazard, in a continued dangerous condition, detrimental to life and health and occupied in violation of law because of the failure of the landlord to remove numerous violations, including six hazardous violations."

Two months later, on November 3, 1961, the building's managing agent, Fass and Wolper, of 604 Fifth Avenue, submitted to the State Rent Commission copies of repair bills totaling $4536.61, allegedly paid between August 9 and October 27, 1961.

In their letter to the Rent Commission, Fass and Wolper tried to get the state agency to restore the rents which had been cut 25 per cent the previous July. The letter read, in part:

You will find that some jobs had to be done over two and three times because of negligence and vandalism on the part of tenants, visitors and neighborhood residents. This entire block, as you know, is infested with narcotics addicts and juvenile delinquents. The landlord of this building has always endeavored to maintain it properly, but a building where even the superintendent has complained of being bombarded with bricks and bottles from the roof and is afraid to step into the halls after dark is understandably a difficult building to maintain.

On December 28, 1961, Fass and Wolper again appealed to the Rent Commission in another letter:

The landlord has plastered, painted and cleared the public areas, removed all rubbish, repaired the landing steps, repaired all rat holes and replaced the front glass door and hall windows. ———— Exterminating Company has long serviced this building under contract and has again increased their service to this building at our request. They report that tenant education for cleanliness is needed in several apartments. We also hired a new superintendent to give better hot water and cleaning service to the tenants. The new superintendent tells us the same thing the old one did, that is, that many tenants give almost no cooperation in protecting their property and keeping the halls and yards clean.

Despite these appeals, the Rent Commission refused to restore the rent cut. The Buildings Department added nine more violations in January 1962. Meanwhile, Fass was found guilty in court of violating the housing laws and ordered on January 22, 1962, by Magistrate Edward J. Chapman to pay the city $650 in fines for seventy-four violations of the multiple-dwelling law. The judge called Fass' operation of the building "disgraceful" and Mrs. Anna T. Withey, then an assistant city corporation counsel, said in court that if Fass had not cleared his property of the violations she would have recommended a jail sentence. Fass asked for an appeal of the sentence.

On March 23, 1962, Fass and Wolper once more sent a letter to the Rent Commission asking that the rents be restored and warning that unless the Commission acted in the landlord's favor there might be financial troubles ahead. The letter declared:

. . . It seems grossly unfair to block restoration of rent on the great majority of the apartments just because a small minority of the tenants are fighting to keep their rents down. The landlord has gone heavily in debt in this building and the delay in restoring the rents has created a very precarious financial position for the owner. We ask that you please expedite the restoration.

In May, the owners, Second Equity Corporation, pleaded with the Buildings Department for assistance. A letter to the department read:

Both our office and the contractor have called you many times
and have been down personally to your office in an endeavor to
obtain reinspection and dismissal of the remaining dozen violations still on your records, in spite of the fact that the work was
completed a long time ago. As you know, the landlord has spent
$10,000 in removing the violations which were basically due to
the fact that the building is in the middle of one of the worst
blocks in the City of New York, being heavily infested by vandals,
narcotics addicts and just plain delinquents. In fact, the landlord
was forced into Chapter 11 [bankruptcy] because of the heavy
expenditures. In spite of his efforts, the Rent Commission reduced
the already low rent roll one-third[3] across the board and refuses
to restore the rents until we obtain dismissal from your office.
Meanwhile, the landlord is again trying to keep pace with the
neighborhood and building occupants who are again beginning
to destroy the property bit-by-bit. It is urgent that the Department cooperate with us in this matter, so that the landlord can
get the rent roll restored and thus enable him to continue to
maintain the building.

The letter was signed by the Second Equity Corporation,
"debtor in possession," because the landlord had in fact
begun a bankruptcy proceeding which eventually was to
lead to a change of ownership in 1963.

In June 1962, the $650 in total fines against Fass was
reduced to $150 by Judge Irwin D. Davidson in an unusual
action in the Court of General Sessions.[4] The judge ruled
that the $650 fines were "excessive." He said in his decision
that the complaint against Fass "reveals that for the most
part the said items are of a minor, trivial and insubstantial
nature. No violations were charged which indicate any
imminent health or safety hazard to the occupants of the
building."

In addition, Judge Davidson noted that the violations
had been cleared at the time of sentence in January and that

Fass had submitted an affidavit stating he had spent $12,000 on maintenance and $15,000 more for a new steam heating plant.

"This property is located," Judge Davidson continued, "in that part of Manhattan which has become known as a slum area. The building department is extending every possible effort to improve the condition of the dwellings located in that general area.

"However, this particular building does not seem to be a slum building, nor has it been maintained as such. An owner who spends such large sums for maintenance as did this owner is not a slumlord.

"The slumlord, a greedy, avaricious type of owner who milks property, makes no necessary repairs, fails to maintain the property, fails to furnish necessary services, and permits the property to deteriorate to the point where it becomes a health and safety hazard to the occupants, should be made to feel the full effects of the law."

The judge concluded: "An owner who furnishes necessary services, makes needed repairs and maintains his property so that no health or safety hazards are created, should not be accorded slumlord treatment merely because the property in question is in an area which has become known as a slum area. In the instant case, the owner and the real estate management company cannot be classified as 'slum lords.'"

During the summer of 1962, despite the court's belief that 311 East 100th Street had been properly repaired, many of the old violations began to crop up again. The Buildings Department, apparently unaware of the bankruptcy proceedings involving number 311, placed ten more violations on the building in June and July and forty-five more in September.

When the Housing and Redevelopment Board's "neighborhood conservation program" was launched on East 100th Street in the fall of 1962, number 311 was among the buildings carefully eyed for inspection. Within a short time, officials anxious to carry out the new housing program placed a total of more than 1500 violations on all of the East 100th Street buildings.

A month later, in October 1962, the Department of Buildings warned the landlord of number 311 of an extremely "hazardous" condition: the masonry retaining wall on the east side of the house was "broken and out of plumb." However, since the wall also bordered the empty lot owned by the city's Department of Real Estate since 1952, it was not clear who was responsible for correcting the precarious condition of the retaining wall.

Should the City of New York or the Second Equity Corporation, debtor-in-possession of 311 East 100th Street, be required to do the job? The question remained unresolved for three months. At the end of January 1963, a ruling was returned by the city's Law Department that the violation was the legal responsibility of the owner of number 311.

But before anybody could repair the sagging wall, it collapsed one day and thus provided its own solution to the problem. Fortunately, nobody was near it at the time it came tumbling down.

In 1963, the count at the outset of the calendar year read twenty-nine violations against the house at number 311. During the year six more violations were placed by the Department of Buildings and one was removed, making the box score in September 1963 thirty-four violations still pending. Finally, in December, a cellar-to-roof inspection of the house turned up sixty-five more violations, including many listed as "hazardous" by the department.

As a result of the continuous violations, in November

1963 the City Rent and Rehabilitation Administration ordered another 10 per cent reduction in rents on all apartments in the building. This rent slash brought to a total of 35 per cent the reductions made in the building. (The 25 per cent cut ordered on July 28, 1961, had never been restored.) By January 1964 number 311 had deteriorated to the point where city rent officials cut the rent once again— to one dollar per apartment per month. An inspector for a private insurance company recorded in a routine report: "This is a dilapidated, filthy tenement with all services broken down. If there is a custodian, he performed very little services. Poor class Negroes and Puerto Ricans contribute to the building's condition by throwing garbage out of the window."[5]

The piles of garbage, furniture, clothing, and other odds and ends which are often found in the alleys and yards of the house at number 311 represent a challenge to even the most dedicated city workers. Technically, they are not housing violations and so they go unattended unless the city's Department of Sanitation steps in.

This department's records show it handed out more than 300 summonses between 1959 and 1964 on East 100th Street for violations of the city health code. The department also reports it sweeps each side of East 100th Street three times a week. With all of this cleaning up, however, the block often looks like a garbage dump, especially during the hot summer days when people heave their trash out of windows.

The Sanitation Department is empowered to clean only in the street and around the building. It is not required to report the dangerously unsanitary health violations which exist in the slum dwellers' apartments. The worst day-to-day signs of the slum are usually found in the reports of the city's Department of Health.

Since 1960 there have been dozens of violations found by the Health Department in number 311—for rat, roach, and mice infestation; rat holes in the apartments; defective gas ranges, lack of hot water and heat; rubbish and garbage in the cellar, hallways, and inside the apartments themselves; as well as the presence of flies and other insects.

A typical cellar-to-roof health inspection of number 311 on March 16, 1963, by Health Inspector Samuel Gartner turned up sixty-six serious health violations (see Table 3, in the Appendix). The roof, Gartner found, was filled with dog feces, ceilings and walls were cracked and leaking, gas stoves were defective, toilet bowls were loose and broken, and in the cellar there were rat holes, fresh rat excreta, and an open sewer line.

The Health Department, like the Department of Buildings, has had little success in the courts against the owners of the building. Fines totaling $150 have been levied against the owners between 1960 and 1964.

Health Inspector Gartner has been in and out of slum buildings as often as most New Yorkers ride the subway. His reaction to 311 East 100th Street? "It's a house of horror. No matter how much you put into this building," he says, "it will always be a slum. The life has gone out of it. It should be torn down."

By early 1964, the house had accumulated 130 violations. It was officially listed by the Commissioner of Buildings as one of the ten worst buildings on the island of Manhattan.

A HOUSE OF HOPE

This is the true nature of the home—it is the place of Peace; the shelter, not only from all injury, but from all terror, doubt, and division.

—*John Ruskin*

ON THURSDAY, APRIL 19, 1906, a pleasant spring morning in New York, the house at 311 East 100th Street was born.

The brand-new six-story building opened its doors on a day when countless other buildings were destroyed by earthquake and fire 3000 miles away in San Francisco. Flags at New York's City Hall flew at half mast as Mayor George B. McClellan solemnly met with officials to map out plans for raising money to help more than 50,000 people left homeless and destitute by the West Coast disaster.

In Albany, Governor Frank W. Higgins issued an appeal for aid to the Californians: "He gives twice who gives quickly," the governor said. In Washington, President Theodore Roosevelt, besieged with dispatches of sympathy from every major world capital, offered aid to San Francisco and urged the Congress to appropriate funds and supplies for the emergency.

Although news of the unprecedented earthquake rocked the world from Manila to Germany and made this a day for the history books, April 19, 1906, could be noted for other events as well. It was also the day on which:[1]

—Mark Twain delivered his last lecture in public and asked his audience to "remember San Francisco, the smitten city."

—Professor Pierre Curie, who with his wife Marie had discovered radium, was killed in a Paris street, run over by a wagon.

—John Davis, an unknown Negro, was shot and killed in Norfolk, Virginia, by a posse in pursuit, after Davis had allegedly murdered a bridge toll keeper because the keeper would not let him pass. The charge was one cent.

—An English Engineer predicted in New York that subways would someday travel 75 to 100 miles per hour and bring the most distant parts of the Bronx and Staten Island to Wall Street in fifteen minutes at a three-cent fare.

—An Aldermanic Commitee on Laws and Legislation opened hearings in Manhattan on a proposed five-cent telephone rate for interborough calls.

—George M. Cohan starred on Broadway in his musical play *George Washington, Jr.* at the Herald Square Theatre.

The stock market was bewildered by the effect of the earthquake—brokers and clients traded heavily and at the close of the day prices dropped sharply; in sports, Brooklyn beat the world champion Giants, 8–5, and the Boston Americans beat the Greater New Yorks, 2–0 and 3–1. The weather: Fair and mild. Average temperature: 63 degrees, compared to an average of 50 degrees for the past twenty-five years.

And on that spring morning, thirty-three hopeful New York families moved into the new freshly painted apartments of 311 East 100th Street.

The building at number 311 had actually been conceived nineteen months earlier when a new-building application,

Plan No. 400, had been filed by the owners, Louis Meryash, of 96 Monroe Street, and Albert London, of 263 Broome Street, at the city Tenement House Department's Manhattan office, 61 Irving Place, on October 5, 1904.

The application for the erection of the new brick tenement house specified it would contain fire escapes opening directly from at least one room in each apartment; a brick bulkhead in the roof with stairs leading to it; iron risers and banisters; steel beams throughout the structure; ceilings of angle irons and terra-cotta blocks; metal-covered door, window, and stair trims; all doors self-closing and fireproofed; all shafts fireproofed.

Each room, according to the application, would have at least one window opening directly on the street or yard, each water closet would have small windows, each public hall and stair hall would have at least one window opening on the street. The cellar would be made damp-proof by means of asphalt, and lighted and ventilated by means of windows and glass doors opening upon the courts and yards. All courts, vent shafts, areas, and yards would be properly graded with cement and drained and connected with the street sewer. Gas was to be the source of light and heat. Sinks would be installed in each apartment and supplied with running water from a roof tank holding 2500 gallons.

The application was signed by the owner's architectural firm, Horenburger and Straus, of 122 Bowery, and it specified that number 311 would be erected as one of five adjacent tenement houses. The first of the buildings was to be built on the north side of East 100th Street, 100 feet east of Second Avenue on a lot 40 feet by 100 feet eleven inches. The building at 311 was the third building to be erected in the row on what was designated as Lot No. 9 of city block

No. 1672. The owner-builders estimated the cost of each building, exclusive of the lot, to be $40,000.

The empty lots had been the property of Philip and William Ebling, who owned the entire block at the turn of the century. The street was completely empty in 1900. The first houses to go up on the block, numbers 321-23-25-27 East 100th Street, had been erected by Ebling in 1901; in 1903, another tenement went up, and in 1906, seven more tenements were completed, including number 311, bringing to twelve the number of houses which were standing when number 311 first began to stir with life.

The street itself, 650 feet long and 30 feet wide with a 15-foot-wide sidewalk on each side, was legally opened on October 7, 1872. On August 18, 1873, a permit to regulate and grade the street from the East River to Second Avenue had been given to S. Meyer Becker. Not until some twenty years later, however, on December 5, 1894, was the street finally approved for regulating and grading. A contract was drawn up on February 25, 1895, and work was completed on June 24, 1895, more than five years before the first tenement was to be erected.

The land on which East 100th Street was laid was once a farm area located immediately south of a huge tract of land purchased from the Tappan Indians in 1669 by John de la Montagne and known as Montayne's or Montagne's Point. It stretched from the East River to what eventually became Fifth Avenue, north to Harlem Creek, and south to some small creeks and marshes which separated the farmland from Montagne's Point.

The first record of ownership of the land which eventually became 100th Street between First and Second avenues was held in the name of Benjamin Benson, a farmer, in 1791. He gave the land to his son, Samson, who died in 1821 leaving the property to his daughter, Margaret, the wife of Andrew McGown. The land then became known as the Margaret McGown Farm, a title to which subsequent owners in this farm area were to refer for many generations.

The McGown farm consisted of over 125 acres of upland and about 100 acres of salt marsh and meadows, located mainly between the Eastern Post Road or Old Harlem River Bridge Road and the Harlem River, starting from an irregular line near 93rd Street and running to Harlem or Mill Creek near the line of 107th Street. The western boundary was near the spot where Madison Avenue was eventually built.

Before Margaret McGown died in 1851, she conveyed her property in seven parcels to various heirs. The last parcel, bounded by 99th to 103rd streets, East River to Third Avenue, had been given to her son, Samson Benson McGown, some years before.

Samson Benson McGown held the property until 1834, when he sold it to Charles Henry Hall. Five years later, there was a judgment against Hall by the Mechanics Bank of New York and a public auction was held to sell the land. From that year the property changed hands twenty-two times up to 1885, when the Ebling family took over all the land in the East 100th Street area. Included among the owners during this fifty-one-year span from 1834 was the New York Street Cleaning Association and the City of New York, in whose name the land was vested for an eleven-month period in 1871–72.

The Eblings sold the lot on which number 311 would eventually rise to Jacob Schattman on January 10, 1901, just before the New York State Legislature passed the historic measure known as the Tenement House Law. Three years later, in 1904, this law was to directly shape the plans for the house at 311 East 100th Street because it prescribed certain improved conditions under which all tenement houses were to be built after 1901. Because of its significance, all buildings erected after 1901 came to be known as "new-law" tenements as compared with the pre-1901 "old-law" tenements.

This significant state law, which also created the Tenement House Department, did not emerge as a major reform overnight, however. The period of tenement-house reform began in the 1850s. The first tenement-house commission had been appointed by the state legislature to work with civic groups, notably the Charity Organization Society, to study programs for the improvement of living conditions in New York City.

The settlement-house movement got underway in the 1880s and virtually all of the leaders in housing reform in the 1890s and early 1900s were persons with settlement backgrounds. Yet, during the period from 1894 until the monumental law of 1901 was passed, there probably was no greater force striving for tenement-house reform than Jacob A. Riis, an idealistic newspaper reporter whose graphic reports did more to call public attention to the evils of slum dwelling than any other stimulus. Riis' dramatic writings were to leave a lasting mark in the battle against the slum in New York.

Born in Denmark in 1848, Riis came to New York City in 1870. He worked as a police reporter first for the *New York Tribune* and then for the *Evening Sun* in 1877. He spent years in the notorious slums of Manhattan's Lower East Side. His books, *How the Other Half Lives, The Children of the Poor, The Battle with the Slum, The Ten Years War*, and others were widely read. The moral indignation Riis personally felt was so skillfully transmitted to the

citizens of New York that they, too, began to feel disturbed
about the presence of the slums around them.

In the early 1890s more than half the city's population
of 1.3 million people lived in old-law tenements. Riis' crusade
against what he termed the "galling bondage" of the tenement dwellers was touched off with the printing of *How the
Other Half Lives,* in which he warned that "public sentiment
has slumbered peacefully until some flagrant outrage of
decency and the health of the community aroused it to
noisy or ephemeral indignation, or until a dreaded epidemic
knocked at our door."

In his next book, *The Children of the Poor,* in 1892, Riis
further declared that "the story of inhuman packing of
human swarms, of bitter poverty and of landlord greed, of
darkness and squalor and misery, which these tenements
have to tell, is equalled, I suppose, nowhere in a civilized
land."

Recognizing that the tenement "has come to stay,"[2] however, Riis campaigned tirelessly during the 1890s for stringent laws to guarantee safe and healthy conditions in the
tenements.

Riis was the most celebrated housing reformer of his
time, but he was not the only one. Indeed, another crusader,
a man who far overshadowed Riis in national prominence,
was New York's Governor Theodore Roosevelt. Roosevelt
helped lead the way to the great tenement-house reforms
after the turn of the century. He appointed the New York
Tenement House Commission to investigate the problem of
slums on April 16, 1900. He named Robert W. de Forest and
Lawrence Veiller, officers of the Charity Organization
Society, the leading philanthropic group of the day, to serve
as chairman and secretary, respectively, of the special legislative commission.

In a public announcement calling for a thorough study of slums, Roosevelt declared:

Every wretched tenement that a city allows to exist revenges itself by being a hotbed of disease and pauperism. It tends steadily to lower the tone of our city life and of our social life. The present movement for better tenement houses is an effort to cut at the root of the diseases which eat at the body politic and the body social. No other reform is more desirable than this and none is more practicable.[3]

Veiller drew up the bill which authorized the Tenement House Commission to make a $10,000 study of tenement-house conditions. Although the bill had the support of Governor Roosevelt, it met some political resistance before both houses of the state legislature passed it.

"The building 'ring' in New York and the corrupt Tammany officials in the Buildings Department especially, were violently opposed to such legislation," Veiller recorded in his 1949 memoirs. "They had no desire to have the conditions disclosed and they especially feared an investigation by the Legislature as to how the building laws were being enforced."

Nevertheless, the bill creating the Commission was passed and signed by the governor, clearing the way for the legislative body to find out why eight previous private and government investigations since 1842 had failed to prevent the evils then present in the tenements.

The study was also to cover tenement-house legislation, a survey of tenement conditions in large American and European cities, enforcement of building laws, fires and fire escapes, and prostitution and "policy" or "numbers" rackets in the tenements.

Veiller aroused the immediate support of the press by

showing them some of the city's worst slums. "I conceived
the idea that it would be especially valuable to the cause,"
he said in 1949 in his memoirs, "if we could take some of the
leading editors—New York had more newspapers in those
days—around the tenement house districts and let them see
and *smell* [italics his] at first hand the actual conditions that
existed." This tour made such an impression on the news-
papermen, Veiller recalled, that ten years after the tour one
of the editors told him: "I haven't got the stink of those privy
vaults out of my nostrils yet."

Finally, after months of tireless research and travel, the
Commission recommended the creation of a new Tenement
House Department and a new tenement-house law. The
department was created on April 20, 1901.

Under the new law, a tenement house was defined as
"any house or building, or portion thereof, which is rented,
leased, let or hired out, to be occupied or is occupied as the
home or residence of three families or more living independ-
ently of each other, and doing their cooking upon the
premises."

The law was interpreted by city authorities as applying
to all multifamily dwellings of the day, including old-law
tenements and "apartment houses." The latter differed
physically from tenements in that they were more expensive
to build and apartments in them rented at a higher price
because they contained separate water closets, set bath tubs,
and separate kitchens. In addition, they were constructed
more elaborately with a more pretentious architectural finish
than the ordinary tenement house.[4]

The new law required alterations of buildings already
erected, including cutting 3-by-5-foot windows in 350,000
windowless rooms throughout the city known as the "black
holes of Calcutta." The law also prescribed far safer condi-

tions under which tenement houses would have to be built in the future (see Table 4, in the Appendix).

For example, the law prohibited owners from keeping cattle, horses, pigs, and goats in or on the same lot with tenements; the storage of combustible materials; and the erection of wooden buildings on the same lot with a tenement house. The law further ruled out the construction of windowless rooms, privies and sinks in back yards, air shafts without ventilation, water closets in public hallways, wooden buildings, rooms of less than 70 square feet of space; owners were prohibited from using more than 70 per cent of any one lot (75 per cent under the old law) for erection of a building; and the height of the building was limited to one and a half times the width of the street on which it stood.

The tenement-house law also required public halls to be provided with adequate lighting; cellar floors to be concrete and cellar ceilings to be plastered; fire-retarding of the halls, bakeries, and other dangerous business spaces in tenements; a flue in every apartment and water supply for every floor; janitor service and fire escapes of some kind accessible from every apartment.

Under the old law, many different types of tenement house had been erected. The more common "dumbbell" type was built on a lot 25 by 100 feet. It extended back 90 feet, leaving 10 feet in the rear for light and air. Each story above the ground floor consisted of two front apartments of four rooms each and two rear apartments of three rooms each. A four-room apartment consisted of a front room or parlor about 11 by 10 feet, followed by a kitchen somewhat smaller, opening onto a 28-inch-wide air shaft. Behind these were the bedrooms averaging 8 by 7 feet. They also depended on the air shaft for light and air. In the public hallway were two water closets—toilets—each shared by two families. Old-law tenements were considered to constitute serious fire hazards because of combustible construction, unsafe fire escapes, and an interior design that accelerated the spread of fire.

When the Tenement House Department officially opened for business on January 1, 1902, de Forest was the first commissioner of the department and Veiller was first deputy commissioner. Seth Low, the distinguished president of Columbia University, had just been elected Mayor of New York City in 1901 by defeating Tammany Hall and, as Veiller himself said later: "The grafters and corruptionists were being swept out of office and decent, clean and honest men put in their place. It was a wonderful opportunity for those of us who had counted on the enforcement of the law and the new piece of municipal machinery to bring about great reforms."[5]

Even with this favorable tide of events, however, bitter opposition began to mount the day the department opened. Owners of thousands of the city's tenements predicted the law would put an end to the building of new tenements in New York City. They failed even to see a glimmer of what lay ahead: within fifteen years so many new-law tenements would be built that 500,000 people, one third of the population of the city in 1916, would be living in buildings built under the new law. And, by 1931, nearly three million New Yorkers would be living in similarly built new-law tenements.

The law had received the firm support of the newspapers which helped to create it. Even before the results could be seen, the *New York Herald Tribune* declared on September 9, 1901, that the "considerable number" of plans filed for new-law tenements at the very outset "means nothing less than a revolution in the present housing conditions of New York, which means, of course, a radical betterment of our civic life." The newspaper even called the new houses "marvelous creations."

During the first eighteen months the law was in operation, plans were filed with the Tenement House Department for the erection of 1227 separate new buildings at an estimated cost of $40.6 million. More than 80 per cent of the new houses went up in Manhattan, including twenty-five buildings in the East Side area from 72nd to 110th streets.

The Tenement House Department's first report, released eighteen months after the department opened in 1902, emphasized even more dramatically the need for the city to replace the old-law tenements with the new-law buildings. In his report to Mayor Seth Low, Commissioner de Forest declared: "Some of the conditions which are found in these buildings surpass imagination. It does not seem possible that human beings can actually live under them and retain the least vestige of health." The story was best summed up by de Forest when he wrote:

The cleansing of the Augean stables was a small task compared to the cleansing of New York's 82,000 tenement houses, occupied by nearly three millions of people, representing every nationality and every degree of social scale.[6]

Fortunately for the builders and landlords who showed an interest in new construction, de Forest declared the new-law house "an unqualified success." He stated: "Not only have the apartments been rented in many cases before the buildings have been completed, but in some instances the apartments have been rented from the plans before the buildings were even started. Such a thing has never before been known to occur in tenement districts."[7]

(Five new-law tenements among the twenty-five in the East Side district were already standing on East 100th Street, housing nearly 500 people. The block was part of the old 12th Ward, a 6000-acre area which stretched from 86th Street north covering all of Manhattan Island from river to river.)

Commissioner de Forest was also enthusiastic about the architecture of the new-law tenement. The design, although hardly brilliant, marked a departure from the "dumbbell" and "railroad-flat" houses, so named from the shape of the building. The "dumbbell" was broad in the front and back and narrow in the middle, while in the "railroad flat" the rooms ran straight through from front to back. In the old types, more than half of the rooms, halls, and stairways were dark and unventilated.

A leading housing official of the day described the new buildings this way:

The new law tenement has brought with it some attention to the artistic appearance and ornamentation of the building on the part of the builders. It is at once distinguishable from its old type of neighbors by its light colored, fresh looking brick or stone work, its ample and even graceful fire escapes, balconies and its architectural featuring of cornices, doorways, window casings and other points of construction.[8]

Veiller and de Forest compiled enough evidence to write a book supporting the claim that the new law had "more than fulfilled the anticipation of the framers of the law." In their volume, *The Tenement House Problem*, the city's two top housing officials of their day stated that "sanitary, comfortable and decent houses are being rapidly built all over the city. Builders and owners who at first were bitterly opposed to the law are now outspoken in its approval and many of them state that the new houses are more remunerative than the old ones. The demand for the new accommodations on the part of the tenants has been overwhelming. Not only have the homes of the tenement dwellers been safeguarded, but also greater opportunities for personal cleanliness and for healthful recreation have been opened to them."

Many years later, in 1936, another housing expert, James

Ford, was to write in his memorable two-volume treatise, *Slums and Housing*, that the Tenement House Act of 1901 "is the most significant regulatory act in America's history of housing. It progressed far beyond its predecessors in its scope, precision and detail."[9]

In the fall of 1903, Tammany returned to power in New York and George B. McClellan, son of the Union general of the same name, was elected Mayor. As a result, de Forest and Veiller were both replaced and the Tenement House Department, according to Veiller, began to play a less important role in the city's development.

"It wasn't long," Veiller recalled many years later in his memoirs, "before it became evident that the department while continuing outwardly its forms and functions, was being wrecked and that not only gross negligence and inefficiency had developed but also gross corruption."[10] Despite Veiller's recollections, however, the department carried on its business and by the fall of 1904, a record number of applications for new-law tenements had been filed with it.

Included among the 498 plans filed in 1904 was one submitted October 5 by Louis Meryash and Albert London for a new-law tenement to be erected on Lot No. 9 on East 100th Street in Manhattan. Its address would be 311 East 100th Street. It was one of 143 buildings soon to be constructed between 72nd and 110th streets on the East Side and it was to be located in what was considered at the time a good part of the city, in close proximity to Central Park and the East River. It was an area of Manhattan, as yet untapped, where fresh air and natural scenery abounded and where Jewish and Italian immigrants, following the Irish and the Germans before them, had recently moved to realize their dreams of prosperity.

It was indeed a time of excitement in New York.[11] The

city was in a state of physical, political, and economic change. On the very day Messrs. London and Meryash went down to the Tenement House Department to file their plans, Mayor McClellan caused a sensation by removing the entire board of New York's Civil Service Commission from office. Three weeks later McClellan opened the "great subway" by riding the first train from the City Hall station underground to 147th Street. During the following winter, the big blizzard of 1905 hit New York, not so severely as the one in 1888, but badly enough to bring all surface travel to a complete halt.

Then followed one of the most notable events since the turn of the century—the famous life insurance investigation in New York which resulted in a marked change in the management of all insurance companies and the prosecution for illegal practices of several top insurance executives. The scandal jarred the entire city and brought on legislative reforms to prevent further corruption in the business.

In the fall of 1905, only months before the tenement at 311 East 100th Street was completed, Mayor McClellan withstood a vigorous election challenge from two opponents, including the redoubtable William Randolph Hearst. McClellan was re-elected. It was the first four-year term for a New York City mayor.

At the beginning of 1906, the construction boom in new-law tenements was picking up steam. There were then under construction and alteration some 5760 tenements throughout the city. Work was well under way on the 926 new-law tenements which were to be completed before the year's end, providing brand-new living quarters for 25,682 families or well over 100,000 persons.[12]

On April 19, 1906, the house at 311 East 100th Street was completed. The property, which had changed hands seven times since London and Meryash filed plans for it in 1904, was now owned by a couple named Hyman and Rose Levin. The Mitral Realty and Construction Company had just put the final touches on the building and it was, at last, ready to take its place among the fine new-law tenements on the emerging East 100th Street block.

Rents in the clean new structure averaged about $15 an apartment, rather high for tenement rentals considering apartments in the old-law buildings were still renting at $6 to $10 an apartment. The rents in this eastern section of Harlem were higher, too, than those in the Lower East Side, where the poorer families still lived. So desirable were the apartments in number 311 and the other new-law buildings on the block that nearly half the families who moved in paid 20 to 30 per cent of their monthly income for rent.[13]

In this young neighborhood the new-law tenements were occupied mostly by Jewish families who had moved from the Lower East Side. Nearly 50 per cent of these families had breadwinners who earned their livings through skilled, manual, or mechanical labor; less than 20 per cent performed unskilled labor; and the remaining 30 per cent worked at clerical or trade jobs or in the professions.[14]

Nearly half the immigrants to the rapidly growing East Harlem area came directly from the depths of the Lower East Side in the hope of starting anew in a fresher and safer atmosphere. About one third of the newcomers came from the nearby neighborhood and fewer than 10 per cent came directly from Europe.

They came for better-quality homes, to improve their social status, to be in more pleasant surroundings, and to give their children everything they did not have themselves. They came not so much because they were crowded out of the older districts of Manhattan as because they were young, enterprising, and in search of better conditions. They wanted to find roots in a new community which had both the assets and hopes of a newborn neighborhood on the threshold of a new life.

As the tenants moved into number 311 on that warm spring day in 1906, life around them held out real hope. The Union Settlement House nearby exerted a desirable influence and the City of New York itself had just completed two recreation centers near local public schools and had added a branch to the public library.

And so, with a flamboyant page of New York City's housing history immediately behind it, the house on East 100th Street opened at a time when the institution of the new-law tenement seemed to be the greatest innovation of the dawning twentieth century.

The new-law tenement, symbolized by 311 East 100th Street, was held up as the solution to the city's housing problems. It was the building that would forever mark the end of slums in New York City. It was the house of hope.

CHAPTER 5

A HOUSE DOOMED

*Neighborhood decay starts slowly, but
when it has gained momentum it has the
force of a hurricane or a great storm at sea.
It destroys values, it destroys families, it
destroys people.*

—Mayor Robert F. Wagner, 1960

THE HOUSE AT 311 East 100th Street, product of the great
housing reforms of the early 1900s, was an immediate success. But the test of time remained ahead for the new-law
tenement.

Would this building be a monument to intelligent and
practical planning in a city which had made so many blun-
ders in the construction of previous tenements?

So widespread had been the acceptance of new-law
tenements by 1906 that few people in New York City had
any premonition of the problems which would soon plague
these new structures. For one of them—the house at 311 East
100th Street—death began at birth.

The tenants of number 311 and their neighbors lacked a
cohesive community spirit—largely because they were new
to the area. Their greatest need was education and development of social and civic interests. East Harlem in these early
days was clearly a neighborhood which, after years of use

by immigrants who had been working their way up, was still in the process of forming a character, a spirit, an inner marrow of its own. It was still in a stage of transition and was not at all certain where it was headed, despite the golden promise of the new-law tenement.

There had been, as Jacob A. Riis reported in 1892, a small migration of poor Negroes to the East Side "with 100th Street as the center,"[1] but until the close of the nineteenth century the East Harlem section appeared to be a neighborhood on the rise. Hundreds of Italian and Jewish families, the heart of the great immigration of the 1880s, had moved up from the Mulberry Bend section of the Five Points in lower Manhattan and an Irish tenement section also flourished in East Harlem. There was a community feeling in those early days. People visited each other frequently. For the most part, they were honest, hardworking, and upright.

Historians of the day published this description of the neighborhood around East 100th Street:

From the East River to Fifth Ave. on all of these streets are tenements. Some are new and ornate, others of the ramshackle sort. In many places there are vacant lots. Between Ninety-sixth and Ninety-seventh Streets and First and Second Avenues are yards of the Second Avenue Division of the Metropolitan Street Railroad. From the foot of Ninety-second Street runs a ferry to Astoria, Long Island. . . . Scattered among the tenements are many small manufactures. All this region is "hill and dale," extremely steep hills and little valleys.[2]

During the first decade of the twentieth century, the expanding Negro population began to move into all parts of East Harlem. Up to then, Negroes had been confined in Manhattan to sections in the West 30s, the West 50s and the West 60s. The district sloping down to the Hudson River above West 59th Street was known locally as San Juan Hill to remind New Yorkers of the heroism of a Negro regiment which had fought valiantly in the Spanish-American War of 1898. These were the days when the clean, richly furnished brownstones of central Harlem were occupied by the white middle class and the more wealthy white families lived on Fifth and Lenox avenues. The newer buildings were grandiose, classically designed, symbols of wealth and prestige.

Gradually, the face of East Harlem began to change. More Negroes moved into the community in 1906 and 1907, after eviction from the site of the construction of Pennsylvania Station; they drifted into East Harlem because even then it was known as a harbor for anyone who was looking for a better life.

The new buildings on East 100th Street, meanwhile, were off to a fast start. Number 311 was operating at nearly 100-per-cent capacity. Hyman and Rose Levin, the couple who owned number 311 when it opened on April 19, 1906, sold it to a Benjamin Rosenfeld that same year. Little is known about these early landlords except that they were in the real estate business and obviously interested in making a profit from the sale of the touted new-law tenement. The pace on East 100th Street quickened. East Harlem continued to be built up and by 1908 East 100th Street was solidly lined with buildings. Over one quarter of all the blocks in Manhattan, in fact, were at least 90 per cent covered with houses by that time.[3]

So rapid was this expansion, however, that the city's short-staffed Tenement House Department could not effectively carry out all the duties mandated it by the tenement-house law of 1901. For one thing, the law had called for annual inspections of all tenements. It was now 1908, the law had been in effect for seven years, and the department had not completed its first "annual" inspections. The first report of the department, published in 1904, recorded the existence of nearly 362,000 dark interior rooms in the city at that time. Progress had been so slow that one critic of the city administration remarked in 1906: "At this rate, it will be 86 years before the work of lighting the interior rooms is completed."[4]

One of the reasons these thousands of dark rooms still existed three years after the new-law tenements came into vogue was that many of the old immigrant families were still trapped in them and could not afford to move anywhere else. It was not so easy as officials had hoped to get landlords to remodel their old-law buildings.

Since there were 82,000 old-law buildings to clean up, it was no wonder that Tenement House Commissioner Edmond J. Butler had little time to assign his men to check the condition of the new-law tenements. He had only twenty-eight inspectors to cover 44,000 old-law tenements in Brooklyn, Queens, and Richmond, a fact which in itself caused a scandal when the newspapers discovered it.

Subsequent to this disclosure, his department was given an additional $50,000 allocation by the Board of Estimate and Apportionment, but it was hardly enough to pay for all of the services and inspections required. It was also virtually impossible for the Tenement House Department to keep track of all new construction and, as a result, many so-called two-family houses were erected and after construction illegally converted to multiple dwellings.[5]

The department's work was hampered in other ways. Architects and owners had developed new schemes to get around the renovation of windowless rooms, and the program to remove sinks and privies from open yards was hindered by litigation in the courts. It was finally settled in United States Supreme Court in favor of the department, but in 1908 nearly 10,000 remained to be cleaned up in New York.

The property interests in the city had grown considerably since the sweeping innovations of 1901, and by now there was a well-organized resistance to the Tenement House Department's enforcement program. To counter this resistance, the city fathers voted Commissioner Butler a $169,000 budget increase—still not nearly enough to do the job. The department was directly responsible for living conditions in each of the city's 840,000 apartments.

Despite monetary and personnel problems, Commissioner Butler continued to sing the praise of the new-law tenement. The commissioner said apartments in the new buildings rented for $14 to $20 a month and "many persons of good standing . . . do not hesitate to take rooms in any new law tenement that might strike their fancy."[6]

The city appropriated more and more money in 1909 and 1910 to prosecute violations with more vigor but the Tenement House Department continued to lose more ground in its race against blight. The department had over 66,000 violations pending, many of which had been waiting for years to be removed.[7] The bureaucracy for which the department's successor, the Department of Buildings, was to become famous had already taken hold in these early days. In addition, the department's work became less and less effective as the politicians gained more control over its operations.

The year 1911 was marked by a national housing conference in New York which spurred renewed interest in the city's tenements. By 1912, reform took hold again and some of the original bite was restored to the tenement-house law through amendments. The Tenement House Department was rejuvenated under Commissioner John J. Murphy.

As New York entered 1913 the city was growing faster than anyone had ever imagined. Some 295,000 apartments, providing housing for 1.5 million people, had been erected under the provisions of the tenement-house law. The city made an attempt to help the Tenement House Department catch up with its responsiblilities by increasing its staff to 800 persons and its budget to $800,000.[8]

Even this dramatic splurge of manpower and money, however, fell short of the mark. The city's Commission on Congestion of Population, appointed in 1911, found an "overloading of land" in many sections, caused by poverty, a concentration of factories and offices, high price of land due to overuse, the city's failure to attract people to outlying boroughs and, by no means least important, lack of definite planning.[9] The report was a strong indictment of all past administrations for failing to plan properly. But it went un-heeded because it was politically impractical to implement its recommendations.

The tenements, old and new, became a growing problem in New York. There were already too many of them and too few city personnel to inspect, maintain, and safeguard them. An English builder of the day, Henry Vivian, recorded this impression of New York City's housing after a trip to the United States in 1913:

I came away impressed more than ever with the evils of the tenement system. No municipality or company ought to en-courage any further erection of tenements. You cannot get out of the individual a strength of character, an outlook and imagina-tion if the man or woman is brought up in a tenement. You do not see the effect in one generation. The workman comes into the great town from the country. He is living on the physical energy of the past. The effect is seen on the children. They lose the capacity of self-development and carving out their lives. . . . The tenement system tends to crush the strong character . . . you should not lose contact with fresh air and nature.[10]

By 1914, it was clear that the housing problems of an expanding metropolis could not be easily solved, at least by any one city agency. And, as the Tenement House Department began to falter again, its opponents stalked it for the kill. Efforts to abolish the department, however, were rebuffed. Commissions to govern building heights and districts were established and by 1916 a movement to make some order out of the planning chaos in New York got a firm foothold and led to the city's first zoning resolution.[11] This divided the city into three categories: residential, commercial, and unrestricted.

Mayor John Purroy Mitchel (1914–1917), a reformer, hailed the zoning law as an "opportunity now . . . to protect the city against the haphazard growth that has resulted in the collapse of districts and obliteration of values."[12]

The 311 East 100th Street tenement in Manhattan was not immediately affected by the new zoning law, but nearby on First Avenue and in the surrounding neighborhood small areas were designated for commercial development. The community was zoned mostly for business, and unrestricted. Only 11 per cent was marked for residential use, thus opening the door for East Harlem to become in later years a hodgepodge of small stores, light industry, and residential blight.

The building at 311 East 100th Street was sold and resold eight times after Benjamin Rosenfeld owned it in 1906.[13] By 1916 it was a far cry from the clean new home it had once been. The tenant turnover was high, a result of the rising influx of Negroes into the community, and the owners had failed to maintain it as dutifully as perhaps one landlord might have if he had lived in it himself for the first eleven years of its life.

During 1916, as the Negroes continued to move into East Harlem, it became apparent to housing officials that all of Harlem would surely become a black ghetto if the migration continued. There were already some 50,000 Negroes in

Harlem and there was no end in sight to the inward movement. The reason for the tremendous influx, according to a
leading housing journal of the day, *Housing Betterment*, lay
in the fact that "probably no race has been so neglected in
the providing of adequate housing accommodations as the
Negro, especially in our northern cities."[14]

The house at number 311 was caught in the crossfire of
population movement, occupation by low-income Negro
families, and an abundance of lodgers, all of which resulted
in considerable damage to the building. The house, like so
many others in the district, was also improperly maintained
and almost completely ignored by city inspectors who, by
this time, had begun systematically to turn their backs on
new-law tenement districts in their efforts to police the still-
bothersome old-law buildings.

The Negroes in New York were on the move, but a
grindingly tough road, studded with obstacles, lay ahead.
Property owners, determined to keep as many Negroes out
of previously all-white communities as possible, formed a
unique organization called Tenants Record, Inc., which
would investigate a prospective tenant's background within
twenty-four hours and provide all details to the landlord.
The object was to bar as many so-called disorderly or dis-
honest tenants from renting apartments as possible. The
plan was well received among real estate men of the day but
it failed as a practical operation because of the difficulty of
keeping track of tenants in a city as big as New York.[15]

During the bitter-cold winter of 1917–1918 when the
United States entered the great World War, a devastating
influenza epidemic broke out in the city. Complaints of no
heat piled up in the Tenement House Department from
tenants inside number 311 and thousands of other tenements.
A government embargo on building materials was called.

The housing shortage became acute. Construction of new-law tenements came to a virtual halt. Only 130 were erected in the entire city. The vacancy ratio from 1919 to 1923 was less than 1 per cent; not until 1927 did it rise to about 5 per cent, still low compared with other cities in America at the time. The apartment shortage grew so desperate that four simultaneous investigations were set into motion by city departments to find a solution. They were unanimous in their answers: no solution could be found until normal building activities resumed.

Capitalizing on the housing shortage, many landlords began to charge higher rentals. In 1914, rents in the tenements averaged $7 per room; in 1916, they were $8 per room, and by 1919 they had soared to $10 per room.[16] A five-story walk-up which had cost, for example, $32,500 to erect six years before was now up to $50,000 because of skyrocketing construction costs.

The tenement at 311 East 100th Street began to reflect the inflation which had taken hold in New York. Rents had risen from a low of $4 per room when the building opened in 1906 to a high of $10 per room in 1918. And the house was rapidly deteriorating because of the never-ending stream of people using it, including many who came to live with relatives in this time of crisis.

The "war housing problem" had become such an issue that it led one civic leader, Frederick L. Ackerman, to urge the city government to adopt a housing goal which, generations later, had still not been attained. It was a historic statement: "Let us write into our municipal program," Ackerman told a meeting of the Women's Municipal League on March 6, 1918, "this rational idea: a slumless city."[17]

The legislators and politicians of that day paid little attention to Ackerman. The call for action went unnoticed and the city's housing problems became more and more complex. As the low-rent housing shortage increased, the lawmakers passed stopgap measures which were to haunt the city many years later: more than 2000 single-family houses were permitted to be converted into boarding and lodging houses.

The rent profiteering which accompanied the doubling and tripling up of families in the city's tenements, however, was enough to disturb even the politicians. So the first rent-control law, passed by the state legislature in the fall of 1920, gave tenants the right to hold occupancy, prevented owners from charging "unfair" rents and gave the tenants opportunity for redress in the civil courts.

Finally, for the first time in the two decades new-law tenements had been rising all over the city, the question which ultimately would have to be asked came from the editors of the magazine *Housing Betterment* in 1920:

Can the type of tenement house which is now being constructed in New York City under the provisions of the tenement house law be materially improved? The type of house can be very much improved, if financial and economic considerations are not considered.[18]

The city remained on the defensive, however, and by 1924 the soundness of the new-law tenement was not even questioned. The fight against the old-law buildings still occupied all the time, money, and energy of the city government. The Charity Organization Society said in 1924 that one third of the city's population was still living in houses which lacked fire protection and hundreds of persons were still being killed by fires.[19]

The Committee on Plan and Survey appointed by Mayor James J. Walker in 1927 reported that more than two million people lived under "distressing conditions."[20]

And Walker himself, though popular with the people,

did not entirely escape blame. "The most flagrant ballyhoo artist in the field of housing was Mayor Walker," critics Paul Blanshard and Norman Thomas, the political reformers, were to write less than five years later. "His heart beats more noisily for the slum dwellers . . . than for any other part of the population. [But] . . . not a single brick was laid or a single plan for a house completed as a result of this prodigious volume of ballyhoo," they said.[21]

Governor Alfred E. Smith moved into the housing story in 1927 by appointing a temporary commission to examine and revise the tenement-house law. This was also the first year in which the number of new-law tenements outnumbered old-law tenements.

In 1929, Governor Smith's commission recommended a new state multiple-dwelling law. In the spring of 1929 it was passed by the state legislature, superseding the city's tenement-house law. The multiple-dwelling law of 1929 set higher standards than had the tenement-house law. It required separate toilets for each apartment, eliminating hall, cellar, and yard water closets. It called for fire retarding of public halls and stairways, prohibited vertical-ladder fire escapes, and set minimum requirements for light, air, space, plumbing, sanitation, fire prevention, and height to be observed in the construction of multiple dwellings.

A few months later, the stock market crash put a quietus on building construction for 1929 and for several years to come.

Meanwhile, the city's disease-breeding old-law tenements were being torn down so slowly that Tenement House Commissioner William F. Deegan was moved to write in his 1929 report to Mayor Walker: "Should the present rate of progress in this direction not be accelerated, the generation living about 2040 A.D. will see the destruction of the last of these buildings."[22]

In 1930, New York's governor, Franklin Delano Roosevelt, made this pledge:

We have a definite goal—the seeking within our lifetime of the day when we can say to the world: New York is a city without slums; New York is a city where every one of its 10 million people can have living conditions which guarantee to them air and light and sanitation.[23]

Roosevelt's dreams of perfection were well known to his constituents. He was a master politician who inevitably won his listeners over by striking the right note at the right time, producing vibrant responses in the hearts and minds of those who heard him. And by winning his listeners over he could then get his message across. An example of his technique shortly after he became governor is this passage from a speech to a group of prominent business men:

You have just cause for pride in what you have achieved—the tall, slim buildings standing clear against the sky. But too often around their feet cluster the squalid tenements that house the very poor—buildings that should have been destroyed years ago, not fit for habitation for any man, far less for the thousands of children that swarm up and down their creaking stairways.[24]

By this time, the old-law tenements had grown so unsightly and filthy that they constituted an alarming health hazard. Infant mortality, tuberculosis, diphtheria, venereal disease, and other plagues increased. The new-law houses, too, began to show obvious signs of decay, especially in the city's most crowded districts, like East 100th Street.

The first violation recorded in the Tenement House Department's file against 311 East 100th Street was dated March 21, 1921, a minor repair. But a decade later, on March 12, 1931, the department declared number 311 an "unsafe building" because a flue in the westerly court was corroded and the sheet-metal chimney above the roof was out of plumb. It was repaired and the violation dismissed on April 11. Nine days later, however, a fire broke out in one of the apartments, causing some damage, and still another violation was recorded against the building. These incidents, which occurred twenty-five years and fifteen owners after the house opened in 1906, were to mark the beginning of a list of unending violations placed against the house in ensuing decades. Herman and Rachel Zacharia, real estate operators, were the owners of number 311 in 1931 and they found themselves saddled with a building which had aged too quickly and a group of tenants who were beginning to voice their dissatisfaction.

The tenants complained and the Tenement House Department sent inspectors to the house. Within a few years, eighteen more violations were lodged against the building which by now was somewhat run-down. East 100th Street had become a haven for minority-group families from all over the city and number 311 had already surpassed its population capacity.

The families in number 311 and on the block at the outset of the great depression came mostly from Jewish and Italian backgrounds, but there were an increasing number of Negroes.[25] Most of the Negroes lived together in two of the buildings on the street. A large synagogue occupied the center of the block on the northern side. To the east on First Avenue, large produce markets had expanded and in the early waking hours each day on 100th Street the clippity-clop of horses' hoofs broke the silence as one horse and wagon after another pulled up to load up with fresh vegetables and fruits which would be distributed throughout Harlem.

To the west, under the Second Avenue El, the trolley cars ran continuously. The streets nearby were crowded with pushcarts piled high with food and delicacies for the Jewish and Italian families. During the day, the block was filled with children playing near the stoops, forewarned by their mothers not to leave the block. There were, even in those days, a few houses on the next block between Second and Third avenues which were rumored to be used for prostitution.

During the summers, the children would pile rubbish and straw in the middle of the block and light huge bonfires; and during the winters the snow was piled so high there were mountains of ice, turned black with dirt and garbage, down which the youngsters would slide every afternoon. People sat on the stoops or they brought chairs downstairs to sit on the sidewalk. In the worst heat they would even bring down their sheets and blankets and, if their fire escapes were occupied, sleep in the streets or on the roofs to get some fresh air. Many of the families from East 100th Street owned the small shops and stores in the neighborhood; a few owned the buildings in which they lived. The block was filled with the humanity of the tenements and, like a mirror, it reflected the pains and the joys of the thousands of people who lived in it.

Mrs. Jean Stern grew up in a tenement on East 100th Street just a few doors away from the house at number 311. She came to East 100th Street in 1923 at the age of sixteen with her family from the Lower East Side.

"We moved," she recalls, "because we wanted to be in a better neighborhood. I remember the horrible rats in Cherry Street. I was once terribly frightened by a big rat. I locked myself up in a room and screamed for hours.[26]

"We moved to East Harlem because we wanted to improve our lives. This was an advancement. There were lots of people on the street in those days, but they were cleaner. There weren't so many people just hanging around as there are now. There was very little crime or trouble of any kind.

"The house I lived in was very nice. We did not have heat but we had a toilet near the kitchen and a bathtub in the kitchen. It was a big improvement over the [old-law] tenement in which we had lived downtown. It was clean. Our house was nice and our apartment was clean. We had a tiled kitchen. We paid about $25 rent for the apartment. It was an exciting place to live, so many people, so many things going on. It was like a little town. Everybody was neighborly. Everybody's door was open. Every time I came home there was something happening. After I got out of high school I got some office work and when I'd come home I would take walks with my girl friends. We would walk over to Fifth Avenue and the park."

The area in which Mrs. Stern lived was known in those days as Little Italy because of its concentration of Italian families, especially on 97th Street between Second and Third avenues. But there were many other groups. The block between Second and Third on 101st Street, filled with Irish families, was nicknamed The Irish Block. East 100th Street, between First and Second avenues, was more of a mixture than these other blocks; it included Italians, Jews, Negroes, and a small number of Spanish-speaking families.

"I remember 100th Street," Mrs. Stern continues, "as a nice place to live compared to the Lower East Side. Downtown I remember a tiny bedroom, a little narrow room, a three-quarter sized bed in which my sister and I slept. It was a constant fight with cockroaches and mice. But after living on 100th Street for a while, I remember wanting to move from there, too. When we used to walk to the park—

Central Park—I remember feeling it was not fair. We would walk a few blocks west and we would find beautiful apartment houses. There was such a difference.

"It was so cold in our building during the winters. We had no heat at all. I remember my mother would light the gas oven and we'd all sit around the oven trying to get warm. I remember the Jewish holidays, too, the little boys with their caps. It was nice. But when the synagogue opened the kids in the neighborhood used to come around and mimic the Jewish boys. We were afraid of the Italian boys. There was more anti-Semitism than there is today.

"I had two brothers. One was not well. He worked on a produce wagon. My mother used to wake him up early. We all had to go out and make some money because my father, before he died, was sick and he couldn't work for many years. My mother had a tough life.

"The block slowly began to run down during the years we lived there. People became careless. They started to throw garbage into the street. It was slow degradation. The whole area began to change. I remember coming home during the winters, hungry and cold. That feeling of cold I will never forget. I often thought to myself: 'It's not fair. Some people suffer so much on this block while others, in different parts of the city, have more than they know what to do with.' The first time I met my husband I was ashamed to take him to my block. I was ashamed to have him see the block or the neighborhood because it was so poor. Once I invited him and just as we drove up to my house somebody threw a bag of garbage down and it hit his car. It was very embarrassing. Eventually we got married, right in the block, in the apartment where I had grown up."

Today, Mrs. Stern lives with her family in the middle-class Inwood section of Manhattan, a vast improvement over

East 100th Street and East Harlem. "When I saw the story in the newspapers about the street I said, 'Imagine, this was my block.' I was ashamed when I lived there and now I'm glad I'm not there any more."

By 1931, one of the biggest wholesale markets in the city—the Harlem Market between First Avenue and the East River—was flourishing around the corner from number 311. It was made up of dozens of small open shops which lined both sides of First Avenue between 99th and 110th streets. Vegetables, meat, and fruits were sold here. In the neighboring blocks of this mixed residential, business, and commercial district buyers could find carpet cleaners, glass and lumber stores, auto-repair shops, wrecking companies, bottle plants, stone cutters and coal, cement, stone, marble and gravel yards.

On both sides of 311 on 100th Street between First and Second avenues, local merchants ran three barber shops, four candy stores, two real estate offices, two drugstores, and two shoeshine shops.[27]

In addition, there were a Protestant church and a Jewish synagogue, both located on the north side of the block—within steps of number 311, as well as a private fraternity lodge. The block then was occupied mostly by Jewish, Italian, and Negro families, but there was also a scattering of British West Indian and Puerto Rican families. A little farther to the west, up and down Second Avenue and on the cross streets up to 110th, were dozens of food shops, wine suppliers, milk plants, pickle-makers, clothing stores, vegetable and fruit shops and, on many street corners, pushcarts carrying some of these foods and goods into the heart of each block.

This section of East Harlem was poor but it was teeming with commerce and industry. In 1932, the area between

99th and 129th streets, First and Third avenues, had a population of 100,000 people. They came from Italy, Austria, Hungary, Germany, Romania, Russia, Poland, and the urban centers of Great Britain and Ireland. A report of the East Harlem Health Center in 1932 declared: "Of late, the district has seen an influx of Porto Ricans [sic], humble folk willing to accept the most forlorn of living accommodations."[28]

As a result of the immigration from 1890 to the beginning of the 1930s, what had once been a leisurely village neighborhood was now a congested, poor, and handicapped neighborhood. Difficulties multipled. The Puerto Ricans constituted a health and welfare problem. Dwellings designed to hold four or five families were made to serve ten or twelve households. "If it were a matter of pride," a report of the East Harlem Health Center said, "East Harlem could boast of the most congested block in the world."[29]

The election of fiery Fiorello H. La Guardia as Mayor of New York City in 1933 raised the hopes of the tenants of number 311 and the other East Harlem tenements that a social point of view would be restored to City Hall. Hope was high for a brand-new program to eradicate slums.

La Guardia was assisted by other political leaders. This was the great era of Franklin Delano Roosevelt in Washington, Herbert H. Lehman in Albany, and La Guardia in City Hall. It was a time when the nation was in the depths of its worst economic crisis. To meet the emergency, federal, state, and local governments joined forces to launch the country's first massive public-housing program. It was eventually to provide decent apartments for half a million poor people in New York City. But in those early days, La Guardia had to battle a new and unexpected problem in New York: the decline of many neighborhoods which only a few decades before had been showplaces of community living.

Fifty acres of housing in Harlem alone were labeled

slums. And, by way of constant reminder, East Harlem—
where La Guardia made his home—was one of the fading
areas. Property values on East 100th Street dipped sharply
after the stock-market crash and, when East 100th Street
was evaluated by the new Fusion administration when it
took office on January 1, 1934, the city's tax records showed
that the house at number 311 was assessed at only $25,000.
(Twenty-eight years earlier, shortly after it was built, the
house had been valued by the city at $47,000.)

Inspired by an aroused citizenry, which included tenants
from his own East Harlem district, La Guardia ordered a
survey of all tenements in the city—for the first time since
1909. The Little Flower said he wanted two laws in particular enforced: fire retarding of public halls and separate
toilets in each apartment. The survey was to be carried out
by Tenement House Commissioner Langdon W. Post, a
popular official, who declared in 1934 that "the interest in
proper housing is as inherent in good government as is the
government's right to build roads and parks. The real estate
people know that unless government takes a hand, the slums
will remain."[30]

The Municipal Housing Authority was created in 1934
with Post as its first chairman. Meanwhile, La Guardia went
ahead with his promise to "tear down the old" by directing
his first deputy tenement-house commissioner, Harry M.
Prince, to issue "vacate orders" in cases where buildings
were endangering the health of tenants.

"These tenements should have been razed 30 years
ago,"[31] the angry La Guardia said of the 67,000 old-law
buildings still standing in 1934. But then something most
embarrassing happened to the La Guardia administration.
Post's survey of the firetraps throughout the city had found
that the city itself was the largest owner of the tenements.

But La Guardia answered back boldly: "We'll tear them down. Every last one of them!"[32] And, in an impromptu street-corner speech at an East Side rally on April 8, 1934, the Mayor declared:

There is nothing that I consider of greater importance at present than the vast program of housing for the City of New York. . . . I don't think for a moment it is going to be an easy thing to accomplish. There is a great deal of opposition and self-interest involved.[33]

Harking back to the same skyscraper theme Roosevelt had used four years earlier, La Guardia told the cheering crowd:

We call ours a great country. We boast of the progress that was made. We are proud to show off and boast of all we have accomplished. We meet distinguished visitors down the bay and proudly show them our skyscrapers, and there are so many skyscrapers that they can't see the housing problem. We can't boast of skyscrapers in New York City as long as we have our unsanitary firetraps.[34]

La Guardia laid down the ground rules and his commissioners were instructed to follow them. "The moment a house becomes unsafe," he told his housing officials, "no man has a right to keep it open."[35] Nearly 1500 buildings were closed in 1934–35. "We were in the depths of the depression and few owners had any money," recalls Harry M. Prince, former deputy commissioner of the Tenement House Department.[36] "Many of the tenements had fallen into the hands of savings banks because of defaults and mortgages. I took drastic action. I actually vacated and closed hundreds of buildings. In other cases, when we threatened them where it would hurt—in the pocketbooks—the landlords made the repairs," the seventy-six-year-old architect said in 1963.

The depression hit East Harlem hard. In the area around 311, a section unofficially bounded by East 99th and East 109th streets, Third Avenue, and the East River, 25 to 70 per cent of the dwellings were rated as "poor" by a Boys' Athletic League survey. Median rents on East 100th Street between First and Second avenues were $17.60 per month; the land and buildings were valued at only $8.75 per square foot.[37]

In 1935, for the first time, a local government body officially attributed one of the causes of slums to racial discrimination. The charge was contained in a report to Mayor La Guardia, from Morris L. Ernst, the liberal civil rights attorney, who served as chairman of a special commission to investigate conditions in Harlem.[38]

Ernst urged the administration to enact a law which would prohibit owners from discriminating on the basis of race, creed, or color. (Not until twenty-three years later did such a proposal become law.)

La Guardia used the findings of the Ernst report to persuade Governor Herbert H. Lehman to interest the state legislature in New York City's housing problems.

The Mayor appointed Nathan Straus, a civic leader and housing expert, special housing commissioner in 1935 to make a survey of European cities and to furnish a plan for the construction of low-rent housing in New York City. In assigning Straus his task, La Guardia resolutely declared:

If there's one thing I hope to do before my time is up it is to give the people of my city, in place of their tenements, decent, modern cheerful housing with a window in every room and a bit of sunshine in every window.[39]

Straus recommended that the city adopt comprehensive housing plans which would be financed, in large part, by the federal government. In his report to La Guardia, Straus wrote: "Piecemeal slum clearance, without a comprehensive plan or purpose, can never constitute a housing program." He charged that 1.5 million New Yorkers were living in crime-festering and disease-breeding tenements owned by men whose only motivation was to make profit.

Hearings opened in Washington in the spring of 1935 to consider a housing bill introduced by New York Senator Robert F. Wagner, Sr. The bill, when it passed two years later, eventually appropriated $800 million for a long-range national slum-clearance program.

New Yorkers flocked to the nation's capital to testify at the 1935 hearings. One mother told the committee:

While the city builds new monkey houses at the zoo, I live with my two boys and my invalid mother in a 40-year-old tenement. My third child died fighting pneumonia in a windowless bedroom.[40]

At the Congressional hearings, the slum dwellers of New York carried placards: OUR CHILDREN MAY BE THE NEXT TO BURN, DEATH TAKES NO HOLIDAY IN THE TENEMENTS. Eighty-seven men, women, and children had died in New York tenement fires during the preceding year and the anguished survivors wanted everybody in Congress to know about it. Over the years, more than 1300 people had died in tenement fires.

Meanwhile, Commissioner Post optimistically predicted that the city's slums could be cleared. He placed a price tag of $1.5 billion on his plan and said the money could come from the federal government at the rate of $150 million a year over a ten-year span.

"We have the resources, we have the materials, we have the skilled workers," said Post. "We have everything which is required to build homes except the whiplash of public opinion which must crack before things start moving." He warned that the Harlem riots of 1935 were not race riots, were not Communist-inspired riots. "The Harlem riot was a slum riot," he said simply. "As long as we condemn vast numbers of our people to live in squalor, in filth and degradation, just so long will we have a perpetual threat to the peace of the community."[41]

On December 10, 1935, a Tenement House Department inspector came to the house at 311 East 100th Street during a routine stop on what had become known as the "Post cycle survey." Up to that time, beginning in 1921, the department had recorded twenty-two violations against the house. The inspector, weeks behind in his schedule and pressed by his superiors, gave the building a cursory look and marked down two more violations. Two rainleaders were missing.

The following year, the city's crackdown spread to more and more tenements. In December, a group of savings banks which owned or controlled some 2000 old-law tenements, fearing criminal liability under the terms of the multiple-dwelling law (which defined owners as agents, lessees, trustees, or any person in charge of the property), decided simultaneously to close the buildings.

Hundreds of helpless families were served with notices to vacate and thousands more were threatened with the necessity of moving in the middle of winter on short notice. This constituted a genuine emergency. La Guardia stepped in with a compromise to halt the evictions. A six-month exemption from criminal liability was allowed owners who signed an agreement with the Tenement House Department that they would either vacate their buildings or bring them into compliance with the law within a period of six months after the agreement was signed. The majority of owners, almost all banks, signed the agreement.

But more than 500 owners filed to vacate their buildings, leaving thousands of families without homes. Coupled with the existing shortage of apartments, it soon became apparent that, despite La Guardia's alert tactics, the housing shortage would grow worse if no new houses were erected to replace those found to be uninhabitable. Less new housing had been built in the seven years since the stock-market crash than was constructed in a single year before that time. While private enterprise had provided some new dwellings for the well-to-do, none at all were built for those with small or modest incomes. Only people who could pay $14 per room per month or more could afford the new homes.

The La Guardia administration made still another move to forestall disaster in the slums. It passed the "prior lien law," an amendment to the Multiple Dwelling Law. This amendment enabled the city to take over neglected slums, make repairs on the tenements and charge the cost as a lien against the property prior to all other liens and mortgages except taxes. Under the terms of the law, a $500,000 revolving fund was created in August 1937. On paper, the plan seemed a good one. But it ran into considerable practical difficulties. Deputy Tenement House Commissioner Prince, who was in charge of the prior-lien program in 1937, recalls:

I had the money to make loans. The department made the repairs. We went in and did the jobs and I got the consent of the owner in every case. But they took us to court and the law was declared unconstitutional on the grounds that an owner was being deprived of his constitutional rights and had not received due notice.[42]

The results of the Post cycle survey brought further discouragement to city officials. In his final report as Tenement House Commissioner, Post regretfully told Mayor La Guardia on December 31, 1937:

The picture thus far obtained from this survey can only be
described as showing an amazing neglect of decent standards of
health and safety over a period of many years. Against this
gloomy background of almost universal violations of the law, the
problem of enforcement appears as a genuinely herculean
task. . . .[43]

With this valedictory, the Tenement House Department
passed out of existence thirty-six years after its inception.
Under the terms of the new city charter, it was merged with
the old Department of Buildings and all five boroughs were
combined under the jurisdiction of the newly created Department of Housing and Buildings. While 1937 marked the
end of the Tenement House Department and the beginning
of a new, more streamlined agency to cope with tenement
violations, it was also the beginning of long-range planning
by city government to eliminate slum areas in the present
and prevent others from forming in the future.

Responding to President Roosevelt's historic proclamation in his second inaugural at the beginning of 1937—"I see
one-third of a nation ill housed, ill clad, ill nourished"—New
York officials began to examine their own city that year.
Mayor La Guardia's Committee on City Planning announced
the results of a series of city-wide studies which it had been
conducting under the auspices of the federally sponsored
Works Progress Administration.

One study showed that East 100th Street between First
and Second avenues housed 2460 residents and lay in a section "destined to provide homes for a large number of low-
income families."[44]

The report described many of the out-of-date old-law
buildings in the area as "economically useless." Even the
newer houses, such as 311 East 100th Street, were viewed as
"hedged in by other shabby tenements" and therefore almost
lost in a neighborhood which was in a "critical condition of

instability that cannot easily be remedied." In conclusion, the report recommended demolition and rebuilding on a large scale—by whole blocks—including the block on which number 311 stood.

On March 10, 1937, for the second time in six years, the Tenement House Department, in response to a complaint, sent an inspector to the house at 311 East 100th Street; he found it an "unsafe building." Brickwork on the front wall and portions of the main cornice were found to be "loose and defective." The violations were dismissed less than a month later when repairs were completed.

Another milestone in 1937 was the creation of the United States Housing Authority. The new agency was empowered to provide funds for local municipalities, including the New York City Housing Authority, to build new homes for 100,000 families throughout the nation.

Federal officials said that the supply of decent homes in the United States was below the estimated normal. Low-rent public housing was hailed as the answer and President Roosevelt himself was instrumental in getting the federal housing legislation passed.

The low-rent housing situation in New York City was critical. Population continued to increase; buildings continued to depreciate. Public hearings on the issue, however, produced the same stalemate that had tied up the city's politicians for so many years in the past. The real estate interests said taxes on real estate were unreasonable and they argued against any control over housing construction; tenants' groups, led by the newly formed Citizens' Housing Council, favored the declaration of an emergency by the Mayor or the state legislature and called for immediate public-housing legislation as the only logical solution to the problem of low-rent apartments.

The city and state governments contributed to the housing problem themselves. A pattern of subsidizing slums, which was to be continued for many decades, emerged as the city and state paid rentals for the 145,000 families who were receiving relief—30 per cent of the families in the old-law tenements.

More public hearings to discuss housing were held in April 1938 by the City Council. It issued a report which said that "slum clearance has been productive of more talk and less action than any other of our modern problems." The Council concluded that the city must have the power to condemn private property "in the public interest" and to rebuild slum areas with low-rent housing.[45]

Other groups were growing more restless. The Charity Organization Society urged that the newly appointed commissioner of the Department of Housing and Buildings, Alfred Rheinstein, be given more money to hire more inspectors to enforce the new building code, adopted in 1938. The city's rapidly growing Citizens' Housing and Planning Council warned that "the New York of today is miserably inadequate as a mechanism geared to perform its functions."[46]

And so the warning flags were up all over the city. The 1938 city charter established the City Planning Commission to develop the New York of the future, but meanwhile the slums were spreading so fast that even Mayor La Guardia was led sadly to admit one Sunday on one of the famous radio programs in which he spoke directly to the public about the affairs of New York:

I must confess to you we have some 30,000 tenement buildings that are inhabited today that are in violation of law, that disregard every provision of the Multiple Dwelling Law as to safety and health, air and ventilation. And yet, I dare not vacate those houses. I cannot order them demolished. Why? Because there's no place that the people living in these houses can move to. There are no homes where these people can find apartments within the rents they can afford to pay.

East Harlem, La Guardia's own home district, was one of those which had become badly blighted. An area to which Italians had come thirty years before, it was now becoming a refuge for the newest migrants—the Puerto Ricans.

The section around 311 East 100th Street was one of the most densely populated areas of Manhattan and housed the largest single colony of Italian-Americans in the country. The 1939 Citizens' Housing and Planning Council labeled this neighborhood "the worst slum area in northern Manhattan, overtaken by dilapidation and deterioration."[47] The CHPC also disclosed that it found one third of the real estate parcels in East Harlem tax-delinquent, one third of the stores vacant, and the population living under "dangerously overcrowded conditions."[48] Property values ranged from $5 to $10.25 per square foot.

Toward the close of 1939, East Harlem social, civic, and financial leaders met to discuss their community's future with Lawrence M. Orton, a member of the City Planning Commission. Among those attending the meeting were Helen M. Harris, a resident for ten years and chairman of the East Harlem Council for Social Agencies, and James Felt, president of the New York Real Estate Board, who years later was to become the chairman of the City Planning Commission.

The group voted unanimously to support the rezoning of East Harlem, encouraged by pledges of cooperation from the Bowery Savings Bank and the Central Savings Bank and other business and finance leaders. It was also suggested that an architectural competition be held for the future development of the area to stimulate the investment of both public and private capital in East Harlem. A tentative area around the house at number 311, bounded by 96th and 106th streets, East River Drive, and Fifth Avenue, was selected for planning purposes.

By 1940, there had been just enough meetings and reports drawn up on the rejuvenation of East Harlem to lead the Citizens' Housing and Planning Council in one of its news bulletins to report optimistically that "today, as never before, the housing movement is enlisting a union of constructive forces strong enough and sane enough to make ultimate victory seem certain in the battle with blight and the slum."[49]

The chances for victory seemed good. There was a 10.8 per cent vacancy ratio in Manhattan, permitting demolition of old slums without causing too much of a relocation problem. One plan for the easternmost district of East Harlem—which included 311 East 100th Street—was submitted by the Savings Bank Association of New York. The plan urged the complete demolition of nearly fifty blocks along the East River early in 1940. The savings banks, which had a stake of nearly $10 million in East Harlem in the form of mortgages on real estate at the time, recommended erecting new housing on the East River and zoning the inland section for business. The other half of East Harlem, they said, should be completely renovated.[50]

Even the courts, which through the past decades had been lenient with chronic housing violators, began to make their power felt. Thomas E. Dewey, the shrewd New York County district attorney, had obtained the indictment of several owners of buildings two years earlier; in early 1940, the head of a firm that owned a building in which four persons lost their lives in a fire was found guilty of first-degree and second-degree manslaughter. This was the first

conviction of its kind and caused the Citizens' Housing and
Planning Council to comment pointedly: "Perhaps we are
approaching the time when it will be just as dangerous to
sell death in a dwelling as it now is to sell death in spoiled
meat."[51]

The City Planning Commission designated East Harlem
early in 1941 as one of thirteen "seriously depressed" neighborhoods throughout the city which were "ripe for redevelopment." A 171-city-block area, which included 311 East 100th
Street, was designated as "an economic loss to property
owners and a financial burden to the city and taxpayers."

Conditions were so bad in 1941 in number 311 that less
than half the apartments were rented. The building was dirty
and in need of repair. It was immediately obvious to any
passerby that this and other tenements on the block needed
some attention.

Before the city could activate any renewal plans, however, the fateful December of 1941 arrived. The United
States was plunged into World War II and New York City's
slum woes, no matter how distressing, were forced into the
background.

During the war, the building industry slowed down and
with the second major housing shortage in the biggest city
in the world since the turn of the century, rents began to
climb. The federal government imposed rent control on all
housing in 1943. The New York City Buildings Department,
required by law to force owners to maintain their properties
during the long construction drought, stepped up inspections. The housing situation grew so bad that Stanley M.
Isaacs, an outspoken City Councilman, warned that it "may
well prove to be a menace to the well-being of New York
and its people."[52]

Several fires in the house at number 311 resulted in violations early in 1944. On February 29, the department ruled the house an "unsafe building" for the third time in thirteen years because, as a result of one of the fires, the plaster partitions and ceilings and wooden beams and doors on the first floor were burnt out. The owning corporation was sent a warning to make repairs. A reinspection was made on March 29 and two more violations lodged against the house, bringing to thirty-six the total number of building and health violations recorded against it since 1921. Still another fire broke out in the building on August 16, 1945, two days after the Japanese surrendered.

By the end of the war, East Harlem had become the concern not only of social workers, planning officials, and politicians, but once again it attracted the attention of financial circles as a potential investment source. A study released by Earl B. Schwulst, chairman of the Bowery Savings Bank and head of the Manhattan Development Committee, said East Harlem offered opportunities for middle-income family housing at a 6.5 per cent over-all return to institutional investors.[53] The committee represented banks, insurance companies, architects, and planning experts. They proposed redevelopment of a 642-acre area starting at 96th Street and stretching northward as a venture to cost more than $70 million.

It was obvious that real estate values had dropped to the point at which it might indeed be profitable to invest here. Using 311 East 100th Street, as a guideline, for example, a prospective buyer would have found the land assessed at $7,200 and the building itself at only $19,800, compared to $10,500 for the land and $48,000 for the house two decades earlier.

The Manhattan Development Committee's plan called for the redevelopment of the area in one operation by creating a giant housing development in superblocks—the project would close off 100 acres of city streets—which would be serviced by the redevelopment company and therefore lower the cost of municipal services for the area. Garden apartments and trees would replace all the tenements on East 100th Street between First and Second avenues, according to the plan.

The grandiose scheme never got further than the discussion stages. But it represented the type of thinking prevalent in the city in the fall of 1945 when New York, caught in a record apartment shortage, was faced with a new housing crisis. Thirty thousand families were already doubled up and 500 discharged servicemen in search of new homes were returning to the city daily.

To meet the emergency, the Citizens' Housing and Planning Council of New York proposed temporary housing be erected in outlying boroughs to fill urgent needs. It also called for a permanent building program with federal, state, and city support, and for the continuation of rent control on existing housing until the emergency was over.

Robert Moses, who had already earned his reputation as the most forceful figure in public works in New York City, called for more subsidized public housing to meet the needs of low-income families, but only as a part of a larger citywide housing program which should include middle- and luxury-priced apartments. And, because of the difficulty of any agency to acquire large parcels of land at reasonable costs, he said the power of eminent domain (the right of a government to buy property for public use) was the "only salvation."[54]

Moses also urged rehabilitation of tenements: "The average brick tenement has a good deal of life left," he declared, "and people can live decently in crowded quarters if they have heat, hot water, bathrooms, fire escapes, as well as light and gas."[55]

Meanwhile, there were fewer and fewer vacant apartments throughout the city. Where vacancies existed, as in such substandard neighborhoods as East Harlem, the racial and national characteristics of the neighborhood were considered drawbacks. Whites hesitated to move into predominately Negro and Puerto Rican areas. And returning servicemen, even though they may have been reared in a blighted section of the city, now wanted "something better."

In 1945, the Citizens' Housing and Planning Council estimated that New York's slums could be cleared by 1955 at a cost of $1.68 billion. Charles Abrams, an attorney and housing expert, in a study made for the Citizens' Housing and Planning Council, called for the city to purchase all of the slum areas and have them redeveloped by private and public enterprise under a ten-year comprehensive master plan which would use state and federal aid.

While these long-range plans were being discussed, Moses launched a major rebuilding program of his own. As City Construction Coordinator, he undertook many new projects—like the construction of New York (now Kennedy) International Airport—which caused the dislocation of many families. Public criticism mounted. It was said that public improvements by him were intensifying the housing shortage. But Moses merely swept his critics aside with this now-famous comment at a house-moving ceremony at Idlewild in the spring of 1946:

You can't make an omelet without cracking eggs. In every big public improvement some people must be discommoded. Under plans which we have, thousands of people have to be moved, but no one will be put into the street.[56]

These were challenging words, but they represented a direct call for action in the city's lagging housing program.

The New York Times declared in an editorial on June 28, 1946:

New York City's housing program has bogged down. No one can dispute this conclusion of a committee of the Citizens' Housing and Planning Council.

The bandwagon for better housing was launched once again and in 1947 Robert F. Wagner, Jr., then commissioner of the Department of Housing and Buildings, told the city's real estate leaders that they must cooperate in solving the housing emergency.[57]

Wagner's proposal? More new housing. In 1948, as chairman of the City Planning Commission, he predicted: "Unless there is a substantial increase in the volume of construction, the housing shortage will continue without end."[58]

During the ten-year span from 1940 to 1950, the federal census later showed, East Harlem's population grew 8 per cent—to 246,000 persons. But the number of apartments remained substantially the same. Result: overcrowding unparalleled in East Harlem's history.

A study by city planner Edwin Friedman showed a steady decline in land values for the 1940–50 period in the absence of any redevelopment other than public housing. "Private investment," Friedman declared, "has proven itself unable or unwilling to attack the housing problem in East Harlem."[59]

In June 1950—only days before the Korean War erupted —the city administration made another try at saving East Harlem. At a public hearing of the City Planning Commission, chairman Jerry Finkelstein said the city was "vitally concerned" with East Harlem's future. The area was designated for clearance, redevelopment, and low-rent housing.

At this point in East Harlem's history, the Citizens' Housing and Planning Council issued a statement that would prove of historic future significance:

What will East Harlem be like in 1975? Will it be an area with wide thoroughfares, parks, adequate schools, health and community services, and housing for various income groups and for people of different races? Will it be an uncoordinated collection of community facilities and of public housing projects tenanted by low-income Negroes and Puerto Ricans?[60]

The CHPC answered its own question by predicting that if this community were permeated with "haphazard improvements, a neighborhood will be created which will look like pieces of a jig-saw puzzle that just don't fit together." It charged that the new low-rent housing was perpetuating the same predominant Negro and Puerto Rican racial composition. Warning that time was running out, the statement added:

Numerous studies have been made of the future of East Harlem by financial groups, builders and others interested in the potentialities of the area. Nothing resulted. The issue is crucial now because of the increased pace of public housing activity. . . . There is still time to plan the rebuilding of East Harlem. The opportunity must not go by default.[61]

The CHPC said at least part of East Harlem could be redeveloped into desirable blocks which would house families of different income levels and different ethnic backgrounds. It recommended dividing the entire section around number 311, from 96th to 125th Street and from Fifth Avenue to the East River Drive, into a series of districts, using a superblock pattern so that certain streets would be closed permanently. Among the districts, it suggested one from East 99th to East 103rd streets and Second Avenue to the East River which could be used "as an initial attempt to attract private funds for housing developments" and for some public housing.

In order for the city to make land available to private investors at an attractive price, the CHPC urged the city to take advantage of the first part of the National Housing Act passed by Congress in 1949, establishing a national housing policy. Title I of the National Housing Act made it possible for municipalities across the nation to condemn blighted land and to sell it to private redevelopers at considerable savings. The federal government paid for two thirds of the land costs and the city paid for one third. The developer paid for the property on the land and for the cost of clearing the property as well as erecting the new housing. In years to come, the administration of Title I housing in New York City was to face bitter public criticism and eventually many of its procedures were changed. At this time, however, it appeared to the CHPC the best answer to East Harlem's housing dilemma.

In the fall of 1950, a group of real estate men who called themselves the Organization of Realty Association of Harlem, Inc., announced they wanted to "promote and encourage investment of capital in Harlem property."[62] Headed by Edward L. Sulzberger, who was to become a partner in the firm of Nassoit-Sulzberger as well as chairman of the Metropolitan Fair Rent Committee, the group consisted of owners of realty-savings banks and mortgage investors. What happened to the plan? "It never materialized," Sulzberger said in 1963. "I couldn't get the owners to cooperate. It never got off the ground. Personally, I felt it was too dangerous to pursue it myself."[63]

The following year, the issue of whether East Harlem might become a permanent ghetto for Negroes and Puerto Ricans became a full-blown political controversy. Robert F.

Wagner, then borough president of Manhattan, said the future of East Harlem was a "problem for the entire city, not just the people who live there." He charged that more than racial tensions and the antisocial results of segregation were involved, specifically that the cost of maintaining the area is reflected in every New Yorker's tax bills and, like every blighted area, East Harlem was "claiming a lion's share of the city's funds for public services and returning a jackal's portion in revenue." The borough president likened the community to an "old jalopy that should be consigned to the junkyard." Referring to the everyday life in East Harlem, Wagner added:

The old neighborhood is dying and the death struggle is not pleasant. There is still some life on the avenues. The stores are almost solidly occupied . . . here and there the modern front of a supermarket stands out. For the most part, however, the neighborhood is tarnished 1906.[64]

There, in one phrase, Wagner expressed the story of 311 East 100th Street. Erected in 1906, it had indeed become tarnished. Wagner brought the picture of a dying neighborhood into even clearer focus when he said:

If you look closely at the ground, and if you have a feeling of what ground ought to be, you will want to close your eyes. There is no trace of soil. The ground is a mixture of ashes, cinders, rubble, broken glass, bottle tops and garbage. This is where the children play.[65]

Wagner conceded that the city did not have any co-ordinated plan for the East Harlem area. He said the city's Housing Authority was "operating strictly on its own" and that the Slum Clearance Committee, headed by Robert Moses, had failed to list East Harlem as an area to be re-developed, despite the fact that the City Planning Commission had designated it as one of forty-three sites that should be cleared. "These two important agencies," Wagner said, "have not tackled East Harlem. No studies are underway; no plans have been drafted. Nothing has been done to interest private investors and to revitalize the area."[66]

The borough president, who three years later was to become the twelfth Mayor of New York City since the modern crusade against the slum in New York began at the turn of the century, said the Korean national defense emergency would cause "enforced delay" of city programs because of growing shortages of construction materials. Nevertheless, he advocated drawing up "more comprehensive blueprints" for the future. "It is not too late to change the pattern," he declared, "and make East Harlem a good example of American living. But the opportunity is slipping fast. . . . East Harlem could become the nation's most dramatic example of replanning for decent, democratic living."[67]

Less than a month after Wagner delivered this significant speech, Mayor Vincent R. Impellitteri was asked by Ira S. Robbins, then executive vice-president of the Citizens' Housing and Planning Council, to take steps to implement the proposed renewal plan for East Harlem.[68] A flurry of letters between Robbins and Mayor Impellitteri continued through March 1952, with no apparent results. The Mayor refused to meet with representatives of the CHPC and told Robbins that "we are doing everything possible . . . to improve living conditions in East Harlem."[69]

But on East 100th Street, the East Harlem Protestant Parish was uncovering some of the worst slum conditions ever seen in New York. During the winter of 1952, the church established three store-front housing clinics. The church distributed more than 1000 questionnaires among local tenants and discovered that hundreds had illegally paid

an average of $500 apiece for the privilege of moving into
their dingy apartments. The parish found more violations on
East 100th Street between First and Second avenues than
in any other block. The "worst block" was beginning to
acquire its dubious reputation.

Mayor Impellitteri, meanwhile, was publicly lauding the
city's new Title I housing program, even though it had no
plans for entering the East Harlem section. "This to us is a
wonderful development," the Mayor declared at ground-
breaking ceremonies for one of the new Title I projects in
mid-1952.

Robert Moses, whose job it was to carry out the new
Title I program, agreed that it was the best answer yet
devised to lick the remaining slums. He warned in 1953
that "we have still, in the heart of the city, some very bad
substandard slum conditions."

On May 2, 1953, the City Planning Commission issued a
revised "master plan" for slum clearance in Manhattan.[70]
East Harlem was among the twenty "unsafe, unsanitary,
improperly planned and deteriorated" sections designated
for redevelopment. The new plan superseded an earlier one
in 1949 and described as "urgent" the need for replanning
the residential development of the twenty Manhattan districts. The 311 East 100th Street house stood right in the
middle of a section of East Harlem bounded by 99th–102nd
streets, First to Second avenues which was neatly marked
off for clearance to make room for a new 1600-apartment,
$24.3 million public-housing project to be called East River
Houses Extension or East River Houses II (East River
Houses I, an older project, was located a few blocks to the
north).

It soon became apparent to City Housing Authority
officials that the money for the proposed East River Houses

II project would be slow in coming and that, even if the money did eventually arrive, erection of such a giant project would cause a major relocation problem because of the high population density around East 100th Street. But it wasn't until 1956 that the City Housing Authority unofficially dropped the proposed East River Houses II plan.

At the outset of the Korean War, one in five New Yorkers was living in a slum. Many landlords, unable or unwilling to face increasing maintenance costs, had permitted their buildings to slip into a state of disrepair. Some, resentful of continued rent controls in New York, merely collected their rents and put little back into their houses. Once again, like an old tune on a new record player, the cries of anguished tenants were heard from the hidden rooms in dilapidated homes throughout the city's 9000 acres of slums.

Even though the city administration had awakened to the need for new housing, the city's tenants now feared mass evictions if such a program were carried out. City Councilman Isaacs, appearing as spokesman for the United Neighborhood Houses, the city-wide settlement-house organization, and for the State Committee against Discrimination in Housing, told a crowded, noisy Board of Estimate hearing attended by more than 1000 persons on January 26, 1954, that 40,000 families would be thrown from their homes with no place to go if the city went ahead with its middle-income and low-income housing projects.[71]

Isaacs, who was minority leader of the City Council for twenty-two years and hailed as the "conscience of the City Council" at his death in 1962, charged that the city's relocation program had been handled "appallingly" in some areas. He urged the creation of a relocation bureau, an idea that did not reach fruition until eight years later, just before he died. He said that "many lives are being ruined" by the city's

haphazard relocation methods and that if President Dwight
D. Eisenhower were aware of the thousands of people being
displaced, he would withhold funds from the federal government earmarked for New York City's urban renewal program.

The city's housing policies came under further attack
two months later, in March 1954, when the City Club of
New York, an alert civic group, accused city officials of
condoning racial discrimination. To meet the relocation
problem, the club suggested using vacant land in Queens for
new housing. The only reason this solution had not been
adopted before, the club said, "is that other city officials have
gone along with Queens politicians who don't want non-
whites and Puerto Ricans in their borough." The City Club
called this exclusion policy "a scandal of the first magni-
tude."[72]

On May 6, 1954, Mayor Wagner joined the mayors of
fifteen other cities in a joint appeal for more public housing
from Congress. Later that same year, the Mayor appointed
more than 100 civic, business, and religious leaders to the
Mayor's Committee for Better Housing. He said he wanted
the city to have a "fresh viewpoint" on the problem.

Early in 1955, the Mayor underscored the importance of
housing in the "workable program" for housing he was
required to submit to the federal government's Housing and
Home Finance Agency. In the program, the Mayor said:
"We cannot solve our housing problem in New York until we
solve the problem of our slums."[73]

In the summer of 1955, the Mayor's Committee for Better
Housing came in with its report, which recommended sixty-
three steps toward better housing—including a new concept
of "spot clearance" of slum pockets as compared with the
old blockbusting technique.

An example of a neighborhood in need of "spot clearance" in 1955 was the section around number 311, an area bounded by East 99th and East 104th streets between First and Second avenues. Nearly all of the buildings in the area were thirty-six years old or more and 50 per cent of the houses were classified as dilapidated or overcrowded.

The median income level of the people living in this district was a lowly $1992 per family per year and several thousand families received aid for their dependent children from the Welfare Department. There were few medical facilities—except the clinic on the ground floor back of 311 East 100th Street, which Dr. Berle supervised.

The future of 311 East 100th Street and its environs lay in the laps of the city planners in the late 1950s but, ignoring previous warnings, the City Housing Authority chose to pump more public housing into the area and turned it into a low-rent Negro and Puerto Rican ghetto. In 1957 the Housing Authority embarked on a giant slum-clearance program which would eventually erect fifteen projects providing homes for 62,000 persons.

The new buildings, however, did replace many old tenements; blocks of filth and darkness were ripped out, letting in sunlight and air. Many slums were removed. Except, of course, 311 East 100th Street and it neighbors.

The Mayor's vaunted Slum Clearance Committee, headed by Robert Moses, began to encounter some major trouble about this time for failing to clear slums like number 311. The Council for Better Housing, a private civic organization, in a scathing report issued on October 31, 1957, characterized the Committee's work as filled with "scandal, haphazardness, and heartlessness." The report charged that the Committee "has not cleared slums. Rather, it has merely shifted slums."[74]

Even Mayor Wagner sensed the near-futility of the battle against the slum. In a rare moment of complete candor one winter day in 1958, the Mayor informally told the author in his City Hall office: "There's nothing you can do about the slums, you know that. They're always going to be that way."[75]

On a broader scale, noted housing expert Charles Abrams pointed up the gravity of the slum problem when he declared that "it is time we realized that, despite our technological superiority in other respects, we remain an underdeveloped nation in housing. The poorest village in India or Africa has at least the advantages of ownership, a more decent climate, trees and a community; an African mud hut is far superior to a one-room Harlem flat into which a whole family has been herded."[76]

On November 25, 1958, Mayor Wagner ordered a "massive new attack" on slum conditions in New York. Eleven five-man "slum-combat" inspection teams were told to fan out through the city in the drive. The new program was to include a tenant-education plan conducted by the Welfare Department and a briefing of all the courts involved with housing and health violations.

In the spring of 1959, Nelson A. Rockefeller, newly elected Governor of New York state, said he intended to keep stride with the Wagner administration in the drive to improve housing. "One of the major fields of concern to this administration," he said, "is the protection of the home, adequate housing at reasonable rents."[77] The Governor cited the practical as well as the political need to continue rent control.

By the summer of 1959, a major controversy was swirling through the city over the Title I program and the city's housing headaches. People wanted to know: where can I find an apartment? why are there so many slums? do we really need public housing? why are they building so much luxury housing?

Prodded by rising public dissatisfaction, Mayor Wagner appointed J. Anthony Panuch, a New York lawyer and leading authority on government reorganization, as his special adviser on housing. Panuch was instructed to make a thorough study of the city's uncoordinated housing agencies and to recommend a comprehensive city policy by February 1960.

During the eventful summer of 1959, as the housing crisis caught the imagination of New York's eight million residents, the city administration made more announcements to placate rising public indignation.

A city-wide neighborhood conservation program, the first of its type in the nation, was launched to preserve buildings in areas which would ordinarily be omitted from urban renewal programs. The conservation program's goals were to slow down the rate of housing blight, to develop stable family life in the communities selected for conservation, and to coordinate city services with community groups in a joint clean-up venture. Three years later, East 100th Street was to become a target of this conservation program.

Panuch himself, at the outset of his investigation, said he was "shocked" by the extent to which slums had "taken over" the city.[78] And Nathan Straus, former housing adviser to La Guardia and former federal housing aide to Franklin D. Roosevelt during the reform days of the 1930s, said the city needed a "completely new approach" to slums. "I'll admit," Straus declared in an interview, "that I've struck out after 40 years."

About this time, an outspoken Housing Court Magistrate, Robert F. Mahoney, publicly complained that there was no

way of compelling "phantom" landlords who had disappeared and left their properties without heat, light, hot
water, and gas to maintain their buildings. The judge, an
independent jurist who had served on the bench during two
previous administrations, urged the state legislature to pass
a law which would require that the rent money be used to
make repairs.

In December 1959, another of Mayor Wagner's many
committees, the Committee on Harlem Affairs, made public
a report in which it was charged "there is no longer any
excuse for delaying action" on an urban renewal plan for
Harlem which, for generations, had been overlooked by city
officials.

The committee, which covered East Harlem in its report,
said there should be more efficient garbage collections,
stricter enforcement of the building and health laws to rid
Harlem of its rats (City Health Commissioner Leona Baumgartner had said earlier in 1959 that there were more than
eight million rats in New York City), and more housing built
in Harlem under the state's middle-income Mitchell-Lama
program.[79] The committee's most salient complaint, echoing
those heard decades before: "Housing congestion is one of
the major causes of racial tensions in the Harlem area."[80]

Combined with all of the discontent which had been
mounting during the course of this year, the report led the
Mayor to announce dramatically in a television talk that
housing was the city's "number-one problem" and to promise that his administration would step up its battle against
the slums. He even boasted: "My administration has not
sat idly by. When someone says to me, 'What are you going
to do about it?' I bristle. I know we have done more about
it than any administration in any city in this country at any
time in our history."[81]

The housing crisis reached its climax on March 1, 1960, when Panuch submitted his report to the Mayor. The independent survey concluded that despite all of the new housing construction of the 1950s, there were still as many slum dwellings—430,000—in 1960 as there had been a decade before. The Panuch report stated:

In our overcrowded city, where low-income minorities fight desperately for living space in its blighted neighborhoods, slum formation has steadily increased. What appeared to be a manageable problem in the 1930s has assumed staggering proportions in the 1960s in congested New York City. . . .[82]

Panuch said the causes of the 1960 predicament in which the city found itself were: the heavy in-migration of low-income minorities; ownership of slums was a "highly profitable, risk-free" business; shortage of inspectors to police all of the city's buildings; public improvements, when erected, required knocking down housing; private building reduced available housing for low- and middle-income families; only a small proportion of slum dwellers who lost their homes because of clearance were eligible, or willing, to go into public housing; the vacancy rate for apartments in the city was far below standard (0.4 per cent in Manhattan); over 33,000 families on relief lived in substandard housing, for which the Welfare Department paid $25 million a year in rents; roomers in good buildings being torn down moved in with relatives and friends elsewhere, accelerating the spread of blight; and rent control, which even advocates of the law conceded resulted in the deferring of property maintenance, contributed to the growth of slums.[83]

In addition, Panuch found that conflicting policies within the city's multiplicity of housing agencies "has all but paralyzed the city's administrative ability to cope with the problem of its renewal. . . ." He said the lack of a central coordinating authority had resulted in "chaotic site clearance" and "uncoordinated demolition" of many vital areas. The solution to the city's housing problems, he said, was "a matter of years, if not decades" away.[84] He recommended the creation of a new Housing and Redevelopment Board to replace Robert Moses' Slum Clearance Committee and to correlate the housing and urban renewal efforts of all city agencies.

Panuch also made a special plea to eliminate politics from housing. He called for an end to the petty rivalry between City Hall and Albany. The approach to housing, he said, should be "nonpolitical and bipartisan."

On the heels of the Panuch report, the Mayor announced a new neighborhood-conservation district in the heart of East Harlem, beginning at 114th Street and running north. The seven-square-block area was called "the East Harlem project." It represented a stab in the right direction, according to community leaders, but once again 311 East 100th Street and the "worst block" were entirely overlooked by the big, sweeping brush of city government.

During the winter of 1960, Mayor Wagner became the first major city leader in decades to claim that New York was not losing the battle of the slums. In a speech celebrating the twenty-fifth anniversary of public housing in New York, he declared:

It is my judgment today that in New York we have checked the tide of decay. It is making no more major breaks in the dikes we have thrown up. No additional neighborhoods have yielded to its attack.[85]

The Mayor's evaluation reversed his administration's previous stand. A year before, in May 1959, his deputy mayor, Paul T. O'Keefe, had publicly admitted he believed the city was losing the battle against blight.

Housing became a national issue early in 1961 when President John F. Kennedy was urged on January 7 by his task force on housing to combine all federal housing and urban development activities into an agency of Cabinet rank to be called the Department of Urban Affairs.

Representative John V. Lindsay, the outstanding young Congressman from Manhattan's 17th (Silk Stocking) Congressional District, gave the housing problem a bipartisan flavor when he said on the floor of Congress in February 1961 that "today in the City of New York, our most crying need is housing."[86]

In New York, all signs pointed to a bitter mayoralty campaign preceding the November election of 1961. Housing would be a major issue. Mayor Wagner, warming up for the campaign ahead, sent off a letter to Governor Rockefeller appealing (for the fourth consecutive year) for support of a receivership law which would permit the city to seize run-down buildings, such as 311 East 100th Street. The bill was not passed until a year later, but the political battle lines were drawn.

Buildings Commissioner Peter J. Reidy and Health Commissioner Leona Baumgartner joined Mayor Wagner in his appeal to the governor for the receivership bill. In a joint statement, the two commissioners who carried the most responsibility for code enforcement said they often found buildings, operated by "ruthless and irresponsible landlords, which are so run down, poorly maintained and filthy, that the families living in them face constant health and safety hazards." They said the city would continue to be "powerless to act" unless the bill were passed.[87]

One of the buildings about which Commissioners Reidy

and Baumgartner were talking was 311 East 100th Street. While the Mayor and his city officials appeared to show genuine concern for the families living in that and all the other "run-down, poorly maintained and filthy" tenements throughout the city, the tenants continued to live in abject misery, completely unaware that a major political battle was shaping up in City Hall and in Albany about their health and welfare.

The families trapped in number 311 may have been aware of stirrings in their neighborhood, however, as members of the East Harlem Reform Democratic club began to encourage tenants to register their complaints with the club's housing clinic. Because Assemblyman Mark Lane's club took an interest in living conditions inside the house at 311 East 100th Street that spring, city inspectors came to the building for the first full-dress inspection in a decade. The eighty-six major violations which were eventually placed against number 311 in 1961 and the subsequent rent reductions in each apartment that year can all be attributed to the club's investigation of the building. And, because it was a "political" year, many other "top" city and state officials became involved with East 100th Street before year's end, including State Attorney General Louis J. Lefkowitz, the Republican candidate for mayor; State Rent Administrator Robert E. Herman; City Buildings Commissioner Reidy; and Mayor Wagner.

On May 1, 1961, the City Planning Commission recommended an urban renewal program for eighteen areas of the city. A section of East Harlem north of East 106th Street was chosen for middle-income residential redevelopment, and a section north of East 125th Street was selected for industrial use. East 100th Street was once again omitted.

The City Club of New York added more fuel to the

growing housing controversy during the same month. Evaluating Mayor Wagner's record, the club declared: "In the field of housing the performance of the Wagner administration has not matched its proclamation."

In June, the Republican mayoral candidate, State Attorney General Lefkowitz, charged "there is a shocking overabundance of blighted and slum tenements in the city." He drew the public support of the Rev. James A. Gusweller, an outspoken Episcopalian priest whose crusade for better housing conditions in Manhattan's upper West Side had caused the Wagner administration considerable embarrassment since 1957.

On July 28, Mayor Wagner visited East 100th Street between First and Second avenues and announced a clean-up campaign. He stood in the street only a few feet away from number 311.

On August 9, State Comptroller Arthur Levitt, vying for the Democratic nomination for Mayor against Wagner, accused Wagner of "visiting the fringe of Harlem once every four years before election and then issuing a press release decrying conditions."

Levitt proposed that the federal and city powers of taxation be used "to take the profits out of slums." He charged that Mayor Wagner had "allowed slum conditions to fester" and that slumlords were permitted to gouge unsuspecting tenants whom the city had failed to protect.

The Mayor found himself under attack from his Republican foes, too. In Washington, Congressman Lindsay charged that the city's Title I housing program was "veiled in secrecy" and was run on a "hit-or-miss" basis. He called for a Congressional investigation.[88] In this demand he was joined by Congressman Paul A. Fino, GOP candidate for City Council President on the Lefkowitz ticket. Fino said that despite the reorganization of city housing agencies after the Panuch report, the Title I program was still using taxpayers' money to build luxury apartments instead of clearing slums and replacing them with new homes for the poor.[89]

Mayor Wagner retaliated with an announcement at the end of August in which he said the city would put into "immediate action" a six-point program to aid tenants and step up building inspections "to take the profits out of slums."[90]

His main object, the Mayor declared, was "a decent home for every New Yorker in a sound neighborhood at a price he can afford to pay. Our goal in housing," he added, "is the re-creation of New York as the first major city of the world without a slum."

He boasted that New York had produced a great deal of new housing under his administration "and this was no accident. I was raised in an atmosphere of concern for housing. My father sponsored the nation's first major housing program in the Senate."[91]

The Mayor singled out East Harlem for a special tour one day in September as the election campaign moved into its final stages. In a prepared speech, the Mayor told a group of local residents:

We have listened to your voice. Your requests, your letters, your petitions, yes even your gripes, give me and my team more specific ideas for improving your community. Together we are renewing East Harlem. Let's keep it up together. An example of what has been done is that 100th Street between First and Second Avenue is now a Police Athletic League supervised play street. . . .[92]

In October, Wagner attacked the Republican-controlled state legislature for failing to pass the receivership bill. He said it was blocked by the "opposition on the part of banks, which hold mortgages."[93] Manhattan Borough President Edward R. Dudley plugged for the bill also. He said he was appalled by the "terrible" housing conditions he found in East Harlem.[94]

The Mayor's overwhelming re-election in November 1961, despite the severe criticism of housing conditions, was interpreted by city politicians as a vote of personal confidence in him as a leader.

He immediately made it clear to Governor Rockefeller that he would honor his campaign pledge to accept the administration of rent control and he once again demanded that the legislature give the city a receivership bill. For his failure to get behind the receivership bill, Wagner chided Rockefeller for "mixing politics with housing."

Wagner used a fund-raising dinner on January 29, 1962, to report to the public on the first twenty-nine days of his administration. He emphasized that "housing is the most critical and the most central of all problems facing us. It is closely interwoven with every good and every evil attached to city life. . . . We are going to remove the blight and slum life from New York City. We are determined to have a slumless city."[95]

On February 20, 1962, in a televised speech, the Mayor admitted that 20 per cent of all existing apartments in the city were "substandard"—lacking essential qualities for decent, sanitary, and healthful living. "There is reason to believe," he said, "that housing blight due both to neglect and natural deterioration is spreading faster than new construction plus rehabilitation."

After the city took over rent control from the state in early 1962 it prepared to enact new local legislation. "We must not play political tennis with it," the Mayor warned, "batting it back and forth between Albany and New York City." He again called for a "constant, unremitting and unrelenting battle" against slumlords and urged the state legislature to pass the receivership bill.

He created the City Rent and Rehabilitation Administration to run the rent control program. In doing so, he announced that the new agency was an opportunity to achieve a "slumless city." It took control of 1.76 million rent-controlled apartments—including the thirty-three inside the house at 311 East 100th Street.

In June 1962, the City Planning Commission announced fifteen more "study areas" for urban renewal. East 100th Street and East Harlem were not listed. James Felt, chairman of the planning agency, was asked by a reporter to explain this omission. A brief excerpt of the interview follows:[96]

REPORTER: Why doesn't the city go into the worst slum areas with urban renewal plans?

FELT: Because we cannot take the relocation load at this time. There are too many people to relocate and nowhere to put them. We want to emphasize rehabilitation and conservation in areas beginning to fall apart at the seams.

REPORTER: Do you concede that you are not going in the worst slum areas?

FELT: That is right. But the city is already in these areas in one degree or another.

REPORTER: Is the city behind or even or ahead in the fight against blight in New York City?

FELT: We feel optimistic. We are gaining. We are ahead of it now.

The next month, Mayor Wagner offered a more optimistic report on the city's battle against the slums. "We have stopped the spread of slums, given more people the chance to live in decent housing and enjoy sunshine and fresh air," he declared.

He predicted that by 1970 the city would overcome its middle-income housing shortage and that the "bulk" of the city's housing requirements would be met by 1980.[97]

Inside the house at 311 East 100th Street, however, there was no such optimism. The tenants saw little sign of hope. Many of them complained to the East Harlem Reform Democratic political club. José Fuentes, housing chairman of the club, in turn grew impatient.

During the summer of 1962 Fuentes asked Borough President Dudley to investigate the slums of East Harlem himself. In August, Jerome L. Wilson, then assistant to Dudley, who later was to become the State Senator from East Harlem, accompanied Fuentes through the area.

Among the 67 tenements they looked at was 311 East 100th Street. They listed these buildings in a letter to Judah Gribetz, deputy commissioner of the Department of Buildings. In the letter, Wilson and Fuentes described number 311 as "horrible throughout."

Analysts probing the East Harlem community for the City Planning Commission nodded their heads in agreement with Wilson's findings in September when a report on the area, compiled within the commission for staff use, described the housing as inadequate. The report also offered this appraisal of the community's attitude:

They do not believe that the city will approach change in a manner which is any different than before—that planning will be "*with* them instead of *for* them." They see East Harlem as a "raped community" on which more housing projects have been imposed than any other community in the city.[98]

This was the prevailing community feeling in September 1962, when Mayor Wagner finally ordered aid for the people on the "worst block," including the families inside number

311. He declared that East 100th Street between First and Second avenues would be designated an "area services project." Fifteen city departments were told to clean the street, remove the most hazardous building violations, step up efforts to care for welfare families, provide more police protection, and set up a narcotics clinic. The Mayor also threatened to use the city's new receivership powers (the bill finally passed in the summer of 1962) to take over buildings on East 100th Street which landlords failed to clean up.

In October 1962, Congressman Lindsay renewed his attack on the city's faltering housing program. In a speech on the floor of Congress, he pressed for an investigation of Title I in New York and complained that too many families still lived in the tenements. He said that "the city administration has been patently neglectful in enforcing housing and building code violations."[99]

Less than a week later, Wagner flatly predicted that within fifty years New York would be a slumless city. In a magazine article outlining his views, Wagner said that by the year 2012 slums "will just be a memory of a rot that afflicted the city long ago."[100]

But in December, Buildings Commissioner Harold Birns said there were hurdles to overcome before such a goal could be reached. He complained that his department could not "adequately discharge its statutory responsibility to assure safe and healthy housing conditions" throughout New York. "This administration," he said bluntly, "cannot ever achieve its goal of re-creating New York as the first major city of the world without a slum, unless the Department of Buildings is given the tools to do the job."[101]

Dramatic changes might have been brought about on East 100th Street in 1962 if a proposal by the city's Housing Authority had been approved. The CHA had made a study of nine buildings on the south side of the block, opposite the house at number 311, for possible rehabilitation. The plan was scuttled, however, when a private appraiser came in with an exorbitant estimate of the cost.

Interestingly enough, the south side of the block was the site chosen for the study, not the north side. What would have happened to number 311 and the other buildings on the north side if the rehabilitation plan had been approved? Gerald J. Carey, general manager of the City Housing Authority, said simply: "The buildings on the north side of the street would have been torn down. They are not good enough to rehabilitate."

East Harlem community leaders during 1962 devised a plan of their own for the area around 311. The plan showed that there was as much concern from within the community over conditions in this block as there appeared to be from without.

Reacting strongly to Mayor Wagner's designation of the East 100th Street area as an "area services project," Peter D'Arpa, president of the East Harlem Merchants Association, held an emergency meeting of a civic group which called itself the Metro North Association. It was named after Metropolitan Hospital and referred to the blocks directly north of the hospital—East 99th to East 103rd Street, East River to Second Avenue, an area which included number 311.

The group sent a letter to Mayor Wagner complaining that the community was not consulted prior to his announcement. The letter suggested the city make use of the "initiative and vitality" of the local residents. The association also complained about the "negative publicity" which resulted from the Mayor's announcement. Several members of the association were particularly upset by a newspaper report which characterized East 100th Street between First and Second avenues as a "jungle."

A survey by the association itself, however, tended to

support this description of the housing there. It found that 69 per cent of the apartments in the Metro North district were either "deteriorated" or "dilapidated" and that more than one third of the apartments were overcrowded. The survey pinpointed conditions on East 100th Street in particular.

In January 1963, Mayor Wagner met with federal officials in Washington in an attempt to seek new avenues for combating the spread of poverty among the slum population. He said the city was "studying" the idea of rehabilitation on a large scale. "Of special concern to us are the sociological problems faced by newcomers to our city," he said. "I am convinced that new and creative techniques can be developed."[102]

In May 1963, James W. Gaynor, commissioner of the New York State Division of Housing and Urban Renewal, challenged Mayor Wagner's prediction that New York would be a slumless city within fifty years. Gaynor said that Mayor Wagner's "goal of a slumless city is at best a political slogan without hope of realization in the year 2000 or in the year 3000."[103]

The next month, the Mayor responded by once more attacking the slumlords. "There is no excuse for the degrading conditions of deteriorated disrepair under which some landlords of jaded conscience force New Yorkers to live,"[104] he said. He declared a "war on slumlords" and ordered the increased use of vacate orders and the receivership law which, until that time, had been used sparingly. He also called for increased inspections of the city's 43,368 old-law tenements and its 49,903 new-law buildings, such as the house at 311 East 100th Street.

"In the past," the Mayor added, "we have waged war against the slumlords. They are still with us. We have not yet won the war." The Mayor could very well have been talking about the "worst block" when he said the war was not yet won. East 100th Street still showed no signs of improvement.

During the summer of 1963, when the unexpected civil rights revolution took hold in New York, the Negroes and Puerto Ricans in the slums began to grow restless. They demanded better housing. It was no longer a matter of listening to promises from City Hall. Negro civil rights leaders said they wanted freedom to move into previously all-white areas. Others demanded that the city take over the slums and make the repairs.

Milton Mollen, the Mayor's chief housing adviser, promised to integrate all government-supported middle-income housing developments. He conceded that city housing officials "must dig deeper" into the causes of social problems in the slums. "We must do this," he said, "because unless we do we will just as surely continue the endless vicious circle of displacing problems from one area to the next—a grim game of not-so-musical chairs, with the bulldozer right behind."[105]

This emphasis on social as well as physical problems was greeted with enthusiasm by most city planners. Mollen received the support of Dr. Robert C. Weaver, federal housing administrator. It appeared as if the city's housing program was beginning, at long last, to take a new and constructive course.

The City Planning Commission said one answer was wide-scale rehabilitation. But its new "pilot plan" for 234 city blocks once again failed to include the "worst block."

Late in 1963, William F. R. Ballard, newly appointed chairman of the City Planning Commission, offered this comment on the goal of a slumless city: "It can be done," he said, "if the people want to do it." Asked if New York was winning or losing the battle against the slums, he replied: "It's hardly holding its own."[106]

In 1964, the New Year had just dawned when Mayor Wagner called for a "pocketbook attack on the slumlords." Governor Rockefeller accused the Mayor of allowing the city's slums to deteriorate to the point where thousands of tenants felt compelled to stage a rent strike.

The unprecedented strike, led by Jesse Gray, a militant civil rights leader, drew the support of tenants in hundreds of Harlem buildings. It was regarded as the most dramatic and effective show of minority group discontent with housing in New York in decades. It struck a responsive chord. The courts and the Mayor supported the strike. City Hall even went to Albany with a plea that rent strikes, in effect, be legalized.

Reacting to pressure for action, Buildings Commissioner Birns made public a list of the owners of buildings in the city which had fifty or more violations placed against them. The house at 311 East 100th Street, with 130 violations, ranked eighth in Manhattan, twelfth in the City.

In Washington, Mayor Wagner told a Congressional committee that one out of every four apartments in New York was in a "deteriorated condition." He urged that the Johnson administration's new housing program be broadened to include more public-housing apartments.

"I can tell you that today the existence of a single building in which human beings live in slum conditions is considered an affront and a challenge to the public conscience, and consequently the responsibility of government," he declared.[107]

The Mayor could very well have been talking about the house at 311 East 100th Street.

Despite the Mayor's view of government responsibility, his own Commissioner of Real Estate, Frank L. Lazarus, threw a monkey wrench into the city's program to rehabilitate slum buildings by warning that the city would "go broke" if it were not selective in choosing buildings for receivership.

Looking for a new way to repair slums, City Hall drew up a plan during the winter under which expert real estate men would provide management advice in slum districts for a fee. A "pilot block" was selected on East 103rd Street between First and Second avenues. Once again, the "worst block" was overlooked.

East 100th Street was also forgotten by the City Planning Commission in April when it announced that some twenty-three substandard areas of New York City would be renewed. East Harlem was not one of the areas listed.

Everybody, it seemed, had ignored East 100th Street— everybody except the residents themselves. They held a symbolic funeral procession on that block and on East 101st Street on April 25.

Six young boys in a makeshift band played Chopin's "Funeral March" with trombones, cymbals, and drums. Community leaders placed floral wreaths on the doors of four buildings, including number 311, which they felt had been particularly neglected.

A local clergyman said that three hundred persons in the four tenements had been "abandoned by their landlords and the buildings themselves are dead as far as services are concerned."[108]

In May, Harlem's version of the New York World's Fair, the "World's Worst Fair," was opened by Jesse Gray, together with many prominent Negro civil rights leaders and entertainers. Placards were placed on dozens of old tenements, sarcastically labeled "pavilions" from the city, state and federal governments.

As summer approached, City Planning Commissioner Ballard, pressing for a master plan, sounded a significant warning when he declared:

Either we plan with wisdom and courage or we must content ourselves to playing "urban roulette" with the lives and well-being of our children and the generations of New Yorkers to come.[109]

And Whitney M. Young, Jr., executive director of the National Urban League, spotlighted the importance of housing in the national civil rights movement when he wrote:

Segregation in our cities is a cancer, eating away at the lives of millions who live in slums, Negroes and whites alike, and spreading blight from neighborhood to neighborhood as the poor struggle outward for added living space and sunlight. Their condition is further worsened by lax enforcement of the building codes, by penny ante fines to slum landlords—all expressing the idea that Negroes don't deserve decent housing.[110]

Housing grew to be a major issue in the 1964 campaign, as it had been in past election years. The rent strike spread; the housing courts and the receivership law were criticized for failing to do enough; the real estate industry, usually aloof, joined the controversy; civil rights leaders launched a new drive against discrimination in housing; rent control, low-rent housing, rehabilitation, and urban renewal once again became major issues.

But even as the housing battle continues to rage on all levels, the tenants inside the building at 311 East 100th Street still live in the same misery they have for decades.

There are no plans for 311 East 100th Street. It is a building that has been pronounced dead.

Once a "house of hope," number 311 stands as a monument to the city's losing battle against the slums. Where sunlight and fresh air should be streaming in there is only darkness. The crumbling building, which sixty years ago housed the dreams of a generation of Americans, now serves only to wall in broken people living broken lives.

The house, originally created to end the fatal influence of old slums before the turn of our century, has itself become a weapon of death which destroys human life.

Who molded this weapon and committed this crime against civilized society? Who is the killer?

Fingerprints of a long line of suspects have been found in tracing the history of a house doomed. Landlords, government officials, community workers, and tenants have all left their mark on 311 East 100th Street.

Each of these suspects has been indicted many times over and each, for generations, has pleaded not guilty. Wherever and whenever the issue has been raised, the question of blame has gone unresolved. Let us therefore call these suspects to trial now, listen to their testimony, and reach a final verdict.

PART TWO

_____

THE
SUSPECTS

THE
SUSPECTS

LORDS OF THE LAND

IN A SHABBY STORE FRONT on a tenement-lined street in the East Bronx, a middle-aged man sits behind an old desk covered with letters and newspapers. On the drab wall to his right hangs a public telephone; to his left the room is cluttered with pieces of a radiator, several wooden chairs, and a broken jukebox. The floor is cracked and dirty. The only light in the room is a small bulb hanging from the ceiling. The man, unshaven, wearing his hat and raincoat, has just come in. It is cold and rainy outside and there is no heat in the cubicle in this ramshackle building at 474 East 146th Street.

"I buy and sell. I deal only in properties. I'm what they call a speculator," the man behind the desk says matter-of-factly as he stares out of the window. "I'll take a building over anywhere. I figure I can get some kind of income for what I put in."

The voice is that of Victor Santini, a part owner of the building at 311 East 100th Street. The scene is his real estate office during the winter of 1963. He says he bought a share in 311 "because I thought I could make some money. I don't know its history, but I'm trying to get it rehabilitated. The rents are low because of the violations. If the rents are restored, it can bring in twelve thousand dollars a year. I'm not going to get rich on this building, but I just want to make my investment. I want to fix it up and sell it, that's all. It'll be tough."

Santini describes his first visit to the house on East 100th Street:

"The other day—Sunday it was—I went to get the rents. One man had a folding knife and he told me he was just sleeping in one of the apartments. When he turned his back I picked up his knife and put it in my pocket. I wasn't taking any chances. The whole place is a mess. It's the tenants who do the destroying. Who breaks the windows? Who stops up the toilets? Who breaks the walls out? Who does all the damage? They do! The street is probably the worst street in New York."

This owner, an admitted speculator, knows some of the problems that lie ahead for him. "You got a lot of headaches with a building like this," he says. "To begin with, the rents are nothing. There are still people paying eighteen to twenty dollars a month and they raise hell if they don't get hot water and heat one morning. Then the janitor gets you by the neck and nine times out of ten he steals. The coal and oil and electric companies got you by the neck. Rent control keeps the rents down on top of it all. In the old days a man bought a piece of property and everybody took care of it. Today the rents are nothing. The house is full of welfare tenants who don't have to pay rents when there are violations. And the Buildings Department gives you a hard time with violations."

Try to suggest to Victor Santini that many of the people who live in this house are handicapped by their environment and he answers angrily:

"Don't tell me these people don't have a chance. If you give them a day's work they'll shoot you. They all have a chance, don't fool yourself. My mother and father went to work, but not these people. They play the numbers. They got the Buildings and Health Departments. They got politicians. They got everything with them. Even those who work are on welfare.

"You think those kids got no chance? They got more chance than I had. I went to work when I was thirteen years old. These people are just bums. They've learned you can get something for nothing so they aren't going to work for it. These Negroes and Puerto Ricans just sit around all day and drink beer. They come up from Puerto Rico to go on welfare. They get up late in the morning and you can see them all over the place during the day."

Turning to 311 East 100th Street, Santini becomes even angrier and his face flushes as he discusses the causes of present conditions in the building. "It's the people themselves," he says. "Do you think that building would look like that if it weren't for the tenants? I say it's their fault. They send their kids downstairs with the garbage and they lose half of it on the way. The people are pigs themselves. This ain't the fault of the landlord or the city. The people do it themselves. They got every opportunity these days to feed and clothe their children. They have more opportunity than we had."

Santini sold his share in the building in early 1964.

Do other past landlords of 311 East 100th Street agree with Santini? Do all of them blame the tenants for the poor condition of the building?

During the past six decades, twenty-seven different individuals or corporations have owned the house at 311 East 100th Street.[1] More than 150 others have assumed direct or indirect responsibility for its physical and financial condition. All have had a hand in shaping its destiny—the private owner and private investor, the title insurance company or bank, the lawyer, agent, mortgagee, trustee, legitimate real estate operator, and the speculator.

"I was the agent in charge of purchasing 311 East 100th Street. It was just another building to us in 1923. We bought it for short speculation," recalls Arthur A. Abramson, a big, jovial man and long-time member of the Raynes Realty Corporation, with offices at 469 Seventh Avenue in Manhattan.

"The rent roll in those days," Abramson continues, "was about five thousand dollars a year, not too bad for the time. We made improvements and then went to the tenants for increases. They paid increases as we fixed up. We put in electrical wiring, white enamel sinks, and heat."

In those early days, the realty firm of Hershkowitz and Raynes maintained its office on East 100th Street, across the street from number 311. "We were in the neighborhood," Abramson says, "it was very pleasant. People used to meet me on the block and say hello. They were all very friendly. My boss, Mr. Raynes, he was the angel for all of them. He would lend money and help the people along. In those days it was harmonious. There was no welfare. People would pay us when they could. I remember we painted each apartment for four dollars a room, but just before the Jewish holidays we did it for nothing—for good will. They expected it after a while and we were glad to do it.

"There were mostly Jewish, Italian, Hungarian, and Irish people on the block. Puerto Ricans weren't even known then. The neighborhood was poor, the rents were cheap—fourteen dollars an apartment—there was no steam, no electric, no gas ranges and walls were papered an ugly green in most of the buildings. There was gaslight in those days and cooking with coal stoves and a water tank on the roof filled with five hundred or a thousand gallons. In the basement, each family had its own coal bin.

"But it was a nice neighborhood. People were friendly and reasonably clean. It was poor but pleasant, a place to which people from the Lower East Side moved to improve their lives. We put in heat in many of the houses, we pulled out the coal stoves and put in gas ranges. Before that they had to work with the black iron sink and the old washtubs, but we replaced them with nice enamel sinks and we scraped the old paper off the walls.

"On the north side of the street we had number 311. We also had numbers 313–315, the buildings that were eventually thrown down because they became a hazard. We bought strictly for speculation, for resale. We thought we'd build up the rents in 311 and then get a good price for it. People were paying six times the rent roll in those days. It was a decent neighborhood to own property. In the street you had a lot of kids playing marbles and stickball. There wasn't the violence of today. In those days the Jews and Italians had a lot of kids who worked. The kids there today don't think of earning an honest dollar.

"Inside of number 311 it was in good shape. We kept it up. I remember, too, there was a speakeasy on the ground-floor store there. It was wide open. Some of the basements of the houses on the block were rented to the pushcart peddlers. They used them to store their stuff. There were a lot of stores which had fruits and other foods."

Hershkowitz and Raynes first moved into East 100th Street, Abramson recalls, after World War I. The firm took over nearly all of the buildings on the south side of the block near its real estate office. It bought the properties from Simon Ashner, a tobacco merchant who had owned them since 1907. It wasn't until 1962 that the Raynes Realty Corporation [Hershkowitz had split up with Raynes many years ago] sold its last holdings on the block. "We had spent a fortune," Abramson says. "We were losing money on those buildings on the south side of 100th Street. In 1953, the city made a big announcement about clearing the area for low-rent housing. After that you couldn't make a large improvement, so everything went downhill. We heard the area was to be taken. We heard it was on the planning boards. But nothing ever happened. The city stopped it. We also took a licking in the 1940s when we got the Puerto Ricans and they destroyed our property. Those buildings were around our throats with rent control killing us.

"We sold these buildings on East 100th Street because they were no longer making money. There's no market at all there today. We had been in there running real estate to make a buck and it had always been a friendly arrangement. We were in business to make money. We bought number 311 to make money. We improved it. Then we resold it [in 1924 to Herman I. Zacharia, a Greek-born businessman who was to become a prosperous manufacturer many years later]. We dropped number 311 like a hot potato in 1924."

Whose fault is it that number 311, a new-law tenement with every promise of providing a safe home for its inhabitants in those early days, has become a living nightmare for its tenants today?

"Rent control didn't budge an inch," Abramson answers. "They decided for the tenant every time. They get the votes from the tenants and there are more tenants than landlords. A landlord gets very little from them for doing anything. They tie your hands every time. I say, let the landlord live, too! They want you to squirm and lie and steal and give them phony bills. When the rent freeze came into existence in 1943 we couldn't do much. Nobody could do much. How could landlords be expected to keep up their properties when they were losing money?

"All of these politicians are interested in feathering their own nest. Whenever I go to the Buildings Department I always ask, 'What's the price?' and these officials are my friends. That's the way it is and I don't intend to change it. Whatever the price is I'll pay. It's listed under 'expenses' on the tax forms and the Internal Revenue accepts it. On East 100th Street, these inspectors are on the payroll. When they started a drive a couple of years ago I was told to pay $50 per building to keep the violations down. The inspectors had to bring in reports of violations. The city is only interested in getting you down to fine you."

Abramson blames the tenants also. "The people are very dirty. They are at fault. There has been so much congestion there over the years. They are jam-packed. Everyone is a cousin. Relief got after them to show electric bills to prove they were legal tenants but they would switch names and they would use other gimmicks to get relief. When the Bronx opened up to the Jewish and Italian families the Puerto Ricans came into 100th Street. They got welfare and flocked to 100th Street. The people there are filthy. They live in dirt. They leave food around which breeds rats. There is no end to the violations they create.

"We don't get anything out of this. Brinkley showed number 311 on television and he said how the landlord made money. But would the owner drop the building if there was a chance to make a dollar? Unless a man goes around in overalls and makes his own repairs, he can't make a buck. I say if a man's making a buck he's not dropping a building. You'll never make any money out of a house like number 311. The only solution is to tear it down, not to come with Governor Hatfield or Mayor Wagner, or some other politicians, but to just tear it down."

The building had only two owners between 1924 and 1946 when the deed was purchased by Mrs. Grace DeVinne Goldsmith, a wealthy Park Avenue woman. Actually, Mrs. Goldsmith had acquired a mortgage on the house in 1933—during the depression—from an investment company. She bought the deed from the 311 East 100th Street Corporation in 1946 and held it until the time of her death in 1953.

Under the terms of her will, the executor of Mrs. Goldsmith's estate turned the building over to two trustees: her attorney, Alexander Halpern, a senior partner in the New York law firm of Pross, Smith, Halpern and Lefevre, of 530 Fifth Avenue, and the Bank of New York.

"My client may have had an interest in this building," Halpern recalled in 1963, "but no knowledge or control." The attorney asserts that Mrs. Goldsmith invested some money in real estate in the early 1930s through a mortgage guarantee company and that she actually "did not know the property," nor had she ever seen it during her lifetime.

"I remember the building was located in a marketing section, a produce market, not conducive to home living conditions," says Halpern. "It also got to be a pretty rough neighborhood. It became a slum property. I think the city has done its best to watch this. When you have private ownership the city can't control the buildings or the type of tenants. The neighborhood just ran down completely. In 1933 this was a distressed area to begin with."

Halpern, a prosperous-looking man with a bent for public service, has played a role in Republican state politics. In 1959, he became co-chairman of the Rockefeller for President Citizens Information Center, the first formal organization to

support Rockefeller for the Republican Presidential nomination. In 1960, Halpern, a resident of White Plains, was appointed by Governor Rockefeller as one of the six nonsalaried
commissioners from New York State to sit on the Port of New
York Authority.

The office manager of Halpern's law firm since 1930 has
been John R. Woods. He remembers what 311 East 100th
Street was like in 1946. "Representing Mrs. Goldsmith, I
went up to look at the house. There had been a fire in the
building and I went up to see if repairs should be made,"
Woods recalls. "We used to make periodic inspections every
year or two. I found the property in such bad condition that
I recommended it be closed. Mrs. Goldsmith owned it at the
time. I found many of the apartments unoccupied in June
1946. The property was in such bad condition we suggested
it should be boarded up. It was a pretty bad neighborhood
at that time. Ten years later, all of the apartments and the
two stores were rented. The total rent roll in 1955 was about
eighty-five hundred per year."

After Mrs. Goldsmith died in 1953, the Bank of New
York, as trustee with Alexander Halpern, took over the management of the building. "We were the owners. We were not
so much concerned with profit but with maintaining the
property and the operation of the building," declares Frederick Dohrman, assistant secretary of the bank. "It wasn't a
Park Avenue building, but for what it was it was well maintained. Violations put on it were promptly taken care of by
our agent. Nothing was allowed to go unattended. The painting was performed as required and we set painting schedules
and violations were removed and repairs made. There might
have been a little delay at times when we had to get estimates
on the work, but in the main it was always performed in a
reasonable time. The social problems there now were there

then, but perhaps not in as aggravated a form. It had no connotation as a bad block.

"It wasn't a blighted area but it could have gone either way at the time. There was talk of the area being taken over by the city for low-income housing in 1953, but that died. The announcement could have had an effect on the building maintenance after that. We did not consider owning this building a routine matter. We inspected it regularly and completed reports on it. The sales manager would also view the building periodically for the purpose of selling it. The fact that we owned others in the area over the years gave us experience.

"We used to have extensive holdings. Many were forced on us in the 1930s during the depression. We have since liquidated the entire portfolio. As a trustee, however, we couldn't speculate on what 311 East 100th Street might bring us. We had to sell it at a reasonable price. In 1955, we got two appraisals, one eighteen thousand dollars and the other twenty thousand dollars. We sold number 311 for nineteen thousand dollars to a firm called Home Properties and turned over the deed."

Why did number 311 deteriorate so much during the past six decades? Who was responsible?

"It's hard to say," Dohrman replies. "It would seem that perhaps the landlords did not give prompt attention to the management problems. Absentee landlordism. Declining rents. The profit motive wasn't there any more, really. You can't put your finger on one item alone. Many things had an influence on the whole area becoming a slum."

On April 29, 1955, the real estate firm of Home Properties, Inc., purchased 311 East 100th Street from the Bank of New York.

"It was in good shape when we got it," recalled Stanley Soltzer, president of Home Properties, in his modern office in the Manhattan skyscraper at 122 East 42nd Street. "We had a staff that ran from building to building to maintain all of our properties. But, basically, these old properties were built with no planning. Age deteriorates plaster and electrical wiring. A lot of them run only seven thousand to eight thousand dollars a year in total rents, and taxes run to half of that. If you consider what is left, after all they are rent-controlled and you have insurance, fuel, and water taxes, there isn't much.

"Years back, the management problems were a little easier. Buildings like this have accelerated in their rate of deterioration. Today we don't go into that area any more. East Harlem is not a bad investment per se, it depends on the type of building. Some are sixty years old and have deteriorated to the point where the property itself can't be maintained except for the complete rehabilitation. The other answer is to have the city tear down the entire area and put up new housing.

"We all know this is one of the worst blocks in the city and whenever the city talks about a really deteriorated street, it picks 100th Street. They should grab it, but I guess they need it as a place to point to. If they didn't have this, they wouldn't have a horse to beat. I say let the community take it over. Some of those people have wonderful ideas."

Soltzer, a forty-three-year-old real estate investor who lives in Scarsdale, has financial interests in numerous properties. He formed a partnership with Jacob S. Lampert, an attorney, twelve years ago. Lampert, who lives in the fashionable Riverdale section of the Bronx, shares the ownership with Soltzer of many first-rate properties in the Bronx, Manhattan, and Westchester. Both are experienced businessmen.

"Even if somebody is sincerely interested in renovating a building," Lampert declares, "they must make an application to the Rent Commission and remove the violations. In most cases, this takes a long time. They have problems just finding the tenants home when it is time for inspections. In the meantime, the landlord must carry the building at reduced rentals. The Rent Commission has to send letters to all the tenants and no tenant will cooperate in getting rents restored. A landlord must go through channels, however, and wait for the tenants' replies before he gets his increase and it remains that way forever. That fact alone takes the heart out of most landlords. If they could collect rents, at least they'd have money. But after a while, they have no heart or spirit to do anything. When their buildings get old and worn out they just fall apart from use. Rent controls in and of themselves create slums. It's a known fact."

Soltzer agrees with his partner. "The people in these tenements are subsidized by the Rent Commission," he says. "There are always violations on these properties. It is a problem to maintain them. It's impossible—impossible—impossible. Nobody can do it. The Rent Commission doesn't understand this. As soon as they reduce rents, they make it impossible to properly keep up a building because the landlord doesn't have much money. Generally, these landlords don't. That's why there are so many foreclosures. There is no market for these properties.

"The tenants contribute to the landlord's problems. They don't respect the property. They break windows. There is an unusually high rate of windows broken and there's a violation every time. When the violations are placed against the landlord, the welfare families don't have to pay rent. No matter whose fault the violation is, the landlord is the one to pay for it. Even if the landlord did have money to spare,

he can't make a repair last. The next day it'll be just as bad
as it was before. And even if the repairs do last, it takes a
landlord six to eight months to get rents restored by the Rent
Commission. No politician who is responsible will admit this,
of course, because it's bad politics. As for the house at number 311, we had this building nine years ago. We sold it to
another man right after we took it over."

"It was in reasonable shape when I bought it," recalls
M. Monroe Fass, president of the Second Equity Corporation, which purchased 311 East 100th Street from Soltzer and
Lampert in 1955 (but with Soltzer and Lampert retaining a
large mortgage of $26,000).

"We had to make repeated repairs of the same items in
311 East 100th Street. Within a two-year period the glass in
the front door was replaced not less than half a dozen times.
A lot of it was the tenants' fault. We have frustrations in any
building where the tenants unfortunately have not been educated to respect someone else's property. All you need are
two or three in a building. The others are reasonably decent.
It's a combination of maintenance and low rents. As a result
of these problems, we had to go into bankruptcy."

But seven years elapsed before Fass, then a fifty-one-
year-old engineer, surveyor, and experienced real estate man,
was forced in 1962 to take the Second Equity Corporation
into bankruptcy. He had bought the building at number 311
under the name of Second Equity Corporation, 570 Fifth
Avenue, chartered back in 1953. Fass had served as an officer
in several other major corporations dealing in general appraisal business, real estate, and insurance. He had a good
reputation among real estate circles in New York, including
the influential Real Estate Board of New York.

After taking over number 311 in June 1955, under the

name of Second Equity Corporation, Fass transferred title a month later to his attorney, Lawrence H. King, whose law office was in Manhattan and whose home was in Yonkers, New York. King was listed as the owner until October 1956, when title was transferred back to the Second Equity Corporation.

"I was born on Henry Street on the East Side," King recalls. "The East Side section was the vital place to be chosen by immigrants as their homes after their long voyages from Italy and Poland and Russia and Czechoslovakia and everywhere else. The East Side was a teeming mass of humanity. These streets appeared to me to be the very essence of a slum area. The conditions that exist today in a sense are the same as those conditions that existed many years ago. In those days you had crusaders like Jacob Riis and the free milk fund. That shows people used to be provided for. There were underprivileged people who were economically depressed. The contrast today is that there is very little economic depression."

Asked why a building like number 311 was still bought by landlords in the 1960s, King responds:

"They are bought for numerous reasons. There are always people trying to get rich who don't know the business. They will buy. There's always the people who think that there are bargains in the real estate field. And to a great extent they are people who honestly feel it's a good and sound way to invest their money. Now I don't say these people are misguided. Real estate is the basis of our economics here in New York. Don't forget the city derives the greater part of its operating income from the taxation of real estate. And the city of course has the most basic interest in preserving the integrity of real estate values in New York."

Questioned specifically about his own role in the operation of the tenement at 311 East 100th Street, King says: "In my practice, I represent landlords who may be deemed in the classification of owners of property considered as slum property, in the general sense that the public understands this word. Among the landlords whom I represent is the owner of the building at 311 East 100th Street. That is a building that is managed by a real estate company which is not among the parvenus of real estate managing agents [Fass and Wolper, Inc., 570 Fifth Avenue, a corporation headed by Fass]. It has managed properties for its existence, which is approximately thirty-five years, and I believe that it is a competent agent for properties and I believe it doesn't want its properties to be considered slum properties. Let us take, for example, a building such as the building at 311 East 100th Street.

"This building was bought on a very sound financing. An adequate amount of cash was invested in the purchase of the building and there was an adequate first mortgage which the landlord expected he could comply with. But in this building, as in the case of many other buildings, there were unexpected catastrophes, such as obsolete boilers giving way, the need to replace an entire line of water pipes because of inadequate water pressure, and the need to replace a roof. Now, these were matters which did not appear to be critical or obvious to the landlord when the building was purchased. In buildings where this sort of disaster happens, rent control has kept the rentals depressed to the point where there is no surplus from the building. If, in fact, the monthly income exceeds the monthly outlay, that money is as a rule put aside to provide for the mortgage payment which the landlord is usually required to make, there being in most cases a first mortgage or in some cases a first and second mortgage on these buildings.

"Insofar as this building at 311 East 100th Street is concerned, when it was purchased I was, as of record, the president of the corporation. This is very often an office without emolument, assumed as a formality for the purpose of executing mortgage instruments. And therefore I am not speaking as a person who has had any financial interest in this property but only as an attorney."

Attorney King was asked if he felt his client, Second Equity Corporation, had properly maintained the building at 311 East 100th Street.

"Well, whether or not my client has done an adequate job is something which I don't feel I should express an opinion about in those very words. I will say that whenever conditions have been called to their attention or wherever they could be seen on examination by them, and it appeared that these conditions either violated the law or were such that were not consonant with good real estate management practice, that they proceeded to correct them."

Perhaps the greatest scourge of the slums are the millions of rats which inhabit them. In New York City, there are an average of more than 700 rat bites reported to the Department of Health every year. Whose fault is this?

"In 80 per cent of the cases," King comments, "it was the fault of either the tenants in that building who insisted on dumping rubbish in the cellar and in the yards or the people of adjacent buildings who, looking for a handy place to dump, would pick on this adjacent property.

"There are tenants who have never arrived at a realization of their duties as citizens. This is not only vandalism in public projects, but it is in private projects. This is at variance with conditions generally in cities in Europe. Not in all cities. In Paris, for instance, you have slums. Take in Amsterdam and Holland. Despite the type that the buildings are maybe three or four hundred years old, compared to our buildings in New York, police have been educated to keep these areas clean. Very rarely do you see them dirty. In New York, however, it is a different story."

Is there any way to wipe out slums?

King offers this observation: "I believe that as conditions exist today, we can make a comparison of our city to a turtle on its back. This is not the ordinary, common or garden variety of turtle. It's one of these big ponderous ten-ton sea turtles, and we need the dynamic and concerted cooperation of all of the many interested groups to get this turtle turned over and back to its gait."

Two years after King turned the house on East 100th Street back to Second Equity, the beginning of a long series of financial troubles befell the owners. They went to the First National City Bank on August 20, 1958, and obtained a $16,687.44 property-improvement loan, recorded as a second mortgage. It was to be paid back in eighty-four installments of $198.66 each.

By 1961, Second Equity found itself the subject of a study by the National Broadcasting Company, which was doing a documentary film on the house at 311 East 100th Street.

Less than a year later, on March 23, 1962, the Second Equity Corporation filed a bankruptcy petition in United States Court for the Southern District of New York under Chapter 11 of the Federal Bankruptcy Act.[2] The petition placed the corporation's liabilities at $405,179 and its assets at $93,200. The attorney for the petitioner was Lawrence H. King. As president of Second Equity Corporation, Fass stated in the petition that sixteen properties owned by the Second Equity Corporation (including 311 East 100th Street) and managed by Fass and Wolper, produced a rent roll of $11,500 per month. He claimed expenses of $10,600, including a 7 per cent management fee of $805 per month to Fass and Wolper, 750 Fifth Avenue. Fass said he had managed the business affairs of the Second Equity Corporation since its inception in 1953, and that the officers of the corporation "receive no salaries and its directors draw no salaries and receive no compensation."

"If permitted to continue in operation," the petition stated, "the debtor will be able to set up a reserve to inure to the benefit of existing creditors and to appropriate to payments under a plan of compromise, and without loss of its assets. Otherwise, a forced liquidation of its assets will have to take place."

Fass gave two reasons for financial troubles: "the effects of the unusually severe winter of 1960–61, which caused exorbitant fuel consumption greatly beyond the norm, and the effects of the campaign against owners being waged by the municipal authorities of New York City, which has required the expenditures of vastly greater than normal sums for maintenance, repairs, and the curing and removal of violations. The additional factor of temporary reduction of rents by the local rent administrator pending removal of violations has also curtailed the ability of the debtor to meet commitments."

The bankruptcy petition charged that the properties "are situated in neighborhoods that are now being subjected to the pressure of such campaign against landlords, there has been a lowering of market value for same." The ten largest creditors, according to official records, had claims which added up to more than $50,000, most of them fuel bills.

Fass proposed a plan whereby the corporation would liquidate all of its properties under the supervision of the court. The money from such sales, he contended, together with the surplus from the operation, would be applied to the payment of claims, either in full or such percentage as would be determined by the court after a reasonable period of time.

On April 5, 1962, the first of a series of hearings on the bankruptcy procedure took place before Judge Robert P. Stephenson, the Referee in Bankruptcy. In the course of the opening hearing, Stephenson asked King for a profit-and-loss statement for all of the properties. Replied King:

"We have an amount of rents that are collected from these buildings. However, rents have been going up. These are rent-controlled properties. When an old tenant moves out, they sign a new tenant with a fifteen-per-cent increase. The rents are still not at a peak; it will go higher as time goes on. We have applications pending on two buildings with the local rent office for increase in rents."

The rent roll for 311 East 100th Street at this time was approximately $860 per month, and there were two mortgages on the property being paid off: $175 per month to Soltzer and Lampert and approximately $200 per month to the First National City Bank.

At another hearing on April 17, Referee Stephenson and Fass had the following exchange:

Q. (Stephenson) Can the debtor-in-possession pay all of its expenses and make money now?

A. (Fass) I believe that is possible. I would say it is probable.

Q. (Stephenson) Has it been making money before it filed the petition?

A. (Fass) It was not making money because of the extraordinary circumstances that took place in the last two years, caused by the heavy flow of violations caused by the campaign for the getting of votes for our present Mayor.

At subsequent hearings Fass testified that when the corporation had first been created, about $75,000 had been invested by a group of investors who formed two "syndicates."

By November 1962, the debtor-in-possession was still operating the properties and, pursuant to a court order, was paying the creditors and the mortgagees. The operating statement showed they were "holding their own." While Fass was fighting off the corporation's creditors, however, the first mortgagee—Soltzer and Lampert—grew impatient and began a legal action to foreclose on the Second Equity Corporation in the case of 311 East 100th Street. This action, which had started on April 11, 1962, was blocked by Fass in December when he asked for a stay of foreclosure, claiming that "such real property is a valuable holding and in information and belief it has an equity of $10,000 or more over the first-mortgage lien held by Stanley Soltzer and others."

Soltzer and Lampert, holders of the first mortgage at number 311, countered by stating in a sworn statement: "The premises have been subject to many violations in the Department of Housing and Buildings of the City of New York in connection with the judgment debtor [and] had been subject to many fines. It is also in a sad state of repair and in much dilapidated condition owing to the mismanagement of the debtor."

By year's end, Second Equity Corporation was declared officially bankrupt and Hyman Lehon, an attorney, was appointed by the court as the trustee-in-bankruptcy, a term denoting that he was to serve as the court-appointed trustee for the bankrupt owner until the properties formerly owned by Second Equity could be sold at public auction.

On January 24, 1963, Judge Stephenson said that Lehon, the trustee, was authorized to retain Lawrence H. King as his attorney for the purpose of "prosecution of rent increases and related matters before the Rent and Rehabilitation

Administration in connection with four buildings." One of the buildings was the house on East 100th Street.

Meanwhile, early in 1963, Paul L. Knobler, an attorney of 234 East Fifth Street, in the Lower East Side of Manhattan, was appointed by Lehon as managing agent of the properties. Following is a report on number 311 as prepared by Knobler for the first five months of 1963:

January–May, 1963

Month	Rent Roll	Received	Arrearage (Amt. the tenants are behind)	Expenses
January	$846.66	$ 632.77	$1323.88	$1156.34
February	846.66	1549.72	255.80	1745.64
March	837.33	566.13	466.77	920.77
April	837.63	706.90	630.92	324.36
May	–––––	82.64	–––––	832.94
TOTALS		$3538.16		$4980.05

Knobler said that the period during which he managed number 311 was not a pleasant one. "You have to cringe," he said in an interview in 1963. "You see the terrible conditions, the rats. It would seem to me one of the reasons it is that way is the owner's inability to collect sufficient rents to keep the buildings in repair. There is no doubt, too, that there are sociological problems. The narcotics addicts terrorize the tenants.

"Once we called the cops and they came but the addicts only moved to the house next door. Oh, the wild parties and drinking that was going on. We tried to give proper services. We had coal-fed furnaces. The landlord's main motivation in a building like this is profit. This problem is too big for an individual man or a corporate owner. This must be solved by the state or a large corporation on a subsidized basis. To rehabilitate, the landlord must get help. An individual owner milks the property as long as he can and then he drops it. It takes a very calloused individual to own and manage properties like this. What amazes me is when the city regards certain areas as in need of rehabilitation they overlook areas like 100th Street and don't regard it as blighted."

Lehon, a quiet-spoken man who maintains a modest office in the Wall Street section of Manhattan at 170 Broadway, gave this account of his role in the management of the house at 311 East 100th Street:

"We were agents of the court," he declared in an interview at the end of 1963. "We came into the picture and we realized we were dealing primarily with human beings. We were not interested in making money. We wanted to run the buildings and give good service and heat. We wanted to satisfy the tenants.

"When we came in at the beginning of January in 1963 the situation was deplorable. It was the coldest time of the winter. We had cranky tenants, as they had a right to be. We found the super had not been paid, the fuel bill hadn't been paid, the heating system had conked out. We were dealing with hundreds of tenants in all of the properties and as soon as we notified them we had complaints of ceilings falling down, rat holes, no water. We had to take care of these things on an emergency basis, but we couldn't borrow money. The Buildings Department began to slap violations on us. This was a nightmare for weeks.

I was receiving summonses for violations that had been recorded for months. I was to be brought into court as a defendant and I was apprehensive about the tenants' safety. The insurance companies wouldn't give me liability insurance. I felt if a tenant were hurt, they might sue me. I had a dread of fire. These are not buildings I would have bought personally. I have bought a lot of buildings but I wouldn't touch this one at number 311. I couldn't sleep with one like this. We found in some of the buildings we took over that tenants had failed to pay electric bills, and tenants had strung wires into the halls and tapped the house current."

As for East 100th Street, Lehon made this comment: "It is portrayed as the 'worst block' in the city. If it is characterized this way, why isn't it made the basis of a demolition program? A doctor looks for the worst problems first and does something about them. It's something to be concerned about. The people have a right to be treated as human beings. Some prefer to be left alone; they would reject help. But they must be educated to accept a different and better way of life.

"Basically, it's a job for the city and for property owners to provide minimum basic standards. I think rent control has been well administered, especially under Mrs. [Hortense W.] Gabel, but she has pressures which make it difficult. Rent control should be relaxed, however. From a trustee's viewpoint our problem was that we could not borrow money because anyone who lent us money would not get priority over the mortgage liens. The mortgagees should have more responsibility. A federal trustee is not protected. The banks should step in and be forced to take the buildings back and manage them properly, or permit a receiver to come in and borrow money and make repairs. The banks have a legal responsibility in this matter. They can't just sit there like a dog in a manger and prevent an owner from making badly needed repairs."

On April 9, 1963, an advertisement appeared on page 78 of *The New York Times* with a head over it which read:

14 MANHATTAN PROPERTIES FOR SALE BY TRUSTEE IN BANK-
RUPTCY. The date of the auction was advertised as Thursday,
April 11, 1963, at 2 P.M. before Referee Robert P. Stephen-
son, Room 201, United States Courthouse, Foley Square,
New York. The fourteen addresses were listed in the ad.
Fourth down from the top of the list was 311 East 100th
Street. Lehon sent out 2000 circulars to real estate agents
prior to the publishing of this ad in March because there was
a city-wide newspaper strike at the time.

The auction began late. There were about twenty-five
men in the room when Referee Stephenson opened the proceedings. All of the prospective buyers were handed sheets
of mimeographed lists which enumerated the fourteen parcels for sale and gave the vital statistics for each. Parcel 4
was 311 East 100th Street, described as a building with
thirty-three apartments and three stories with an assessed
valuation of $40,000, rents amounting to $12,182 per year,
and mortgages of $25,453.

Hyman Lehon announced that all bids were to be "net
cash" and above the mortgages. "You are taking the right,
title, and interest of the trustee in bankruptcy," he said
matter-of-factly, "subject to all violations." He then stated
that he had received a flat offer of $8000 cash for all prop-
erties except one, and opened the auction for "bulk bids"—
that is, bids for all of the parcels in one lump sum. One real
estate man, after an exchange of bids, won out at $11,000,
but this was soon eclipsed by the individual bids, which
totaled $26,900 for the fourteen buildings.

Only one man bid on 311 East 100th Street. When Lehon
read off this address, E. Shelton Reed, a Negro real estate
man, of 321 West 125th Street, said casually:

"I bid one hundred dollars."

There was silence. Nobody else bid. Seconds later Lehon
announced.

"Sold to Mr. Reed for one hundred dollars."

That was all there was to it. Reed pulled a $10 bill out of his wallet and handed it to Lehon as a down payment.

E. S. Reed, Inc., took over the building officially on April 30. "I went down and looked at it," said Reed a few months later in an interview. "I found the building in bad shape. The lot next door to my building is owned by the city and the party wall had fallen in. It was in terrible shape. There were leaks and broken pipes in the building and the water lines were bad. I did fix a lot of leaks.

"Before I bought it I drove there and I was afraid to get out of my car. I just drove right on. I didn't want it. But I bought it because I figured what's the sense of letting it go bankrupt for the sake of a lousy hundred dollars. Why let the trustee get stuck? They wanted to get rid of it. Nobody bid on it but me. The first fifteen or twenty days I did a lot of work on the building. I put a whole team of men there. I put in new water lines. I broke about even. I'd say 311 East 100th Street is about as bad as any occupied building I have ever seen."

Reed was born the same year—1906—that his newly ac-quired property was opened. For thirty years he served in the United States Army and he retired in 1956 with an honor-able discharge. He presents a "substantial worth centered in real estate holdings," according to an evaluation of his finan-cial stability made in 1963 by a reputable independent rating company.

He is president of three real estate corporations, all char-tered under New York State law. His business operations gross him between $80,000 and $90,000 a year, he says, "but I still can't make a decent living because by the time I get through with my expenses—including paying off inspectors—there is little left." Reed maintains a neat but ordinary-

looking office on the second floor of a two-story commercial
building at 321 West 125th Street, the most active crosstown
thoroughfare in Harlem.

Ask Reed why the property he purchased on East 100th
Street turned into a slum and he replies:

"I think what happened," he says, "is as long as it had
white tenants the building was kept better. But most landlords, especially whites, want to collect as much rents as
they can when they get colored tenants in. So they bleed
the buildings, put big mortgages on them and get rid of
them.

"The cause of the slum is race prejudice. When they put
in colored tenants and started bleeding the house, that's
when it started. I don't think a white landlord would admit
a house was bled. I bought most of my houses from whites
and I know every one was run down by a white man. He
may not intentionally bleed it. He may say, 'They will tear
it up anyway,' but he lets it go. I come along and buy it and
I got the headache. More white landlords let their buildings
go down than colored landlords. I know white landlords who
wouldn't dare go visit their houses. They go to Connecticut
someplace. You can't even find them to give them violations.
I put everything I get out of my buildings back into them
because I want to keep them. I don't want any of my tenants
to live under conditions I wouldn't live under myself."

Reed also blames some tenants for causing slum conditions. "A lot of people," he declares, "don't have any gump-
tion. They're just satisfied. They throw garbage out of the
window and they throw everything out of the house onto the
fire escape. There are many tenants who don't go to work.
If they'd get jobs they'd get ahead and they wouldn't have
to live in the dilapidated places. If these people would get
some good jobs, they could get better housing. I feel the
tenants—especially those with children—are more than fifty

per cent at fault. I'm getting to the point where I'm inclined to reject families with children. On 100th Street they are a problem and there are a lot of bums, too."

The Negro landlord also complains about rent control, city agencies, and "politicians" in his assessment of the responsibility for slum-making. "One reason number 311 is in such bad shape," he explains, "is the low rents. The past landlords didn't get much out of it, so they didn't put much back into it and the tenants tore it up. There's no money in that building. The heat bill alone is six hundred dollars to seven hundred dollars per month. Some of the apartments rent for as low as thirteen-eighty a month. That's terrible. Rent control is to blame. The rent roll is only nine thousand dollars a year for thirty-three apartments. That is not enough to break even. Even a man who has bled his house to death doesn't have enough income to do the work. There's nothing you can do about it.

"As for city agencies, I personally think they're all working against the landlord. None of them cooperate with the landlords. They're very inconsiderate. Hortense Gabel is too harsh with rent control. They want to give you violations and fines and don't give you a chance to fix up. There is also a great deal of overlapping authority. I could get a violation from four different places. I'd rather deal with one agency at a time. They differ among themselves. Each inspector has a different requirement. This makes it twice as hard. There should be one inspector, a construction inspector, with the authority."

Reed collected rents on number 311 for the month of April 1963, but just as he started to make the badly needed repairs fate stepped in again. Still another legal action was going on behind the scenes which was to affect the management of the house.

Unknown to Reed, the foreclosure action which Soltzer

and Lampert, the first mortgagees, had started a year earlier came into court before Referee William S. Evans and on June 6, 1963, the building was awarded to Stadium Towers, Inc., a trade name for a realty investment firm registered on March 29, 1963, by Soltzer and Lampert.

This unusual and somewhat tangled legal situation left the deed to number 311 in Reed's hands, but Stadium Towers, Inc., because it held the first mortgage, also appeared to have a solid claim on the house. After a month of confusion, during which the tenants were asked by both parties for rents, Reed stepped out of the picture.

"I don't feel badly," he said later. "I didn't want it. It was getting too hot for me anyway. Everybody was closing in on me. The Department of Water Supply, Gas and Electricity wants the whole house rewired. I put more into it than I got out of it during the time I owned the house. I wanted to continue payments on the mortgage, but they [Soltzer and Lampert] foreclosed. They got a referee's deed. But they didn't have a clear title."

Stadium Towers held title to the house for only eight days. On June 14, 1963, title passed to a real estate firm which called itself Respectfully Yours, of 505 Fifth Avenue.

In the fall of 1963, 311 East 100th Street once again changed owners when the Corose Realty Corporation, of 474 East 146th Street in the Bronx, took over and became the twenty-sixth owner since the house was opened in 1906 to assume responsibility for its maintenance. A twenty-seventh owner bought the house in December.

There will, of course, be more landlords—perhaps in 1964, and certainly thereafter. The house, as long as it stands, will spin from one owner to another like a broken top without direction or purpose, leaving the tenants bewildered and without hope.

CHAPTER 7

THE PEOPLE WITHIN

ON MAY 4, 1962, a thin, quiet-spoken Puerto Rican man stood up at a hearing on rent control at City Hall. The problem of relocating tenants when new buildings are erected to replace old ones was being discussed.

"We in East Harlem," declared José Fuentes, a member of the East Harlem Reform Democratic Club, "have many problems that are more pressing to us than the problem of relocation of tenants that are to be evicted.

"We are rat-bitten and cockroach-infested. We are living in filthy slums. And we are paying high rents for the privilege of doing so. In East Harlem we have one of the worst slum conditions in all of New York City, and our [Reform Democratic] housing committee has been struggling for over a year to correct the abuses in housing in our area. I cannot adequately describe to you the terrible conditions under which the people of East Harlem are compelled to live. I know the conditions because I live there.

"The housing committee ardently worked to correct the landlords' violations of state and city laws. Our committee organized the tenants in over fifty-eight buildings in the past year and we were able to compel the landlords to do some repairs, but it is really very discouraging, and we need laws with some teeth in them."

Fuentes demanded stronger laws to prohibit landlords from getting rent increases when they only give a building "a lick and a promise." He urged that no rent increase be handed out if even one single violation remained on the building. "It is frequent," he charged, "that when the landlord puts in a new refrigerator or stove, or puts in a new electric wiring, or replaces the plumbing, that the rest of the building and the apartments are in a deplorable state—windows broken, plaster falling, doors broken. The new refrigerator was put in because a rent increase would follow; so, too, are the pipes and wiring installed. Each of them grants the landlord a rent increase, but he does not repair the parts of the building and apartments which do not give him rent increases."

He described as "terrible" some of the apartments in which the Welfare Department places its families on relief. "They pay the highest rents," he complained, "and obtain the very worst apartments."

One of the buildings visited by members of the East Harlem Reform Democrats was the tenement at 311 East 100th Street. It was subsequently inspected by city officials, but only after complaints had been lodged by its tenants, assisted by an attorney from the political club. Many of the tenants had to be awakened from a lethargy. However, once they were stimulated to register their complaints, their indignation mounted.

Here is how the people within feel about their home on East 100th Street:

Marcellino Rodriguez, the plodding former superintendent of number 311 who tried for two years to cope with its maintenance, blames the whole mess on the landlord. "The landlord is supposed to fix the building," he says. "But he is not right with the people. Some tenants need a plumber or a painter. The landlord say: 'I send a plumber.' But he don't come for two or three weeks after. In my apartment I plaster and paint and plumber. The landlord say he pays me but he don't pay me nothing.

"The whole thing no good. Building no good. The halls no good. The door out front no good. No glass in the door. The mailboxes no good. The boiler no good. I said to the landlord, 'the boiler no good.' I asked him to check boiler. I work all day there. I live in the boiler. I put coal in the boiler, too much. He fix nothing. He pays me a hundred and twelve dollars a month. I no live on this. This no good for my family. It's small money for my family."

In 1961, soon after he had taken the job as building super, Rodriguez recalls receiving a letter from the then managing corporation, Fass and Wolper. The letter read, in part:

Dear Mr. Rodriguez:
  We received the following violations. Why did we get these violations? You are supposed to be taking care of this house. Please let us know immediately. Plastering and painting of public area. Broken hall windows, broken landing steps, roof littered with garbage, no glass in front door, no hot water, dirty public area around building.

"It's not my fault," Rodriguez cried. "When I work I clean out the whole area around the building. Before he sent this letter to me I tell him, 'It's not my fault.' He knows that, my boss . . . the manager, Rabin, he gives the orders to me. He owed me about a hundred and twenty-five dollars. I do not know the landlord's name," Rodriguez says when you ask him about the owners. "All I know is Fass and Wolper [the managing firm]."

Rodriguez' wife, Petra, also blames the landlord. "He never did nothing for anybody," she says bitterly. "The bathtub kept backing up. I called him. A workman came and broke the wall over the tub. They came around and replastered. But nothing was fixed. The landlord asked Marcellino to fix things up and he didn't pay him. He used to fix windows that were broken and save the landlord the bill and the landlord would pay what he felt like. Marcellino would pay for the glass and the supplies and the landlord would not pay him back. The landlord never came around. Marcellino never saw him. The landlord never cared and he still doesn't care."

As angry as this woman is at the landlord, she also criticizes her own neighbors. "The people here dirty the house up," she says. "My husband complained he had to clean the stairs and no sooner had he finished when they would throw the garbage out of the windows and in the halls all over."

As for city government, Mrs. Rodriguez declares: "I have seen inspectors here. They come around. I usually see them walking around the yards and all that. They ask questions, they write in their books. I don't know what they're doing. Then they go away and nothing is any different."

Juanita Pachecho, the Puerto Rican woman whose infant child was killed in a fall from a fire escape at number 311, is just as unhappy about conditions in the house as is Mrs. Rodriguez, but she blames Mrs. Rodriguez' husband, Marcellino, for at least part of the situation. "Sometimes the super no collect the garbage," she says. "He don't clean the building. We have too many cockroaches—sometimes in the clothes. This building bad. For our apartment the landlord get too much money." Mrs. Pachecho pays $18.62 per month.

Mrs. Anna Maria Vargas, who has lived on the third floor for two years, answers the "Who's to blame?" question this way: "This building isn't worth two cents," she says. "I mail in the rent and I never see the landlord. The super doesn't do anything, either. The stoves don't work. I can hardly get enough flame on mine. I had to buy my own refrigerator. I haven't asked for a new stove because I don't want my rent raised. Recently, they lowered my rent, but that was because after you live in a house for six months they automatically lower your rent." [*Author's note:* This is, of course, incorrect.][1]

Mrs. Vargas turns some of the blame on the tenants, too. "Many times after the super cleans up," she explains, "I find papers in the hall and a lot of garbage. Why should he clean up all over again? Sometimes I see garbage flying out of the window when I walk downstairs."

Ask Mrs. Vargas who her landlord is and she replies: "I have never seen him. I don't know what he looks like or what his name is. When I first applied for an apartment here I got an application in the mail and filled it out. I got it from the super and I sent it to the landlord, but I have forgotten his name and I have never, never had anything to do with him at all. He has a month's security of my money."

Mary Williams, who lives on the fifth floor, remembers the house when she first came to East 100th Street in 1946 after the war. "The house was pretty good then," she recalls. "It was in good condition and the agent we had, if anything went wrong, he did see that it was fixed. He painted for us. We didn't have to paint for ourselves like we do today.

"Later on," she continues, "another agent took it over, in about 1955 or 1956. Well, he didn't do too much. Since we started complaining, he do a little more. But like for instance the stove I have, he wants more rent for a new stove and that we don't pay because we can't afford it.

"I had to complain for a year before the landlord would

fix my toilet and the tub. We also have trouble with mouses and roaches, the usual thing. I have plenty holes. Under the Frigidaire we have a big slat to hold the Frigidaire to keep it from going through to the apartment below. The landlord must know it. I have complained. But nothing is ever fixed.

"Once I saw the landlord. I brought him upstairs and I showed him my door was going to fall on my head. I showed it to him. And I showed him the stove. He saw it. I told him I was going to set the house on fire. He said he was going to send somebody to fix the door. But it's been a year now and nobody's been here for the door. I don't know the landlord's name. I pay my rent by money order and send it to the agent.

"The landlord never supplied us with an ice box. When we first moved in we had to buy our own. After the ice box we bought a Frigidaire. I knew he was supposed to give us a stove. I told that to the inspectors who came here. In the eighteen years I have lived here there have been a few inspectors but where they come from I don't know. They just come in and look around. But I don't blame the landlord and the inspectors only. I think it's the tenants, too, because if the landlord would fix up the place the tenants would feel like it's a home and would take care of it. But they see he's not fixing up the place and they still have to pay money for it so they get to the point where they don't care. That's the problem. Then they start to make it a mess, too, and everybody's ruining the house."

Tell Mrs. Williams that the landlord of number 311 can get as much as $1000 per month from the rents and she responds with a laugh: "I think somebody should spank him because with that much money he ought to be able to do a little bit of work, more than he's doing now. That's an awful lot of money to don't do no more than he's doing."

Francisco Matos, the construction worker who has been unemployed for many months because of a shoulder injury, shares Mrs. McWillie's reaction. "The landlord has money," Matos says. "Crooks make money. The landlord is crooked. He paint only two times in the seventeen years we are here. He rob us. The man has got the money. We are poor. The building is coming down in two or three years. It's impossible to meet the man who owns the building because it's a company. I saw different people. One time comes a man, another time comes another one. It says Fass and Wolper, Inc. This means people in a corporation. The landlord doesn't fix the building even if the violations come after him. The judge listen to the money. All the time we lose the case. The money is more."

"The landlord no gotta care," Matos continues, pointing to his dilapidated apartment. "Three years no steam. Hole in the ceiling, he no fix. All the time we got a rat, sink broken, pipe broken. The water coming in through the one big hole in the roof of my room. You can see the sky through the hole. I fix it myself. He don't pay for that. Four year, no paint the apartment. He's supposed to paint in three years. Broken window I got to put glass in. . . ."

Matos' wife says the house is much worse today than it was when she arrived with Matos in 1947. "When I came here I paid thirteen dollars rent. Now I pay twenty-five dollars. Now the building is falling apart. The landlord worries only about picking up the rent. The landlord is in a lot of trouble. He was taken to court. He made small repairs but that's about all. In our corner room you see the sky." Asked why the house was in such bad shape, Mrs. Matos replies: "I can't tell exactly. I believe it's because of the personalities of the people living here. Also, I can't understand why the government hasn't done anything to fix it up.

There are a lot of good people here, too. But the government has done nothing to help any of them."

The one man in number 311 who should know about its change in the past fifteen years is William Davies, the burly forty-four-year-old Negro superintendent who took care of the premises before Rodriguez arrived and after Rodriguez abandoned his family and left the house. Davies lives with his two children and his sister in apartment 9 on the second floor. He does not pay rent and he receives $110.50 a month in salary from the landlord.

"If it were left to me," Davies, a native of Spartanburg, South Carolina, drawls, "I'd say it was the tenants' fault. If the people would cooperate there wouldn't be all the mess. Why can't these people bring garbage down instead of throwing it out of the windows? If they didn't feed the rats with garbage, there wouldn't be any rats. You take these people—they pee on the stairs. If you put these people somewhere else and tore these buildings down they'd do the same thing somewhere else. This street is the worst in the city, and I say it's because of the people in it."

If it is so bad, why has Davies remained in this one tenement for the past fifteen years?

"I stay here," he explains, "because I'm stuck with this joint. I got no wife and the kids go to school around here. I'm super and this gives me a chance to wait for the kids after school and make them supper and look after them. I also got the store on the ground floor."

The block is bad, Davies says, because it attracts families who cannot find lodgings elsewhere in the city. "What brings people here," he says, "is that nobody else in the city will take them. They come here and their kids write all over the walls, dump garbage and throw bricks. They fight all the time and ruin the cars parked on the block. I'm telling you, it ain't the landlord that tears up this building. The landlord don't live here."

Davies defends the landlord. "When Fass and Wolper had this building," he says, "they did a lot of work on it. They done a very good job. But they claimed bankruptcy and when the building went into receivership, that's when the trouble really started. They would not let me do anything, except keep the hot water and heat going. And when the junkies came and took over the empty apartments, they ruined the house. We had a number of landlords who said they owned the house in 1962 and 1963. They all tried to collect rents—get what they could from the building. Then they ran. They grabbed a few rents and run away with them."

Has the city government helped? "Yup, they kept it clean if you piled up the garbage for them," Davies replies. "The big trucks came in and picked up a lot of stuff. But they kept bumping up against the big wall next to the building. Then the wall collapsed. That man [Everett W.] Reid [director of the city's area services project on East 100th Street], he was a hundred per cent. If everybody do what he tells them, we'd be all right. The Mayor's interest is good, but the Mayor, the cops, nobody can help this street if the people don't help themselves and teach their kids. They don't do nothing for their kids."

Mrs. Shirley Smith, a neighbor from the house at 322 East 100th Street, probably knows more about living conditions on the block than any other tenant. In 1960 she organized the East 100th Street Tenants Association and helped Assemblyman Carlos Rios and officials from the city's area services program. The group was concerned mostly with lack of heat and hot water.

"We never got any complaints from people in number

311," the thirty-seven-year-old woman reports. "We got a lot of people when they had problems but the people in 311 kept to themselves. If they had problems, they didn't tell us about them."

Mrs. Smith, whose husband, George, forty-three, earns $100 a week as a warehouse manager, lives with her husband and two children in a four-room apartment for which she pays $25.30 per month. "We have stayed here all this time," she explains apologetically, "to save our money and buy a house. We're buying one in Richmond Hill and we plan to move out of here very soon."

Who created the slums on East 100th Street? "I couldn't say it was the people who have lived here a long time," she replies. "It's the people who come into the neighborhood— the drug addicts, the bums—who made it bad. It's been this way as long as I can remember. I've been here twenty-nine years and I've seen the street get worse. I don't think the city is doing anything because when the addicts are in the hallways the city don't pay them no mind and if you want to go into your house you have to knock them down and the police don't do much better.

"The landlords have blame, too," Mrs. Smith continues. "They leave the cellar doors opened all night long and people go there and when we have trouble with heat and hot water the supers can't go into the cellars to put the heat on because the addicts block the doors and the supers are afraid to go in there. But the landlord is only responsible for certain things and he can't do everything. The addicts and the people don't have no consideration. If the landlord does make repairs, the children break it up, the drunks break all the windows up.

"The politicians don't help much. They come up, but only at election time. I have called Carlos Rios but he don't come in a hurry. To the Puerto Rican families maybe, but not to the Negroes on this block. After election, nothing happens. The addicts just keep coming back. They are the worst part of the block. They go into the hospital for cures but then they come right back in a few days and do the same things. They should be put somewhere where they can be helped. It's a waste of the city's money. They're the first ones treated at Metropolitan Hospital but they don't get any better. They get worse. They rob people around here and make this place terrible. This block has gotten worse over the years. Oh my goodness, yes. Nobody seems to do anything about it."

After listening to Mrs. Smith's story, an observer could assume that she would be glad to leave the block. Curiously, however, this is her response: "I'll miss it when I move from here. I have a lot of friends here, you know. I've been here a long time—since 1935. That's a long time."

CHAPTER 8

THE PUBLIC SERVANTS

"MY NAME IS BILL GESWINE. I have a foot post on 100th Street. It runs from First to Second Avenue. You might say the block is a mass of humanity stacked one on top of the other. The general attitude of the people on the block is disrespect for police. They move in mobs, maybe because they live in mobs. We have a lot of trouble here, arrests for narcotics, gambling."

A husky, broad-shouldered man who speaks in an abrupt, clipped manner, Geswine explains with a shrug of his shoulders:

"A patrolman going into a block like this takes his life in his hands, but that is what we get paid for. But it is not an easy block. They have social workers here. I guess they do a lot with these people. I am not paid to understand it. I am paid to protect property, enforce the law and protect law-abiding people against these elements that we have right here in this block.

"But these people don't seem to understand that we are here to protect them against wrongdoing. As far as when we patrol the block, we have had men hit numerous times by the debris. They loosen chimneys, throw bricks down, Coca-Cola bottles, and beer cans. We have had men hurt.

"In these buildings you will find one thing. You will find the filth, you will find dirt throughout. And then you will find one family on the third floor rear that have a clean apartment, that scrub their halls, and live in all this mess. Yet, they are a member of the same community.

"So it gives you a little pause to think that maybe this little segment, these little people in this building, are trying to break away from what they are exposed to, or maybe they were never that type of people to live in those conditions.

"The buildings in themselves, really, they are too far gone. They have superintendents which are on the run. They don't pay them much. The superintendent has no enthusiasm in the building. In fact, he is one of the neighborhood, one of the type.

"I imagine a social worker would say that the people don't have a proper opportunity or a chance or that they should be treated better. I don't know. I think the people in the area if they had a better understanding of community life and their responsibility to the city as citizens and if they wouldn't stand behind or just turn their heads on these wrongdoings, try to help us, try not to condone these wrongdoings in the block, we would be able to get a better solution to the whole thing. They seem to think whether they are good or bad that we are against them.

"If there is an answer to the problem, the congestion, the attitude of the people, might all be the answer. But still in all, they are citizens in the city and they still have a right to the community regardless if it is crowded.

"There is a sanitary problem within the buildings and we give summonses to the landlords. But the people don't cooperate with the landlords; actually they are both at fault. I wouldn't say there is any one element at fault, no more than there is any one element, race, or creed in the block. It is just a mass block.

"It looks very clean now because the Department of Sanitation has given it more attention lately than they ever had and they made it a play street for children to play in, which is very good. If you want to, sometime come up and take a look at it. But wait until after the primary, because then it will be dirty again."

Patrolman Geswine's testimony, during the summer of 1961 before the Democratic primary, was corroborated by his superior officer, Captain Charles J. Markloff, the commanding officer of the 23rd Precinct at the time.

"All those people," the captain declared, "can't be in the apartments at one time. Many of them are out on the street. They don't know what to do. And when they don't know what to do they get into mischief. They have gangs, troublemakers, tension groups, and those things are all conducive to higher crime rates."

In 1963, when the precinct changed command, Captain Pearse Meagher declared: "The people on this block don't meet their responsibility. Everybody there wants something for nothing. The landlords want us to protect their property rights, but they won't complain against tenants. They're afraid of reprisals.

"As for dope addicts, this is an enforcement enigma. These boys are getting therapy. We want to enforce vigorously, but we must understand therapy at the same time. There is also the social problem. Most of these people, living in an area which has been reconstructed with public-housing projects, do not qualify for such housing. They are not basically a family unit.

"Now what has happened to people dislocated from other parts of the city who don't qualify for public housing? They have to stay in these slums or follow the rooming-house trail. In my view, this is not a police problem. We are only an enforcement agency and a symbol, even to the people on East 100th Street."

Fire Captain Nicholas Zogg, of Engine Company 91, a veteran of many years' experience in the East Harlem neighborhood, put the problem this way:

"When we issue orders to have fire department violations corrected in slum buildings, we find it very difficult at times to have the violations order corrected by use of a summons. In order to serve a summons we have to serve it personally upon an individual responsible for the building.

"A large number of times we find these buildings listed in corporation names and it is difficult to find one individual in the corporation who can be held accountable for this particular violation and who will accept the summons."

Lieutenant John Fedyck, of Ladder Company 43, on the other hand, feels "it's more the 'inhuman element' than anything else." He blames the block's troubles on the tenants. "When you see hallways littered and yards full of garbage, you often wonder whether any type of landlord—even the best—can keep up with them. Every once in a while the city has a drive on the block and we notice large piles of rubbish. But it's difficult to see the results. The people go right back to their bad habits."

Samuel Gartner, the health inspector, is another public servant who holds tenants primarily responsible for slum conditions. After a tour of the house at 311 East 100th Street in 1963, he observed:[1]

"No matter how much you put into this building, it will still be a slum. Why? Because of the type of tenants. They break glass. They break everything. They are destructive and mischievous. They are drug addicts and prostitutes. They go up to the roof and on the way they destroy the inside of the building."

Gartner feels the city itself should not be absolved from blame. "City departments," he says, "go after landlords just for publicity. They come up to 100th Street only at election time. I say do a job all the time. What I hate is the politician who goes into an area before election and blames it all on the landlords. It's not the landlords' fault. It's the fault of the city. During the day the tenants, many of them, are on relief. They sit around and drink beer. Let the city give them some work to do so they're not parasites. Let them clean up their own street. The neighborhood conservation program is not sufficient and not efficient."

Gartner believes that city departments actually help perpetuate slums by trying to drive landlords out of business. "A landlord has nothing but headaches," he explains. "He is discouraged from making improvements because even though he is entitled to a rent increase after the building is fixed up, he must borrow the money from the bank to make repairs. But even if he does fix up, it takes so long to get rent increases approved by the Rent Commission that he winds up losing more than he makes. And many of the repairs are destroyed again and again by the tenants. I would absolve the landlord. I would say it's fifty per cent the city's fault and fifty per cent the tenants'."

The inspector pointed to 311 East 100th Street, where the landlord gets no more than $10 per room per month. "You can't run a building on that kind of income. So who is to blame? The city doesn't let the landlord of this slum collect more money. He can't make the building go. How can the city expect him to be a slave to this?"

Harry C. Harris, director of the city-wide neighborhood-conservation program, coordinates all of the inspectional services of various city agencies in the conservation districts. More than any other city official, he bears full responsibility for what the city has done—or failed to do—on East 100th Street and inside the house at number 311.

"There is no question," he says, "that since we moved into the 100th Street area the property owners have tried to comply with the laws. The improvements are substantial, which is not to say you have Park Avenue houses. The big thing here is age and neglect and the abuse by landlords and tenants. But by prodding and keeping at it we can at least maintain buildings on a minimum basis."

Harris testifies that the city spends about $35,000 a year in this particular slum pocket, about 5 per cent of his annual budget of $800,000. Part of the money goes for a three-man social-work staff headed by Everett W. Reid, who has an office on East 110th Street. When Reid first came into the block in the fall of 1962, he called a meeting with Shirley Smith, chairman of the 100th Street Tenants Association, and landlords from twenty-five of the twenty-seven buildings on the block. The group was briefed by Milton Mollen, chairman of the city's Housing and Redevelopment Board, under whose auspices the conservation program functions.

"We were only a three-man staff," Reid recalled in an interview in 1963, "so we told them we needed everybody's cooperation. But we found a lot of animosity on the part of the tenants. They felt this was a political thing, especially since we had come into their street just before the elections of 1962. They said to us, 'What's the sense in you being here if you leave after election?' And the over-all community felt we should get the tenants to clean themselves up.

"We tried to get the tenants to work with us. There was a lot of apathy on the part of the tenants and the police. They didn't like to clean up and they would not inform to the police. When the people see the junkies there they don't have much faith in us. But when it comes to pointing a finger, they refuse.

"A lot of people stay in this block," Reid continued, "because they're wise enough to know the city will have to do something. They say the buildings are so bad that eventually the city will have to do something and the tenants will have to be relocated. The people on this block want the buildings torn down."

Harold Birns, New York's Commissioner of the Department of Buildings and a former assistant district attorney to New York County District Attorney Frank S. Hogan for fifteen years, is in charge of enforcement of the building laws. Asked why houses like 311 East 100th Street remain uninspected, sometimes for years, Birns replies:

"The complaints flow into the department at the rate of more than five hundred a day. We have all we can do to keep up with this crushing tide of complaints. Many buildings are not inspected until the tenants complain."

Is the city administration doing enough?

"In my opinion," Birns responds, "no society can call itself civilized if it fails to provide the machinery by which healthy living conditions will be guaranteed to all within its borders."

To emphasize his point, Birns says he puts his staff on notice several times a year. He tells them he will not tolerate cracks in the inspection machinery. One time when he was swearing in a group of new inspectors in 1963 in a City Hall ceremony at which the Mayor presided, Birns, a normally quiet-spoken man, told the men sternly: "If you cannot perform your duties capably and conscientiously, if you view your position as an opportunity to get 'fringe benefits'—or, to be perfectly blunt, take graft—my advice to you is to get out and get out now—there is no place for you in city government."

Mrs. Hortense W. Gabel, administrator of the city Rent and Rehabilitation Administration, is a skillful politician and a former housing assistant to the Mayor. She agrees with Commissioner Birns.

"I would say the great bulk of property owners are not very sophisticated but they are not crooks," she testifies. "I would say there is a small group—and it's too bad the real estate lobby doesn't try to separate this small group out and not defend it unwittingly and ignorantly—who cause most of the slum troubles in any city."

Mrs. Gabel, who has spent more than thirty years in the housing field in New York, says emotionally: "East Harlem and all the East Harlems of this nation are a symbol of the profound moral failure of the people and the governments of this country. They tell us, and they also tell the world, that we have failed in the most primitive obligation that any decent society has: to provide decent, safe, and sanitary shelter in decent neighborhoods for the community's families.

"There are really two kinds of people who operate slums—professional slumlords who milk deliberately and the poor devil who is anxious to invest three thousand dollars in hard-earned money," Mrs. Gabel continues. "He frequently spends his time trying to collect rent for a first mortgagee who is likely to be a very respectable bank; a second mortgagee who may well be a businessman who has turned his funds over to his lawyer and has no knowledge of where his money is going; a third mortgagee who can be an unscrupulous broker who has sucked the owner in. The professional slum operator probably makes the highest profit of any businessman in the country."

In Mrs. Gabel's view, most of the city's judges, although personally honest, contribute indirectly to poor housing conditions. "Judges," she explains, "are still loath to impose jail sentences on slum owners. They have the feeling almost that this is a civil crime. Now this is changing more and more in

New York and other cities. The judges are beginning to realize that a jail sentence is one of the few ways to go beyond the pocketbook motive, but we have a long way to go to convince sincere, well-meaning judges that a man who operates a slum, deliberately milking it and exploiting it for costs and ruining the human values of the tenants, is really a criminal."

Mrs. Gabel testifies that she is sympathetic with those tenants who must live in the slums. She explains their dilemma this way:

"So often people say to me, 'Nobody has to live in a slum.' To my way of thinking, this indicates a complete lack of understanding of the problems of people who are forced to live in slums. The overwhelming majority of slum-livers in our city are minority people. They are Puerto Ricans and Negroes.

"If they do suffer the color barrier and the language barrier as well as barriers of coming very quickly from a rural society and being shoved into an industrial cold climate in the North, they cannot get out even if they want to. Negro families of means in Harlem often send their children to private school to escape some of the impact of the slums. But they can't get out. The discrimination problem, the lack of know-how in living, the deprivation of these families, economically and socially, condemns them to the slums. They can't move out just because they want to."

Welfare Commissioner James R. Dumpson is the man in the city administration responsible for moving relief families in and out of 311 East 100th Street. "People do not move out of slum areas on their own as frequently as we would wish. Frankly, there is no place for them to move. We put them in houses like number 311 because we cannot put them out on the streets," he says.

"But, of course, there's another reason," the commissioner adds, "and that is that people who have had to live in slums for long periods of time have lost the will to change. They become beaten down, they become frustrated. They get a sense of complete loss about the direction of their lives, and many of the efforts that they might make in terms of moving out to different housing are completely lost to them."

The welfare commissioner says he is forced to put welfare families in slums because "there is no greater unmet need in the City of New York today than the lack of plentiful supply of good low-cost housing. Before we can substantially reduce costs in public-welfare operations a solution must be found to the housing problem."

Dumpson disclosed in testimony at a hearing before the Temporary State Commission on Low Income Housing on October 29, 1963, that there were hazardous violations in more than 9000 buildings in which welfare clients lived. Of the 80,000 families on the welfare rolls, Dumpson said, 40,000 need rehousing badly. "If we could move these families into decent housing at fair rentals, we would do so tomorrow. But such housing does not exist."

The commissioner blamed the slow rate of public-housing construction for the welfare-housing dilemma. The number of welfare families in public housing has remained unchanged since 1959. Families on relief occupy only 10 per cent of the 100 low-rent public-housing developments throughout the city. "It will take fifty years to meet the housing needs of the present welfare population at the present rate of construction," Dumpson said.

Ira S. Robbins, a member of the New York City Housing Authority and one of the staunch supporters of public housing in the 1930s, concedes that part of the blame for houses like number 311 lies with the city itself.

"In 1901 there were 82,000 old-law tenements. In 1964 there are still 43,000. In other words, we haven't demolished as much as the public thinks we have. Our job is to get rid of the old tenements. We have done only half the job.

"We have also had the influx and overcrowding of low-income families in buildings which are sixty years old. It's also partly due to our tax system—we haven't evolved a system of taxing profits from slum ownership. This is partly due to court decisions which give slum owners high prices for overcrowded slum buildings in condemnation proceedings.

"There is also the greed of some property owners, the need for tenant education on the use of housing, and the problem of a shortage of housing for low-income families. All of these are tied up with the problem of poverty and slums."

Milton Mollen, an attorney, is chairman of the Housing and Redevelopment Board and, as head of the Mayor's Housing Policy Executive Committee, he is the number-one housing official in New York City.

"We are essentially struggling," he says, "with the accumulated effects of three hundred years of neglect and exploitation—both of buildings and people. There is no single cause of slums. They are the product of many forces acting together—physical, economic, social.

"To begin with, the buildings are old and decrepit. Many were built in the least desirable area of the city. Into these buildings crowded wave upon wave of newcomers. Most were forced by poverty, prejudice or both to take whatever housing was offered them, at least until they could work their way up the economic and social ladder to command something better.

"Then their places were taken by new groups. The years of abuse, from overcrowding, from unknowing tenants, from exploiting landlords, have only worsened the basic inadequacy of the tenements. In a vicious cycle the bad housing conditions under which slum families live tend to magnify the very disabilities and problems which brought them there in the first place. These problems spill over into the streets and aggravate the neighborhood blight."

Robert Moses has served New York City for more than forty years. The one-time secretary of state under Governor Alfred E. Smith has been a member of the City Planning Commission, Parks Commissioner, and has held a dozen other posts—including that of chairman of the Slum Clearance Committee. He describes the genesis of the slum in this way:

The general pattern of the development of slums is almost always the same. They begin with the overcrowding of existing buildings and the addition of tenements built by conscienceless speculators to a considerable height on little land, without reference to light, air, sanitation, and other standards of decent living and safety. The place of a single family in a reasonably comfortable house is taken by a number of families, and in the tenements people are packed in like chickens in a coop. Wave after wave of newcomers inhabits these rookeries. As soon as one generation achieves enough prosperity to get out, it moves on and another with lower standards and income takes its place.

By the time civic and social workers succeed in impressing upon the old-line politicians the enormity of this process, the neighborhood has degenerated to such an extent that it becomes a question whether anything short of complete clearance is worth attempting. In the meantime local political hacks satisfy the customers—or at least prevent open revolution—by handouts of coal and wood, groceries and Christmas baskets. Property owners, real estate developers and their allies, banks, estates, and even churches, are content to collect their rents and close their eyes to the implications of their investments.[2]

Moses says the blame for what has happened in neighborhoods like East Harlem lies with the men who created the buildings at the turn of the century. "New York's leading real estate operators," says Moses, "at the turn of the century have now passed on to what is conventionally known as their reward. I devoutly hope this reward will be adequate, because they were without question the most malignant influence on the city and its surroundings in my lifetime. Their disservice to the community should be noted from time to time so that it will not be repeated. These men created our slums of today."

They left a "slimy trail" behind them which eventually had to be "mopped up" by public officials with public funds, Moses continues. "Almost every city has them but I claim without pride that we had the topnotchers in New York. The fact that they were often extravagantly admired and praised as pioneers by their own generation and regarded as leading citizens by the next is one of the saddest commentaries on our urban civilization. It is, thank God, an era that is over, but we still have a tremendous price to pay for it—a price we are paying every day in the form of high taxes, bad living, economic dry rot, humiliation, disease, and crime. Real estate operators are only just beginning to recognize their responsibilities."[3]

Former Assemblyman Mark Lane underscores Commissioner Dumpson's point that the families in 311 East 100th Street cannot simply pick up their belongings and move away. But he feels there is another, more compelling reason for their plight. When he was in office in 1961, Lane charged:

"Almost all of the people living in this area are Negro and Puerto Rican, members of minority groups. Other portions of New York City are just not open to them. Recently I traveled through Georgia, Mississippi, and Alabama, and as bad as things may be there I found no area in that portion of the country more sharply segregated than the assembly district which I represent in New York.

"In the heart of my district in East Harlem is 311 East 100th Street. It is a bad building. It is overrun with rats and roaches, no heat in the wintertime, no hot water the year round. One of the basic reasons for the suffering of the people on 100th Street and many other communities throughout the United States is the huge profits which are realized by unscrupulous landlords who charge rents which are not compatible with the services they don't render.

"You find landlords who pile tenant upon tenant, and see there are apartments overcrowded. But nevertheless they seem to escape criminal prosecution. And really there is no crime greater than, it seems to me, forcing these people to live through a winter without any heat, allowing fire escapes to be broken so that children may fall, sometimes to their death, allowing children to be bitten by rats."

Lane says such conditions are permitted to exist because landlords "hide behind a corporate front of one kind or another, and the law finds responsible only some poor little superintendent someplace because he is the only one that can be located. The tenants don't know where the landlord is when they have to make complaints. In the last ten or eleven years here in East Harlem I have represented some five or six thousand families living in conditions similar to the ones at number 311. And, in many cases, it has taken us many months even to discover who the landlord is. The landlord just has an address, post-office box. That is the only contact the families in the buildings have with the landlord.

"There have been efforts over the years to bring about stringent regulations to see to it that landlords who are criminals—criminals—are severely dealt with. But unfortunately the huge and powerful real estate lobbies here in New York and in other cities seem to always prevail when there is an effort made to pass decent legislation to regulate these practices and to prohibit them."

Carlos Rios, a Puerto Rican who succeeded Lane as assemblyman from the 10th Assembly District, is equally vehement against the owners. "If we will count the times we have taken landlords to court because of their abuses," he says with a smile, "I would like to have that number in dollars. We have been fighting these conditions for many years. We recognize the buildings are old, but this is not an excuse.

"In some respects," Rios goes on, "I will agree the tenants need to be educated. In the same way there are good and bad people in a family, some of the tenants don't deserve to live here. I have seen with my own eyes the landlord put glass in a window and two hours later the glass is broken by a tenant. I know this is a problem for East 100th Street landlords. Tenants break pipes and steal them to sell. But this still doesn't let landlords off the hook.

"The best way to solve the problem is to take the landlords to the court. We have the laws, but we need better enforcement. The city makes a survey, but after that is done, what is the result? If you pass by two months later, you will see the same violations."

Rios and Lane both stress race prejudice as the underlying reason for the immobility of the slum population. "We have the same discrimination as there is in the South," says

Rios. "Landlords don't want Negroes and Puerto Ricans living in their buildings, so they wind up here in East Harlem.

"But the people who live in these slums are crying for better housing. They are citizens, they are humans. They carry the burdens of the city and they are living in the worst conditions. Families pay hundreds of dollars for a pigsty. We have seen people downtown paying the same amount of money and they have everything. For this I can only blame the landlords."

Jerome L. Wilson, state senator from the 22nd Senate District, which covers East Harlem, says economics is the root cause of slums.

"The chief problem," Wilson says, "is the pure and simple lack of money. East Harlem has the lowest median family income of any neighborhood in the city—$3700. How can a family feed, clothe, and keep themselves on that amount? They can't, obviously. The needle and the bottle for the susceptible provide the temporary answer.

"Who is to blame for this? Primarily, I blame government and the voters' all-too-great willingness to turn away from the problem of poverty in our midst. The laws about minimum wages are ludicrously low. Unemployment, which is perpetually at crisis proportions in this neighborhood, is ignored. We need WPA, CCC, the Marshall Plan, the Peace Corps, the Army Corps of Engineers, the Air Force, and the Marines to afford employment opportunities and decent wages for the people in East Harlem. Give the people the tools for decent living, to paraphrase Winston Churchill's wartime plea, and they will finish the job."

East Harlem is also part of City Councilman Robert A. Low's district.

"Overcrowding is perhaps the single most damaging element in the housing picture today," he says. "Despite the
construction of some one hundred thousand units of public
housing—more than has been constructed in the rest of the
United States—a serious housing shortage continues to exist.

"Discrimination has added to the problem, because it has
had the effect of containing our newcomers with their large
families in the worst housing. Opportunists have moved in
as landlords to take advantage of this critical situation. Many
have been more interested in taking out quick profits than
in maintaining their properties and they have permitted them
to deteriorate. When finally brought to court by the city,
they have pleaded inability to make the necessary repairs
because of the rent limitations set by the city.

"In some cases, the deterioration has been accelerated by
tenants unaccustomed to, and unprepared for, city living.

"The city has been slow in meeting the problem on three
counts: first, in failing to develop, in cooperation with landlords, an effective maintenance and rehabilitation program;
second, in failing to consolidate and streamline its code enforcement procedures; and, third, in failing to activate a
meaningful tenant education program."

New York City's five borough presidents have set up local
"planning boards" composed of volunteers in each community. Each board meets once a week to discuss the specific
needs of its own neighborhood. The boards include businessmen, social workers, artists, writers, civil-service workers,
laborers, and many more.

Do these planning boards succeed in doing the job for
which they have been created? Is the planning board in
East Harlem helping solve that community's problems—
specifically the decline and fall of East 100th Street?

Listen to Henry J. Stern, assistant to Borough President Edward R. Dudley, who replies:

"The people of East Harlem are completely unaware and apathetic. They don't know what's going on. And these so-called leaders who attend the board meetings are caught up in a political struggle for local power. What's needed is real community participation. One reason the area got to be so bad is that few people cared enough to stop what was going on around them."

Stern agrees with Senator Wilson's view of the controversy. "If these people had jobs," Stern says, "they would live better. They earn so little they can't provide for their families."

As for the condition of the housing, Stern says "there's nothing to do with the old tenements except let them rot, unless you have new tools and a new approach, the case-work approach, family by family, door by door. The fault in East Harlem is the fault of the city's social services. Although it's spending more and more money, it's falling further and further behind. We continue to look to government to solve all of our problems. We give government more and more money to spend, but in government few people do much work. You only get paperwork and discussion.

"In private industry you have the check—is it working? Is it making money? Is it pulling its weight? In government nobody does this but the city administrator's office. In government where you have so many Civil-Service workers the only concern is working less and being paid more. They know nothing about the people in this city who get beaten up or the merchants who have to pay bribes."

Ask Stern about the landlords' place in this grim picture and he replies:

"You cannot expect people in this capitalistic system who

buy buildings for profit to be guided by anything but profit. You can't improve the buildings. The slumlords don't provide the services, but the decay of the buildings is due to age and deterioration and vandalism as well as the owner's neglect. But you can't realistically expect owners as a class to improve buildings unless the law tells them to. Rent control is partially responsible, too."

In the final analysis, Stern admits that government has failed in the battle against the slum. "Social workers are among the most ineffective people in society—that's why they're social workers. Many devoted social workers are overwhelmed by what they see in East Harlem. This is not like building a highway. It can't be done just by putting in more manpower. The city under Mayor Wagner is committed to slum clearance in theory, and while the Mayor and the city are in a state of rightness and decency, they have a sense of futility. This is essentially their attitude. The city doesn't have the resources, the programs, or the taxing power to raise funds to tear these buildings down and put up new ones."

Deputy Manhattan Borough President Earl Brown, a Negro politician who, as a city councilman, was a sponsor of the city's first Fair Housing Practices Law, admits that "city government talks about doing things for the people, but we must do things *with* [italics Brown's] them. We must win their confidence on the basis of equality."

Brown's long experience in politics leads him to blame his own Democratic party for the city's present housing ills. "Stagnation of slums," he concedes, "is due to the one-party system in the past fifty years in New York. The great tragedy of politics in New York City is that the politician here has vegetated and has let society's needs pass him by. He has remained static, small-minded, completely opportunistic."

Brown believes the "politics of housing" has become so important today that "no official will ask a tenant to move." He charges: "The city traditionally has done the least for those who need the most and the most for those who need the least. This includes health, police, and education services—right across the board. As soon as a neighborhood declines, the city ignores it. The city, through indifference, lack of courage and political cynicism, has failed through the years to protect itself.

"It has tried valiantly to keep the people in the slum houses out of sight. It has neglected such areas as East Harlem and East 100th Street where you find a slothful, indifferent air on the part of police. They consort openly with racketeers in this district; cops have been in the numbers racket and they are practically pimps for the whores there.

"I contend that in great urban areas cities must put their best in the worst places. Then they can go to a landlord and he may respond. Otherwise, he believes he's part of a system he knows to be a racket. This requires extraordinary political courage, but we must do something because the tab is too high. Now, no private agency can handle it alone. The city's neighborhood conservation program does a 'lick and split' job with a million and a half dollars a year. It needs at least ten million. We're building up a political football. Every neighborhood group comes in now and says, 'I want one [neighborhood conservation project], too.' I say, let the city concentrate on one area and have something to show for its effort."

Brown does not hold the Mayor personally responsible for the city's apparent lack of progress during the past decade. "I sincerely believe that Bob Wagner has more sympathy for people than any guy I've run into in city gov-

ernment," Brown says. "He's done more than anybody else—
but it's still not enough. Kids go to school in an area like
East Harlem for years and they still can't read or write. These
are some of the things that tell the tragic story of a blighted
area.

"In New York, it's popular to espouse the cause of more
housing. But no thought has gone into it. It's been a willy-
nilly program of spending money and putting up brick and
mortar. The agencies that plan housing are motivated only
by press, politics, and pressure. These are the ingredients
which build housing in New York. This is why I felt frustrated and could not sleep at night when I was a member of
the Housing and Redevelopment Board."

Although critical of official efforts to eliminate slums,
Brown believes that owners and mortgagees of slum tenements are also at fault. "They are partners in human misery,"
he says. The deputy borough president is just as critical of
some tenants. "Many tenants come to New York as immigrants with completely nonurban mores and attitudes. Many
try hard to keep decent homes, but some collapse. They are
the prostitutes, dope addicts, and others who completely dis-
integrate. These are the people who have spilled into East
100th Street. This is the hard-core problem of New York
today. These are the people who infect each block."

Manhattan Borough President Dudley himself has made
many trips into the slums of Harlem. He has often publicly
proclaimed that he was appalled by the terrible living conditions he saw. On one such tour of East Harlem—in October
1961, just before elections—the borough president hinted at
what he believed to be one flaw in the city's effort to rid
New York of slums. After visiting three tenements in which
tenants told him they had no hot water for months, he
stated:

"Maybe by continually sending these same landlords into the courts they will realize how serious the problem is and not let them off so easy. Unless the courts start to cooperate, we are in bad shape."[4]

"It is a mistaken belief that slums are made by the people who live in them," says Mayor Robert F. Wagner. "The fact is that the people who own slum properties are often much more responsible for slum conditions. By this I mean the slumlords, that small body of landlords who are out to squeeze every last dollar out of the property as quickly as they can, regardless of the consequences in terms of human lives, suffering, and sickness. It is against this small minority that battle must be given—constant, unremitting and unrelenting battle."[5]

Wagner implicates a building's mortgagee as well as its owner. "In every housing case there are at least four parties," he says, "the owners, the tenants, the city and the mortgagee. We proceed criminally against the owner. We educate the tenant. We improve the procedures of our municipal agencies to meet slum threats. But the fourth party, the mortgagee, sits in the background collecting his interest and amortization, unconcerned with the violations which take root, knowing but ignoring the fact that under his mortgage he has the legal right to foreclose if there is failure by the owner to comply with the building codes."[6]

Ask Mayor Wagner why the city has not succeeded in wiping out slums and he replies:

"On the whole, over most of the current century since government was forced into the field of policing private housing and then furnishing housing with its own funds, private industry refused to admit its failures and government's own actions were slow, hesitant, and faltering.

" 'What have you done about it?' people ask. We have

pushed our public-housing program faster than it has been pushed anyplace else in the United States. We have teams cracking down on the worst of our buildings . . . and most recently we have embarked on a program of neighborhood-conservation districts . . . we are enlisting the help of the people of community centers in individual districts to spruce up and keep up and clean up the area and houses in which they live. To these districts, to help avoid the spread of slums, we give the coordinated efforts of city agencies such as health and welfare, sanitation, buildings, police and fire departments. Rather than sitting on our hands in connection with the slum problem, we have probed, we have studied, and we have acted."[7]

State Comptroller Arthur Levitt has taken issue with the Mayor's actions. Striving to unseat Wagner as the Democratic candidate for Mayor in 1961, Levitt campaigned during the summer of that year up and down the streets of New York with one main theme: Wagner was a "housing hoaxter" and he, Levitt, would take the profits out of slum ownership.

The comptroller hit hard at the Mayor in speech after speech, opening deep wounds within the Democratic Party, much to the delight of their mutual opponent, Republican Attorney General Louis J. Lefkowitz. Levitt blamed Wagner for failing to cope with the spread of slums. He declared:

"He has done little to solve the city's housing woes, but has done much to brag about his accomplishments." Levitt criticized the Mayor after Wagner's much-publicized trip to East 100th Street in 1961 for going into Harlem only at election time. "The city must start erecting middle and low income housing at an accelerated pace," Levitt declared, "Mayor Wagner thought it more important to build luxury houses for the wealthy, while the people of Harlem, as well as other areas, live in intolerable conditions."

Levitt eventually lost his bid to wrest the Democratic nomination away from the incumbent, but by his attacks against Mayor Wagner on the subject of housing gave the Republicans ammunition.

State Attorney General Louis J. Lefkowitz also capitalized on slums as an issue in his 1961 campaign and accused the Wagner administration of a "dismal failure" in combating New York slums. He contended that "lack of vigorous, decisive enforcement of the laws now on the books" had brought the city under Mayor Wagner to the point where its slums constituted "its greatest shame."

Lefkowitz placed the blame for number 311 and all the other slums like it in the Mayor's lap just before the election when he charged:

It is only with the smell of election day that Mayor Wagner even makes the slightest showing of interest in the problems of slum housing. He will not fool anyone into believing that he really cares about the slum problem which he has forgotten or ignored in nonelection years.[8]

Another state official who mixes politics with housing skillfully is James W. Gaynor, New York State housing commissioner. Commenting on Mayor Wagner's goal of a slumless city, Gaynor told a luncheon of the Citizens' Housing and Planning Council on May 14, 1963:

A slumless city has been a pervading and recurring symbol in the history of New York. At the start of the twentieth century, it was the ideological force behind the enactment of the Tenement House Law. In the thirties, it evoked the first public housing programs. Today, more than six decades after the turn of the century, it remains an elusive and unrealized end. In fact, it has tended to become a blurred vision of a golden era occurring some time after the year 2000.

Gaynor does not argue with the goal. He takes issue with the methods used to achieve it. He criticizes the Wagner administration for leaning on what he calls the "myth of clearance and code enforcement," the mistaken belief that the city's slums can be eliminated by stepping up enforcement and tearing down buildings. But this strategy, Gaynor says, is failing because "the goal of full enforcement, like the goal of the slumless city, continues to be postponed and deferred. We are not meeting the demands of families displaced by demolition, nor are we meeting the requirements of families still remaining in substandard units. In sum, we are not actually running hard enough to stand still in our approach to the goal of a slumless city."

Gaynor believes the erection of low-cost housing to replace slums is not the answer. He warns that the city must "break away from the present pattern of economic and racial segregation that is one of the distinguishing characteristics of low-rent housing." The state's housing chief is also critical of the city's failure to "budget" future land use—to plan ahead. "We are planning," he says, "merely to meet our present problems, rather than scheduling future growth."

Representative Adam Clayton Powell, whose Harlem district includes the house at 311 East 100th Street, offers this reply to the question of why large segments of East Harlem have been permitted to remain slums. "It is definitely because the City of New York refuses to enforce the laws which would put these buildings out of existence," he says. "In thirty days, these pockets of poverty—these ghettos—would have to be closed down because each and every building has many violations that are just not enforced."

New York Governor Nelson A. Rockefeller blames the New York slums largely on the city's failure to enforce its

For 5000 people, East 100th Street is home. (*Credit Walter Albertin*)

Number 311 East 100th Street: symbol of all slums. (*Credit Phil Stanziola*)

At the front door of poverty. (*Credit Phil Stanziola*)

(Left, above) "I live here because I can't move."—Mrs. Petra Rodriguez.

(Left, below) 1906 kitchen in 1964.

(Right) The slum child . . . the most pitiful victim.

(Below) "All the time there are rats here."—Mrs. Candida Matos.

(*All credits Phil Stanziola*)

Companions of the tenement. (*Credit Phil Stanziola*)

Window on a world of want. (*Credit Phil Stanziola*)

"All I live for is my next fix."—Eddie, a dope addict. (*Credit Walter Albertin*)

housing code. In 1963, he attacked the Wagner administration for failing to inspect annually all of the city's multiple dwellings.[9] He called the city's failure to inspect every tenement at least once a year a "tragedy, particularly in this area where human problems are so importantly related to the conditions."

"The excuse is given," Rockefeller declared, "that they haven't got the personnel. But I think also politics comes into this because I don't think it's very popular to make these inspections and I think an awful lot of sliding is going on which is really allowing human misery to continue when there is no reason for it to continue and when the people have spoken through the enactment of laws."

Re-emphasizing the charge that code enforcement is lagging badly, the Governor added:

"The tragedy of this situation is that so often it's a lot cheaper to pay the fine than it is to make the correction. And when the owner of the building knows there's a good chance he won't be inspected again for half a dozen years, this is an easy way out and the result is that the city is just not doing the job that the people have mandated through the law and elected officials to carry out."

The Governor subscribes to the theory that by opening up employment, the slum dwellers' lot would be much improved. "I think the important thing is that we've got to have more and better jobs for these minority groups because if they don't have the jobs they haven't got the money to pay the rent and therefore, hand in hand with assuring them equal access to housing, is the opportunity to earn the funds to be able to pay for it."

How does Rockefeller feel about Wagner's prediction that New York City will be a slumless city within fifty years?

"Well, my reaction is, it's a long time after he's in office," the Governor replies. "I hope we won't have to wait fifty years frankly and in my opinion, we have the tools in the middle-income field now . . . we ought to get them in the low-income field, and in the rehabilitation of housing. There's no reason to wait. Why don't we shoot for ten years from now? Make it realistic. Let's do it for the people who are living here and now and not have to wait for their children and grandchildren before we can achieve goals which are essential in a modern free society."

Governor Rockefeller also lays partial blame on rent control. "While rent control was necessary for the government to regulate rents during the long apartment shortage in New York City," he says, "we must also face realistically the stark fact that rent controls actually multiply and perpetuate the blighted living conditions we all desire to have eliminated and replaced by new and improved decent housing facilities.

"There can be no disagreement among responsible leaders in public service that the people of the City of New York deserve vastly more progress toward decent housing and an end to conditions, born of the housing shortage, that have made rent control necessary for the past twenty years."

Another Republican governor, Mark O. Hatfield of Oregon, visited East 100th Street in 1959. "My impressions were gained in talking to gang leaders, merchants, and residents of the area," he reports, "and in spite of the dreariness and monotony of the buildings and the architecture, there was a brightness and sparkle reflected in the eyes and words of the people.

"I felt a most warm welcome and eagerness to share an idea, an experience, a comment, a deep appreciation for being looked upon and accepted as citizens, human beings— like citizens and human beings elsewhere," Hatfield continues. "These people are not different—their environment is different. They possess the same vision, hunger, dreams, ambition as people anywhere else. Their mores are conditioned by their life's experience but their souls, hearts, and minds are basically the same as mine—one living in the Far West in a small community.

"Environments are not going to change overnight. In fact, I believe it to be an oversimplification to place the total problem of social living in the area of environment. I believe that many of the social problems of this area could be attacked through (1) realizing that these people are basically no different than any other people, (2) that their needs in many ways are spiritual, and (3) not isolate them from contact or concern."[10]

Dr. Robert C. Weaver, the country's top housing official, testifies that "the development of any slum area is a consequence of many factors. First, of course, it reflects the fact that our cities are dynamic and changing; that people move, and that in our society prestige addresses become status symbols.

"In general," continues the administrator of the Housing and Home Finance Agency, "this process is accelerated in cities like New York where there is a constant immigration of large numbers of persons, many of whom are unfamiliar and unprepared for urban living. Decline of areas is further accelerated by their neglect. This may take the form of inadequate public facilities, such as police protection, garbage collection, maintenance of streets, and the like.

"In New York City another principal factor has been overcrowding. The economics of the situation are clear. They reflect a general housing shortage, a lack of standard low-cost housing, and artificial limitations upon the mobility concentrated upon ethnic minorities.

"One situation which is often overlooked is the fact that the filtering-down theory does not work the way its proponents would lead us to believe that it should. To wit, occupancy of housing designed for higher income groups, built many years ago, is seldom readily adaptable to the needs and requirements of low-income people. Many buildings which are structurally sound become, in the passage of time, architecturally obsolete."[11]

Attorney General Robert F. Kennedy is the highest government official in the nation who has seen the "worst block" and 311 East 100th Street with his own eyes. He reports:

I've seen these kinds of things before. I went to East 100th Street when I worked on our juvenile delinquency program. I think if people made enough money and had jobs—full employment— these kinds of things would improve. If enough opportunities were given to the people, the side effects we find in the slums would improve.[12]

CHAPTER 9

THE SOUL-MAKERS

THE REVEREND WENDELL H. ELMENDORF, JR., a young pleasant-mannered Protestant minister who graduated from Williams College in the peaceful Massachusetts countryside, came to New York in 1955 and stationed himself in a tiny flat on the ground floor of 311 East 100th Street.

When he first moved into number 311 the clergyman wrote an article and mailed it back to Massachusetts for printing in his college alumni magazine. "I found my new home sometimes exasperating," he wrote, "but always fascinating; my neighbors warmly affectionate, and briskly spontaneous and unpredictable."

Elmendorf's approach to religion was down-to-earth. "A bull session with a group of boys under a street lamp late at night," he said, "often provides a better opportunity for exploring the deeper phases of the Christian faith than a Bible class. A personal talk with a boy, perhaps not enrolled in the parish program, can often plant the seeds of a changed life more readily than a sermon on Sunday morning. A glass of beer in a local bar may prove more effective than a confessional booth in a church."

The clergyman points to narcotics and bad housing as two destructive aspects of East 100th Street. "I suppose the worst thing that the slum conditions produce," he says, "is the feeling of despair that many of the people have. They turn for help and see only a maze of red tape in the various agencies of the city. And very often it seems as if no one has the heart to care for their problems, and they seem to be reduced to a number on an apartment house, in a numbered building, on a numbered street between two numbered avenues in a city that is known throughout the world for its vast numbers that live here.

"One of the mistakes we often make," he continues, "is that we blame our slums on the people who live there. But they didn't create the slums; they didn't build these tenements; they aren't the ones who own them and let them run down beyond a state of repair; they didn't create rats and garbage. It is not their fault that the landlord doesn't provide enough receptacles that contain the refuse. They are not responsible.

"Often the people who live in these houses are crushed by overwhelming problems. Men can't find jobs that pay enough to support their families. The welfare department provides some, but often you have to try to come to grips with the red tape there. It is too much and too confusing. And a person can be cut off from his welfare support overnight and be left with nothing to pay his rent or pay his food bill. A mother copes with the overwhelming problems of a son who is becoming addicted to narcotics. She is ashamed to admit it and doesn't know where to turn for help or what to say or what to do. But these are conditions which they did not create."

Who is to blame? "The slumlord bears the primary responsibility," Elmendorf says, "but we have all turned our backs on the slums, and for that we are all to blame, and the infliction of the slum is something that is the responsibility of every American."

Elmendorf says the "racial question" is at the base of the slum. "This has been brewing since the Civil War," he says bitterly. "The people in 100th Street tell me how they have been hurt. The most eloquent are the teen-agers who see the TV commercials blaring how to get ahead and they grow up and find the world is different than what they were told, so apathy comes at an early age. These are the recruits of Malcolm X. The appealing thing about Malcolm X is the racial supremacy idea. When the underdog is told 'You're better,' it falls on welcome ears."

East 100th Street is reputed to be one of the biggest centers of narcotics traffic in the city, but it is only "small stuff" compared to the bigger operation throughout Harlem, according to the Rev. Lynn Hageman, an associate of Elmendorf's in the East Harlem Protestant Parish, who operates a clinic for addicts on East 103rd Street between First and Second avenues.

"We feel a deep responsibility for the two hundred to three hundred addicts who live in the immediate vicinity," Hageman says. "Some wind up in jail, some in hospitals, and some work and support their habit legally. The police leave us alone, but not the kids. The addicts make things pretty miserable; they steal from their own families and the whole neighborhood suffers. The fact is, the addicts are not a horribly lovable bunch. They are a fairly miserable lot. A few broke into my office recently and stole fifteen hundred dollars' worth of equipment. We have a good idea who they are."

Why do they become addicts?

"You can call it the culture of poverty and subculture of the criminal. These two come together where you have the rejected. It infects youngsters because of the meaninglessness of life, their sense of having no value or role as a social participant. Yet they possess the quality of youth which all

America holds up and admires. But in them this quality just lays there and rots. Those who experiment in narcotics find a role and status as a consumer and they get satisfaction. They find meaning in it, costly and painful, but still they get a sense of purpose from it."

The Rev. Norman Eddy, a Congregationalist minister and a member of the group ministry of the East Harlem Protestant Church, organized a committee to work on the narcotics problem in 1956 and it became a regular neighborhood program of referral and aftercare. In 1962, testifying before a Senate subcommittee investigating illegal narcotics traffic and its effect on juvenile and young-adult criminality, Eddy said his committee had seen more than 2000 separate individuals who had come to the clinic voluntarily. He estimated that at that time this amounted to 10 per cent of the 22,000 addicts then in New York City and almost 5 per cent of the estimated 45,000 addicts in the United States.

"The tragedy behind these figures," Eddy told the Senate committee, "is that our operation is so tiny; we cannot give any real help to any but a few hundred who live in our immediate neighborhood. The fact that so many crowd into our office each day is mute testimony of the desperation of the addicted, the scarcity of facilities to help them, and their real eagerness to be helped.

"Our program is complex," Eddy continued, "as we aim to be able to follow the addicted individual from the first time we meet him in the hospital or prison, back out on the street, into his home life, and, hopefully, through his period of rehabilitation. If he has a slip, we stand by and help him begin again. Our aim is to alleviate suffering for the many, to help some to abstain from narcotics completely, and to help many others to learn to manage their habits without resorting to crime."[1]

Herschell Ross is employed by the New York City Youth Board to win the confidence of the boys with whom he works on the streets and to reach them by setting an example.

"After knowing many of them," says Ross, a big good-looking Negro who trained for his post for many years, "we try to help individual youngsters with their problems. We get to know the parents, teachers, and what the boys do all night. I have gotten to know the Magistrates gang in East 100th Street, for example. They are essentially Puerto Ricans. It seems in this day utterly impossible but some of those boys can't even read the name of the streets up here. We have this throughout East Harlem—youngsters can't read or write.

"We try to broaden the scope of these boys," Ross goes on. "One day recently one of them told me, 'People on welfare can't go to college, can they?' They seem to accept their spot down there and they think they can't rise above it. I feel they have not been properly motivated so I try to take individual kids and get them to realize that by going to school new doors will open up to them. We had one kid who finished high school while in jail on Rikers Island. I visited him every two weeks. He told me, 'Herschell, you're my friend.' That meant he trusted me and I was about the only one he trusted because most of the time he would tell me, 'Herschell, people are no damn good until they prove themselves.' This kid got out of jail and he got out of high school. Then one day I got a phone call from the police to come on over to his apartment. He had taken an overdose of narcotics. He was dead. This was the one guy I thought I could save."

Ask Ross whose fault it is that most of these boys, even with help from sensitive men like himself, still wind up as educational and emotional casualties. He tells you:

"I blame it on the complacency of the people in the houses and the people in responsible positions. The people in East 100th Street, for instance, don't know that there are services available for them. If somebody could come in and point out to them what demands they could make of city agencies—of police, sanitation, and building departments; if they could organize themselves and make such demands they would cut down on the narcotics. The people themselves are permitting this. Compare this with Park Avenue. If these elements started to come into Park Avenue, you would hear some loud complaints and the city would act—fast!"

Ross is convinced the police in East Harlem make little effort to help the people. "One day I was walking down the street—the cops didn't know me—and two cops came along and pushed me into a paddy wagon with three addicts. They threw me against the side of the wagon and searched me. They roughed me up—then I told them to lay off and told them who I was. There's no doubt that cops tend to look down at the groups living in the slums, just because most of the slum dwellers are Negroes or Puerto Ricans."

The attitude of the youngsters toward the "outside world," Ross says, is fatalistic. "They feel they're just not 'lucky' and if they do want something, it's usually a Cadillac or a hundred-dollar suit or a pair of thirty-dollar shoes. The racketeer is the richest person they know, so they want what he has. These kids rarely go outside of East Harlem, though, because they're insecure elsewhere. They know the streets here. They feel more comfortable. It's less anxiety-producing."

Ross says there are fewer of the traditional fighting gangs in East Harlem than there were a decade ago. Now he is apt to find gangs composed of both Puerto Ricans and Negroes and the rivalry is based more on neighborhood than on race or religion, as it was in the old days. As for 100th Street, Ross says it is not the worst he has ever seen. "The reason that every official in the city pays so much attention to it," he says simply, "is that there are a lot of votes on East 100th Street. I would say a lot of people are trying to do something on that block but it's the supreme effort that is missing. I'm coming to the conclusion that the street should not exist. They say don't bulldoze the street and break up the community, but I'd rather see that since nothing's being done."

For five painstaking years, Dr. Beatrice Bishop Berle, wife of former Undersecretary of State A. A. Berle and an internist associated with several of New York's best hospitals, operated a family medical clinic in a converted apartment on the ground floor of the building at 311 East 100th Street.

The purpose of Dr. Berle's clinic was to find out if by establishing family medical service in a slum environment it would be possible to help people to resist the physical and mental pitfalls around them. According to Dr. Berle, the premise was that "in a neighborhood-oriented, neighborhood-integrated medical facility, both physicians and patients would come to share a common knowledge of the environment in which they live and the manner in which they perceive life's difficulties."

"The primary need in a neighborhood like this," Dr. Berle believes, "is a better form of social organization. Even if you had better buildings and more doctors, you would still need to take a closer look at each individual. Look at the census figures on this block—fifty per cent of the people over twenty-five don't have better than an eighth-grade education. How can they get a better job out of that? It perpetuates itself. The best medical care might even be detrimental. If you spent a great deal of money keeping alive premature twins of a fifteen-year-old girl who has a sixth-grade education, for example, you know these children just don't have any future."

The perpetuation of the slums, Dr. Berle continues, is inevitable because of the migration to New York from a primitive environment of families who don't have the tools to more than make a living in the city. "They come to New York because they think they can do better—and they do. They don't starve here. They have running water, rotten housing, and rat bites, but it's still better than what they had before."

She charges that even though many people in the medical field treat poor families, "what we haven't learned to cure is the person with no money. We may take care of his physical needs, but we cannot salvage his other ones. What is needed is a personal interest by the doctors themselves. There must be a different type of medical care.

"Once that 15-year-old girl has the twins you must take care of them and then we get into community organization and education on a large scale."

As for tenement owners and the city departments, Dr. Berle comments: "Sure, many of the owners are speculators. They operate on a shoestring. I suppose if the city did a job the buildings would be cleaned up. I looked over the area services project and I have to laugh at what the city does— in one building the window is broken, toilet flooding, rats, and water leaking from the ceiling above. They called it 'area conversation'—it was, indeed.

"It will be interesting to see if they do anything on East 100th Street. The city said they had sent somebody to the block but the Buildings Department is using IBM processing.

But it takes too long to get the results of the violations. I gather that in order to do something, the various departments are involved. But before they get around to doing anything, a family could freeze to death."

However bad the physical condition of the building—such as number 311 in which her own clinic operated—Dr. Berle adds: "I'm less concerned about this because society can solve this—it's not just the building, it's the people. We must have some way of motivating people. This is more of a problem." She sums up her convictions about what is lacking in number 311 this way:

"You have to care and you have to be highly imaginative in social organization," she says. "Nobody says it better than James Baldwin in his *Fire Next Time* when he talks about the gift of one's self. This is what our civilization doesn't have enough of."

A public-health nurse, who served as one of Dr. Berle's assistants during the five-year experiment, describes her reaction to the people who walked through the doorway of the clinic in the rear of 311 East 100th Street:

"Very often we run up against problems which are beyond ourselves," she admits. "And often I think of trying to get people better homes in public-housing projects. I think the Department of Welfare workers also have a sense of frustration while they are trying to relocate these families.

"Of course, in very crowded quarters a little cold might become a family epidemic, because everybody takes the germs from the rest of the family. Not only that, if one of the children can't sleep at night when it is so hot and wakes up and cries, the total family is awakened; and if the father has to go to work the next day, he is quite tired."

What is the deeper root of these hygienic problems?

"Many of the problems we see," she declares, "have their origin in discrimination. The people in East Harlem are living there because they cannot live in some of the white communities. We deal mostly with Negro and Puerto Rican families, and there definitely is discrimination right here against them. Also, the families are quite large and landlords go up and say, 'We don't want such a large family.'"

Her impression of the block? "When I walk towards the street coming from the West Side," she testifies, "and see practically every child out because of the summer heat, I am convinced it must be the most crowded street and the most congested area. One might wonder why these families are not making more of an effort to get out of 100th Street. I think I know a partial answer: they are limited to where they are; they do not have enough money; they are discriminated against; and they do have large families."

The nurse said that above all she detected a strong resentment on the part of the tenants toward the landlord. "One of the causes of their resentment," she explains, "is the fact that in some cases five people—husband and wife and three children—sleep in one bed, and when you see something like that, everything is out in the open. There is no privacy for the parents; and the children if they become a little noisy might be a nuisance to somebody else. And it's generally not a very health-inducing environment. Also, nutrition is not as good as we like to see it. Often the reason for this is again the budget which these people have."

Dr. Leonard Covello, former principal of the Benjamin Franklin High School in East Harlem and an educational consultant to the Commonwealth of Puerto Rico, firmly believes that the primary reason for juvenile delinquency in East Harlem is that the public schools have failed to do their job.

"Education," he says flatly, "is still the crucial question. The schools don't give a child a sense of his own background or build any pride in him. For decades the schools have not encouraged enough youngsters to identify with their own backgrounds. Instead, many of them have grown up feeling ashamed of their race or religion. What they need is something to counteract the feeling of anonymity. The public schools have not done this.

"The city government has a responsibility, but it's the community-centered schools that should be the focal point of a youngster's life outside of his home. The student should be involved in the planning and carrying out of community projects. Students should be encouraged to go out into the community, not kept within the four walls of the school. We talk about social competence and yet the Board of Education has failed to help the students participate in community life."

Dr. Covello describes his impressions of East Harlem today: "You walk through a block and into the doorway of a building. It is dark and gloomy. Families with children seem to live in fear. On the streets there are so many healthy-looking youngsters, but with no productive work for them. Many seem to be roaming the streets.

"I remember East Harlem many years ago," he continues in contrast, "when the Italians were coming to America. There was a free spirit then, except for 108th Street, which we called the 'murder stable.' On that block the criminals hung out. We had our East 100th Street in those days, too.

"But the bulldozer has destroyed much of the old community life. This has hurt small business, the little store. It was much safer in those days. Now the area is stagnant. To me it's depressing to walk along these streets at night today—all those projects, one building the same as the next. I don't like it."

Michael Decessare, once a student of Dr. Covello's, is now principal of Junior High School 99 on East 100th Street. The school building occupies the block between 99th and 100th streets on the East River, just one block east of the "worst block" between First and Second avenues. Decessare has 1600 students in his school, two thirds of whom are Puerto Rican and one third Negro.

"The fact that they come from the worst slums in the country has an effect on them," he declares, pointing out his office window to East 100th Street below. "Here we have some of the worst housing I've ever seen. Informality reaches a point where it's demoralizing if not immoral. The economic level of these people is far below the families in public housing. The types of crimes are unique—related to alcoholism, narcotics, prostitution. Their clothing is poor. Many are on welfare. In our school, we try to cling to rigid standards which were set up when this was a girl's school run by a strict Irish Catholic."

Richard L. Levenson, an attorney and member of the East Harlem Reform Democratic club, was the one person most responsible for setting off the chain of events which eventually caused the city and state to investigate the building at 311 East 100th Street in 1961.

As a volunteer political worker, he went into East 100th Street and into the house at number 311. He told the tenants that they should exercise their rights under the law. He showed them how to fill out forms and urged them to appeal to the rent commission for rent reductions because the landlord had failed to provide proper services.

Levenson's contact with the families in the house was limited to conversations about housing conditions. He says the city's program to assist East 100th Street is "practically worthless." "Neighborhood conservation," he says, "results only in the eviction of tenants. It would take a committee a year or two years to deal with one side of the street—with consistent daily attention. The city's policy is to ignore it, however, because of the relocation problem. There is no hue and cry to do something about East 100th Street, despite all the publicity."

The attorney holds that tenants and landlords are both accountable. "Landlords who own buildings in East Harlem know what they are getting into—they want to pull out as much as they can as fast as they can. I have very little sympathy for them. The tenants come from huts with dirt floors and no bathroom or toilet facilities, with chickens and pigs wandering in and out of their homes. You throw them into a highly complex urban setup and they're supposed to know how to live. They don't. They do destroy the landlord's property."

"East Harlem's biggest asset," according to William Kirk, headworker of the Union Settlement House and chairman of the East Harlem Council for Community Planning, "is the people who comprise it—and their growing ability to sustain their joint undertakings." Kirk believes the best way to reform a community is from within. "East Harlem," he says, "is a community which does not stand still."

He is skeptical about city government's role in aiding East Harlem citizens. "Though much lip service is given to the thesis that communities should participate in those vital questions that affect their well-being, no sustained equation has yet been found to carry this forward," he says.

Why has East Harlem become so run-down over the years?

"Nobody has the answer," Kirk replies. "You can't fault

the city administration in terms of intention. The city is not unmindful. It has not failed. Up to the present time, however, a formula has not been found to get the best creative mixture between the highest potentials of the community and public effort. It is as complicated as possible. You have to approach this humbly—with humility and with humor. But there are no miracles. There are a whole lot of people working and a whole lot of groups and nobody speaks for East Harlem. It's beyond any one person."

If anyone is to blame for East 100th Street, Kirk hints that the City Housing Authority, by designating the site for public housing in 1953 and then failing to erect new buildings, gave what amounted to an open invitation to property owners to let their buildings run down because they were to be condemned anyway. "Have you ever known a neighborhood that has stayed on an even keel after that type of announcement?" he asks.

Preston Wilcox, a staff member of Columbia University's School of Social Work, formerly served with Kirk as chairman of the housing committee of the East Harlem Council for Community Planning. He was also a former director of the East Harlem Project, a joint social-reform venture sponsored by two settlement houses.

"People have an attitude toward this area," he says. "They give us second-class service. They don't believe the people here have any potential or capacity. The area is a product of second-class treatment. Actually, if given the opportunity the people here will do as well as anybody. I believe the people have a right to grow and if we have any rapport with them it's because we believe in them.

"We get city services, probably more than other areas, but the results here are not as good as elsewhere. This means the community is not reflecting the city's services. What's needed are services which are not merely handed down to the people but which help them to get on their own feet."

In the housing controversy, the city makes the landlord the whipping boy for political reasons and fails too often to reach the tenants, according to Wilcox. "There is no effort to get the tenants to take on responsibility. This shows no respect for the tenants. The neighborhood is judged by outside, middle-class standards. For instance, one of the problems of neighborhood conservation is that it has failed to draw on the interest of the people whom it is supposed to be helping. With the social revolution going on now and the Negro demanding his civil rights, this is the biggest problem. To get people to change their attitude toward this area."

In 1963, the East Harlem Project issued a report[2] in which plans were announced "to continue rebuilding the shattered human fabric of that corner of Manhattan bounded by 96th Street, Fifth Avenue, the East River and Harlem River."

In view of past renewal in the East Harlem community, members of the Project said they felt that many of the area's problems came, ironically, with the replacement of tenements with public housing. "A mammoth housing program," the report stated, "designed to help this overcrowded area, provided air and plumbing but destroyed the social structure that largely held the community together. Stores disappeared, neighbors scattered, and the traditional gathering places vanished.

"With the old ties gone," the report continued, "an estimated 60,000 strangers [tenants in the public-housing projects] rattled around eleven hygienic developments— lonely, rootless, apathetic and hostile. Lacking any vitality, all decisions were left to others—even those vitally affecting their own welfare. The over-all effect spawned a breeding ground for crime, delinquency, everything that makes an unhealthy city."[3]

The group's report sought no scapegoats for the neighborhood slums. "City Hall," it stated, "does its best for East Harlem. The trouble is that city officials are often out of touch with local conditions. This sometimes leads to arbitrary, unrealistic decisions by City Hall, or (and just as dangerous) a lack of understanding and a mood of resistance by the neighborhood. There are plenty of people in East Harlem able and anxious to plan their own future—if only the city will give them a chance."[4]

The failure of the city's neighborhood conservation program was mentioned in the Project's report. It cited the example of how the city, with all good intentions, could not do much to bail East 100th Street out of the doldrums, even after an announcement in 1962 of a broad "area services" project. "The city made a sweeping announcement implying (to the neighborhood at least) that the 99th Street to 105th Street area was slated for early demolition. The area is admittedly one of the worst anywhere, but with no concrete plan offered—and no thought given to the relocation of the residents—the city's announcement only made conditions worse. Local leaders already had been working on a realistic plan of their own for the area and the East Harlem Project has taken the lead in encouraging these leaders, welding them into an even tighter organization, and getting their plan into a form that can be presented to the city as a practical alternative to the morale-shattering ukase it had recently issued."[5]

Miss Helen M. Harris, director of the United Neighborhood Houses, served as head of the Union Settlement in East

Harlem during the 1930s. There was great hope for East Harlem then, she recalls.

"We used to feel you could count on the fingers of both hands the buildings between 96th and 125th streets that were worth preserving. The rest could all come down and you would have an excellent opportunity to do the kind of community planning the community dreamed about—low, middle, and luxury housing, with parks and schools.

"During the 1930s it was quite evident that a large proportion of the old tenements were in the hands of the banks, so the East Harlem Council for Social Planning called a meeting of the banks. To our great surprise they all turned up. They were surprised, too. They became interested in the possibility of planning for East Harlem. The City Planning Commission had just been established in 1938 and East Harlem was the first area they chose to study. They made Union Settlement House their headquarters and they did a very thorough study. They recommended East Harlem for development. The banks set up a committee headed by the Bowery Savings Bank. The banks were cooperative and were making plans, but the thing that put the kibosh on these plans was the war. After Pearl Harbor nobody could build anything and the whole effort went by the boards."

In the 1930s, according to Miss Harris, "East Harlem was a multi-mess of nothing. Land was cheap. There was nothing worth saving, if not in the 30s, certainly in the 50s. No money was put into rehabilitation. The City Housing Authority was desperate for land to build low-rent housing for doubled-up families.

"So for better or for worse—East Harlem thinks it's for worse—the City Housing Authority moved in and built where it could. Then the community raised on its hind legs and said, 'Enough, enough, too much.' So the city quit, except for middle-income projects and a few schools. There still remain a lot of tenements that nobody has pulled down that people live in. Our problem in East Harlem is that we haven't been able to devise a variation from design which would cut out the vast, sterile-like project. We have no neighborhood amenities. We have lost the corner drugstore and the grocery store and some other important community landmarks. I don't know how you work this out.

"I am not one of those who believes it is better to live in broken-down slums than in new buildings. I know the new housing is better. People who live in the new low-cost housing projects are simply enchanted. It's not always as bad as enemies of public housing like to think.

"Current events have been the villain in this story rather than anybody's intended plans. When we sat on cloud nine with the Bowery Savings Bank and their committee, we were really planning and we were going to wipe out the whole lower end of East Harlem. The Housing Authority was the only one to come in, as it turned out, and they haven't found any solution to the slums that remain.

"I believe in doing things with people in a community, but I also believe there are times when the city must move in and do what the majority of city and private agencies feel has to be done. I think that if the people all got out into the middle of the street and said, 'We don't mind living in these tenements,' the city should not listen to them or go along with this. Most people don't want to move, but that's no reason for letting the city fall to pieces. I think citizen participation requires leadership and it's up to the social agencies in the community to give it. I think they're trying."

Peter D'Arpa, a retail wine merchant and a member of the East Harlem Merchants Association, has operated a store in East Harlem since 1926. He blames the decline of East 100th Street on migration.

"That section," he remembers, "used to be integrated. The majority were Italians. There were a few Jews and a few Negroes. Then, when the city put up Washington Houses [a public-housing project nearby] these people moved out. There were vacancies but they weren't filled by these type of people.

"The undesirables were moved in here. That was the beginning of the sickness of the section as a whole. It was a social phenomenon which took place. The people who came into 100th Street couldn't qualify for public housing. They had to choose between the sky and this shelter on 100th Street. All of them are good people, but when they are brought together sickness spreads and morals are corrupted. I'm not blaming the people, you understand—we, as part of New York society, are responsible. We have let them down."

I. D. Robbins, president of the City Club of New York, has been active in East Harlem and many other communities of New York. His club has long served as one of the most constructive critics of city government.

"What happened to create pockets of evil slums in East Harlem? It is dangerous to oversimplify," Robbins says, "but the city never had a total plan for East Harlem. It left behind what was really not worth saving.

"Perhaps this is one place where the bulldozer approach might not have been so bad. There is not enough public housing to take care of the people who can afford to live nowhere else. The Housing Authority, for good reasons, does not give shelter to families whose histories show an anti-social pattern.

"Such families, even though a small percentage of the

total, tend to live together in whatever places are available to them, often on the periphery of the projects to which they have been denied admission. They usually can't afford decent places and can't get leases.

"The City of New York does not enforce its housing laws. A slum is said to be caused by too many poor people living in too small a space. If they weren't poor, they'd have enough bargaining power to insist on having the space maintained. If they weren't overcrowded, the deterioration which characterizes a slum would not occur at a rapid rate. If this is true, then the most important section of the housing code is the one that deals with overcrowding. Unless the City of New York is disposed to enforce that section, we cannot protect the remainder of the community from the social troubles associated with slums.

"New York itself is changing into a low-wage, sweatshop-industry city. People who can't earn enough at their jobs to maintain high standards tend to adopt low standards. Racial and ethnic discrimination in various forms has probably played a part in the growth of East Harlem slums, too."

The Citizens' Housing and Planning Council published in 1938 a report which stated that the tenants were not co-conspirators in the crime of creating slums.[6] The city's most influential civic housing group declared: "There are many persons who still believe and state that 'people make the slums.' Generalizations of this sort are repeatedly heard at public discussions devoted to housing and social work. The very thought that families of low income who now dwell in slum buildings will occupy the nice new homes being built with public funds fills certain minds with forebodings of deepest pessimism. These individuals point out that a visit to the slum areas of almost any city furnishes evidence of carelessness, indifference and uncleanliness among families living in these areas, and that both the people and the buildings seem steeped in dilapidation and dirt.

"Upon superficial view such assertions seem convincing," the report continued, "but careful study of the subject and of the fundamentals of human behavior reveal its basic fallacy. Human habits if not nature can be changed by a little patient instruction. Normal human beings respond to the environment in which they are placed."

Roger Starr, the present executive director of this housing organization, offers this testimony in the case of the house at 311 East 100th Street:

"The blame is spread between a number of different elements. The building was no good in the first place. It was sold off and sold off down the line until it ended up in the hands of people interested only in a quick return. People who moved in were without too much pride or they wouldn't have moved in in the first place. The problem of enforcement of building codes is overwhelming. The house deteriorates as fast as it is inspected or repaired.

"There is no one guilty party," he continues. "The reason you have blocks like East 100th Street and houses like number 311 is that nobody with an interest in the property has sufficient motivation to change it."

PART THREE

THE
VERDICT

THE SILENT PARTNER

All that is necessary for the triumph of evil
is that good men do nothing.

—*Edmund Burke*

WHO TURNED the house of hope on East 100th Street into a house of horror?

The testimony of all the suspects leads to one inescapable conclusion—no one person, no one group of individuals can be blamed for the making of this slum.

The verdict is that all on trial are guilty, to a greater or lesser degree.

Above all, the government officials and the landlords are guilty because they abused the power to create and maintain this home.

Second, the tenants are guilty because they have failed to uphold the sanctity of this home.

Third, the community workers are guilty because they have failed to reach deep enough into the dark rooms of this house and bring sunlight to the people inside.

THE CASE AGAINST THE PUBLIC SERVANTS

After sixty years of trial and error, New York government officials have failed to come up with a housing program imaginative or large enough in scope to eliminate the house at 311 East 100th Street.

We are now spending $1 billion a year to build new housing in New York. Nowhere in the world are more slums being cleared. Nowhere are more homes being built. New construction has reached an all-time high.

Yet, there appears to be little hope in sight of winning the centuries-old battle against the slum. One million New Yorkers still live in squalor, And one in every four apartments in New York is officially designated as being in a "deteriorating condition."

Why is this? Why should there be more than 90,000 tenements still standing in the richest city in the world in this year of 1964? After decades of planning and building and urban renewal, why should so many Americans be housed in what are generally regarded as some of the worst slums in the world?

Part of the answer to these questions lies in a long list of broken pledges which each city administration made to the people when it came to power. In the early days, it was the promise of public housing. A great many projects were built. Today there are more than a half-million persons living in public housing in New York. Still, it has not been nearly enough.

In more recent years, it has been the failure of the much-publicized Title I housing program which, for many needy families in New York, was a great personal tragedy. Designed to clear slums and build housing for those most in need, it did neither. We have seen how it was mismanaged and corrupted by public officials and private builders seeking money and power. Only since 1960 has it been geared toward genuine middle-income housing, and even that moderate price range is out of reach for hundreds of thousands of poor families.

Furthermore, the Wagner administration's frequent call for a war on slums has, thus far, brought little dramatic change in the worst rookeries of New York. Mayor Wagner has not made a notable record in housing. He has a history of so many promises and so few achievements in the field of slum eradication that a large segment of the public was skeptical when he announced his newest "war against the slumlords" in 1964. Here is why:

In 1947, as commissioner of the Buildings Department, he publicly took responsibility for the "safety, comfort, and very lives" of New York tenants.

In 1948, as chairman of the City Planning Commission, he called for a bold program to clean up the slums.

In 1951, as borough president of Manhattan, he warned that the "City of New York is inadvertently building a new racial and economic ghetto [in East Harlem] that will last well into the twenty-first century."

In 1954, after being elected to his first term as Mayor, he appointed a committee of 100 prominent citizens and pledged a "fresh view" on housing.

In 1958, he announced he would clean up Manhattan's West Side slums.

In 1959, he said he would act on a recommendation from his Committee on Harlem Affairs that "there is no longer any excuse for delaying action" on housing conditions in Harlem.

Also in 1959, he announced that housing was the city's "number-one" problem and made public a program which, he said, had been "sweated out for months." It called for rent reductions, stiffer court fines, and more inspections.

In 1960, Wagner renewed his pledge to step up the housing program, and boasted: "We are doing more, I believe, than the rest of the country combined."

In 1961, the Mayor announced a "massive attack" on slums and a six-point program to help tenants.

In 1962, at a public hearing, he vowed to drive slumlords out of business in a new war on the real estate villains. He called for "more and tougher" weapons and promised to "press vigorously" against the tenement speculators.

Also in 1962, he predicted that New York would be a "slumless city" in fifty years.

In 1963, after a meeting with President Kennedy in Washington, Wagner declared: "I am determined that adequate means shall be developed to enable us to mount a new and ever more effective attack on slum conditions."

In June 1963, he pledged a seven-point program "to hit the slumlords where it hurts—in the pocketbook."

And early in 1964, the Mayor once again declared war on the slums and called for another "pocketbook attack on the slumlords."

Mayor Wagner's record, of course, is history. But no matter how ineffective his administration has been, it certainly cannot be shouldered with the complete responsibility for a process which started decades ago.

The demise of 311 East 100th Street started even before its plans were drawn by architects and converted into brick and mortar. Poor architectural and city planning was apparent everywhere in the late 1800s and early 1900s when most builders, unfettered by government controls, had their houses designed in conformity with the tiny lots on which they were freely allowed to build. Rapid obsolescence was implicit in the design of the new-law tenement at 311 East 100th Street. Its sixty-year life has been merely the carrying out of what was a mistake to begin with.

Even when legislative controls did come into vogue in the late 1920s and early 1930s, enforcement fell far behind most of the laws. Not only did the slums continue to exist, but they expanded and new slums were created. The city had a hand in this process, too, because of its mistaken laissez-faire policy on zoning for many decades.

Law after law was passed in the early part of this century, but not one city administration stood up to the direct cause of the mushrooming problem: the overpopulation and over-use of existing land. They passed the Tenement House Law of 1901, the Multiple Dwelling Law of 1929, newer and more stringent laws in the 1930s, 1940s, and 1950s. Yet in the 1960s New York is still pockmarked with rows and rows of tenements, back to back, block upon block. The builder built and the city government simply tried to find new ways of catching up with him. Never was the city ahead in the race to prevent blight.

So lackadaisical have been the city's planners that in the past sixty years not one administration has put down on paper a "master plan" for the City of New York. The city did not even have a planning commission as an arm of city government until 1938. Planning Commissioner William F. R. Ballard dedicated himself in 1963 to the task of drawing up a long-awaited master plan as one of the goals of his new administration. But is it not a sad commentary on municipal government in New York that such a pledge has to be made after more than half a century of building new mistakes on top of old ones? Is not the very existence of the house at 311 East 100th Street today a constant reminder of how the planners have failed, even after saturating the low-income areas of the city with low-rent public housing for three decades?

A few fervent crusaders have brought genuine hope to the slum-dwellers in the past. But now the public servants in housing spend their time improving their image with press releases and promises instead of taking vigorous action.

They point proudly to the fact that they have tamed the

dreaded bulldozer which Robert Moses and others before him used. But in doing so, they have also made a mockery of urban renewal by sidestepping the worst slums, such as number 311.

In their zeal to please the public, our housing leaders in the 1960s have permitted slum clearance to come to a virtual standstill, construction of low-income apartments to lag far behind the city's needs, large-scale rehabilitation to remain only a dream.

There is hardly enough housing going up in New York at rents which most people can afford to begin to solve the present housing shortage in two decades. There is hardly enough practical planning now under way to sustain the city for another generation.

Housing in New York continues to be erected in a pattern which perpetuates racial and economic ghettos. Officials in charge pay little more than lip service to the goal of an "open city" or an integrated city. And housing developments continue to be planned in the same bureaucratic, time-consuming way that they were in the past.

In the 1960s most of New York City's housing officials lack the one quality which is needed above all to wipe out the house at number 311 and all the others like it—political courage.

Instead of doing the job at hand, individual commissioners in New York seek power and prestige. Because they aspire for higher office, many of their decisions are political rather than in the public's interest. This practice has brought personal popularity to some of the men and women in housing, but it has also spelled trouble for the city's housing plans.

Politics has played altogether too large a role in housing

in New York. As a result, municipal government has no long-range program to house its citizens.

Two modern-day housing officials concede in their testimony that the public servants' efforts have fallen far short of the desired mark. "As long as we permit any family to live in the squalor of an East Harlem slum," said Mrs. Hortense W. Gabel, city rent administrator, "we have failed not only these people but our country and the moral standards we're so proud of boasting about." And Earl Brown, the deputy borough president of Manhattan, declared: "The city, through indifference, lack of courage and political cynicism, has failed to protect itself. . . . [It] has traditionally done the least for those who need the most and the most for those who need the least."

For the underlying reason behind the corruption of city government by special-interest groups and men seeking political power, we need not look any further back into history than Tammany Hall itself in the early part of this century. "Tammany," Riis once wrote, "has placed murderers and gamblers in high seats. That is the Tammany which you have to fight at every step when battling the slum."[1]

The tail of the Tammany tiger has been twisted many times, but never have the thieving and plundering and the influence-peddling which characterized it in the old days been completely tamed. The one-party system, with a few exceptions, has had its shortcomings in New York. Even under the best Democratic mayors, corruption has penetrated all echelons of city government.

Inspectors in the various housing agencies have come under close scrutiny from time to time; on a few occasions, grand juries have returned stinging presentments against the city Department of Buildings. But the inevitable cycle of payoffs between the public and their elected or appointed

officials continues. In the specific case of 311 East 100th
Street, there is no evidence beyond that of real estate agent
Arthur A. Abramson's testimony of payoffs. But it is a safe
conclusion that East Harlem is no different in this respect
than the rest of New York.

The shortage of inspectors has led to weak code enforcement. The shortage of apartments has led to an even weaker
housing program over the six decades. Were it not for the
lack of modern apartments in New York, 311 East 100th
Street would long ago have been relegated to the wrecker's
ball. The inordinate length of time it takes a city housing
agency to approve a site, a building plan, or a housing
development has hurt the cause of decent housing.

Of course, even the production of new housing does not
solve the slum problem, or even come close to eliminating it.
In East Harlem, for example, thousands upon thousands of
low-rent apartments have been erected all around the house
on East 100th Street. Yet, the "worst block" in the city remains. Why? Because the same city officials who claim they
are making great headway against New York's slums cannot
tear down number 311. They cannot demolish this building
because, as former City Planning Commission chairman
James Felt has testified, there is no place for the tenants to
go.

In East Harlem, under the banner of reform and urban
renewal, many thousands of poor families have been up-
rooted in the past to make way for the towering public-
housing projects. But this kind of large-scale blockbusting
approach with the bulldozer no longer is viewed as helpful
to a community which looks upon itself as "raped" by such
a process. One of the paradoxes of the rebuilding program
has been that while it replaced old slums with modern

apartments it created a new ghetto of low-income minority families.

The city was warned several times that flooding East Harlem with public-housing projects would cause the Negro and Puerto Rican groups to solidify, but the pleas of the community leaders, the planning experts on the Citizens' Housing and Planning Council, and others apparently fell on deaf ears. For this refusal to take cognizance of the community's desires, the mayors and city officials involved must be held responsible. Their sin was not so much one of commission, but one of omission.

Just as damaging to the cause of sound homes have been the rent control laws which state and city governments have levied upon the tenants of number 311, allegedly for their own protection, for the past twenty-one years. In their zeal to gain political favor, the politicians have permitted the law to oppress the owners of number 311 to a point where they claim they are unable to properly maintain or rehabilitate the building.

By keeping the rents down to a legal maximum of $30 to $40 per month (and far less with the 25 or 35 per cent rent cut because of violations), government has discouraged any of the owners of number 311 to make any substantial repairs. While it is true that there may not have been a burning desire on the part of past owners to upgrade the house in the first place, whatever interest they may have evinced was certainly stymied by rent control.

The Department of Welfare also helps perpetuate number 311 as a slum. It pays an average of $2500 per year in rents and more than $3500 annually for food, clothing, and other needs of the tenants receiving public assistance in this one tenement.

Welfare Commissioner James R. Dumpson has testified he has no alternative but to pay the rents. Otherwise, he says, the families will be evicted. But is this true? Is there no other alternative? Must the city continue to subsidize slumlords indefinitely? If this is so, it is most certainly cause to find our public servants guilty of the crime of contributing to the making of the slum.

For years, welfare officials have knowingly played into the hands of the speculators at 311 East 100th Street for what has been called humane reasons. Families needed a roof over their heads and because most rent-controlled apartments elsewhere were reserved by landlords for nonwelfare tenants, welfare officials seemed to have no choice but to place these families on relief in number 311 and tenements like it. The basic flaw in this reasoning is that it is impossible to rehabilitate either the buildings or the people in them. The worst part of the Welfare Department's annual $400 million operation is that poor families are often treated without respect or compassion by the very social workers who are supposed to help them.

The city's neighborhood conservation program also lacks trained social workers; the Health Department, which early in 1964 announced a million-dollar campaign to eliminate rats from the slums, sent only four community workers into the worst neighborhoods to enlist the support of tenants; the Department of Relocation is very short of social workers to help families adjust to new neighborhoods. In all of these programs, there is not enough emphasis on the specific needs of a specific family and too much time spent on filling out forms and gathering data.

There is a police problem, too, which often goes unmentioned in any report on the social ills of the slums. As the testimony of the cop on East 100th Street indicates, most of the people in the slums do not trust the men who are stationed in their neighborhood to protect them. In return, the police do not trust the tenants. This mutual distrust results in a maximum of illegal activity and a minimum of law enforcement. Racketeers flourish while the police have their backs turned.

As for the Board of Education, it is apparent that the majority of youngsters in the public schools are not aware of the plight of some of their own classmates. The teachers and the administrators have failed to impart to the students, particularly in the white neighborhoods, a genuine sense of social conscience. Recently, an official body of the New York City school system told public school teachers to avoid "speech patterns" that create feelings of inferiority.

Thus, a slum was not to be called a slum but "an older, more overcrowded area." Low-income or underprivileged children were to be called "children unable to secure much beyond the necessities of today's world because of the modest finances of the family." Children who live in slums and who do badly in school were to be characterized as "children with untapped potential or children with latent ability."

While the intent of such word devaluation may be well-meaning, it is just another example of a misguided attempt by the city's educators to avoid facing reality. By softening the impact of slum evils, the educators only encourage those who should care about injustice to overlook it. A slum is a slum and should be so labeled.

Another arm of government which has failed properly to do its job is the judiciary. As we have seen, reports of code-enforcement agencies which have inspected 311 East 100th Street are studded with violations. Yet when the landlords were finally brought to the bar of justice, they were not dealt with severely. Jail sentences are rare in the courts, even for the worst offenders.

Housing Court judges in New York carry a big stick, but

they have rarely used it. They have handed down many tongue-lashings, but few property owners wind up in prison. The jurists who ruled on the guilt or innocence of the land- lords of number 311 meted out light sentences. Fines in Manhattan average out to only thirty dollars.

Too often the politics of a landlord or his lawyer spells the difference between justice or the defeat of justice. Too many court decisions are influenced by political considera- tions. The fact that judges must receive the endorsement of political parties, and become a part of a political hierarchy according to the present system, puts them in a serious conflict-of-interest position even before they put on their robes.

The inevitable link between housing and politics is what makes the indictment against public officials even more damaging. "The man in the slum," Riis once said, "votes according to his light, and the boss holds the candle. But the boss is in no real sense a leader. He follows instead, always as far behind the moral sentiment of the community as he thinks is safe."[2]

If politicians were not so outwardly dedicated to the cause of good housing and the goal of a decent home for every American family, perhaps they could be forgiven for indulging in a little political sport. The periodic call to do away with the slums, however, should be far more than just a convenient political slogan.

Even if the government leaders who came to East 100th Street were sincere, even if each of them meant every word he said, it was already too late for them to win the confi- dence of the tenants of number 311. The Public Servants' past failures and broken promises have made the slum- dwellers cynical, distrustful, and uncooperative instead of hopeful and willing.

THE CASE AGAINST THE LORDS OF THE LAND

The history of the growth of the slum at 311 East 100th Street began with the growth of New York City. As the population increased and land values rose, more and more people who owned land gave in to the temptation to sell it off in parcels at high profits. The new landlords, anxious to get the most out of the land they purchased, sought ways and means of improving their land.

In the case of the old Margaret McGown Farm, this land was bought by individual owners in separate parcels. As the city-dwellers started to move to the northern part of Manhattan Island, the race to build a new community on standardized plots of earth, usually 25 by 100 feet or 40 by 100 feet (as was the case with 311 East 100th Street), was on.

This was the beginning of the boom in real estate in New York. It was also the beginning of the new-law-tenement slum as we know it today. At first it appeared to be the soundest and most reasonable investment possible. The builders of the first new-law tenements on East 100th Street undoubtedly expected they would bring an end to the old slums against which Jacob Riis had so vigorously crusaded. At the same time, many people bought new-law houses because they wanted to hand on to their children what was then considered one of the soundest investments in the country. The bankers and the mortgage brokers shared this view. They, too, lent large amounts of money for first mortgages. They were in effect the financial power which made possible the erection of what eventually were to become the slums of the 1960s. In the olden times there was no stigma attached to the ownership of a new-law tenement.

However, the building at 311 East 100th Street was sure to fail—partly because East Harlem itself never realized its full potential and partly because from its inception its owners viewed the house more as a real estate investment than a home. Within the first ten years of its life, it had ten separate owners. It became the object of speculation soon after its doors opened on April 19, 1906. Number 311, like many other new ventures in real estate in the early 1900s, was an attractive prize for a person looking for profit.

As a form of enterprise, real estate speculation thrived in the early days of the new century. Many fast-buck operators were indeed helped by a lack of city or community planning and by lack of code enforcement. The municipal government was already overburdened with the tragic aftermath of the older, disease-breeding tenements of the 1800s.

From the outset, the land on East 100th Street was exploited for the landlord's rather than the public's benefit. For centuries the courts had safeguarded the private rights of property ownership. And so many an owner held a justifiable legal position behind which he hid while shutting out his neighbor's sunshine. Profiteering and vested interests were protected by the law while the tenants suffered.

Riis warned of such landlord abuses as far back as 1902 when he wrote: "Vested rights are to be protected, but no man has a right to be protected from killing his neighbor."[3]

Many of the owners of number 311 through the past six decades have been "absentee landlords" and, as such, have contributed to the building's gradual deterioration. Many of the landlords never even visited the property themselves. They put it in the hands of agents or superintendents who proceeded to mismanage the building.

These men in turn assumed the owners' interest was purely to continue or increase the income from the building. They saw their job as merely collecting rents (and making their salaries). As a result, many of them made few if any repairs unless violations were listed against the building by municipal agencies and either they or the landlords were threatened with legal action.

They applied the age-old principle of slum ownership—give as little as possible, gain as much as possible. Much of the landlords' own testimony supports this thesis. Arthur A. Abramson, the Raynes Realty agent who operated the house at 311 East 100th Street more than forty years ago, admitted frankly: "We were in business to make money. We bought number 311 to make money. We improved it. Then we resold it. We dropped number 311 like a hot potato in 1924. We just wanted to build up the rent roll and sell it, that's all."

The late Mrs. Grace DeVinne Goldsmith, the Park Avenue real estate investor who acquired a mortgage on the building in the 1930s, "had an interest in this building, but no knowledge or control," according to her attorney, Alexander Halpern. "She did not know the property" was his testimony, indicating that absentee landlordism played a role in the management of the house during that period.

The building has changed hands many times since Mrs. Goldsmith had it. Landlords have testified they spent considerable money on its maintenance. Yet city and state agencies found it in such a bad state of repair that it was declared a danger to the health and safety of the tenants. Finally, when M. Monroe Fass and Second Equity Corporation appeared in Federal Court at bankruptcy hearings, it was established that more than a dozen other persons besides Fass had invested in his real estate corporation for the purpose of making money on their investments.

E. S. Reed's testimony provides important evidence that his fellow landlords before him had indeed milked the property. Reed echoed an age-old charge when he testified:

"The cause of the slum is race prejudice." Others before him have raised the question of racial bias as a factor in the perpetuation of poverty. As far back as 1890, Riis defined the pattern of prejudice by landlords when he wrote:

The color line must be drawn through the tenements to give the picture its proper shading. The landlord does the drawing, does it with an absence of pretense, a frankness of despotism, that is nothing if not brutal. The Czar of all the Russias is not more absolute upon his own soil than the New York landlord in his dealings with colored tenants. Where he permits them to live, they go; where he shuts the door, they stay out. By his grace they exist at all in certain localities; his ukase banishes them from others. He accepts the responsibility, when laid at his door, with unruffled complacency. It is business, he will tell you. And it is. He makes the prejudice in which he traffics pay him well, and that, as he thinks it quite superfluous to tell you, is what he is there for.[4]

Since the days of Riis, landlords have excluded Negroes from districts such as Park Avenue south of 96th Street, just below East Harlem and East 100th Street. The unwritten conspiracy of property owners has divided New York and other cities in America into golden ghettos for the rich and grimy ghettos for the poor. "If this pattern continues," warns Charles Abrams, "our house will become more divided against itself than it was 100 years ago."[5]

History also reveals that the banker, as the financial source of the building industry, is equally responsible for the continuation of number 311. Thirty years ago, as commissioner of the New York City Housing Authority, Langdon W. Post publicly blamed the banks for blight. He said they were the largest single group of owners of slum tenements in the city, having replaced the wealthy families and private entrepreneurs who had owned them at the turn of the century. For decades banks have kept the slums alive by blindly issuing mortgages without evaluating the condition of the property in terms of the damage it was doing to human lives. But the cloak of respectability has protected them from the shower of public criticism of slum ownership.

The banker has permitted real estate to get away from his control and into the hands of the speculator. He cannot be blamed for all of the vile conditions which are found inside 311 East 100th Street today, but neither can he be found innocent simply because he was not on the scene of the crime. He is certainly guilty of complicity.

The landlord, his agent or rent collector, the banker and the investors are not alone to blame for this crime. Under the terms of the Multiple Dwelling Law in New York, the term *owner* includes others who are also legally responsible. The title of *owner*, according to the law, "shall mean and include the owner or owners of the freehold of the premises, or lesser estate therein, a mortgagee or vendee in possession, assignee of rents, receiver, executor, trustee, lessee, agent, or any other person, firm or corporation, directly or indirectly in control of the dwelling."

The verdict of guilty holds for all of these people involved in the building's history. The voices of the past have clearly told us, as Riis wrote more than sixty years ago, "that murder is murder, whether it is done with an axe or with a house."[6]

THE CASE AGAINST THE PEOPLE WITHIN

Tenants alone do not make slums. But they often compound the problem. While lawmakers and civic leaders are busily occupied with other duties, the immigrant population of New York City through the generations has been left to shift for itself.

In the early days, many immigrants came from farms and were not trained for urban living. In the nineteenth century it was Europeans who crowded the shores of New York and placed their meager belongings in the first shelter they could find, usually some hovel in the Lower East Side.

These were the people first accused of making the slums in the United States. Foreign immigration was the major cause of overcrowding of tenements in those early days. The movement and pressure of the immigrant population strained the housing facilities of New York long before the turn of the century. By 1900 there was little room available for any more migrants. Yet they came from all parts of the world. They were consigned to rat-traps and dingy cold-water flats, and they became the prey of real estate speculators and moneylenders. The slum-dwellers of 1900, according to Riis, were largely illiterate, and about 95 per cent of them either immigrated from abroad themselves or were only first-generation Americans.

Though they did not conspire to make the slums, the tenants were in on the crime from the start. Here is how Riis, the foremost critic of the landlords in 1890, described the problem in his day:

The causes that operate to obstruct efforts to better the lot of the tenement population are, in our day, largely found among the tenants themselves. This is true particularly of the poorest. They are shiftless, destructive and stupid; in a word, they are what the tenements have made them. It is the dreary old truth that those who would fight for the poor must fight the poor to do it.[7]

Political romanticists prefer to view all immigrants as newcomers who drive New York forward with bursts of creativeness and imagination which enrich the city. New York, they say, derives its great strength from its diversity, from the many foreigners who have landed on its shores. Out of the slums, they point with pride, have come some of the city's and the nation's most outstanding citizens. It is always interesting to note how many men running for public office claim they were raised, educated, or had friends in the Lower East Side of Manhattan.

Happily, there is some truth to this fanciful belief. Some great men have emerged from the slums. Some have been capable of overcoming even the most sordid environment. But they are the exception—not the rule. More often, the child of the slum does not grow up unscathed by poverty and neglect. Eddie, the addict who has spent his life inside 311 East 100th Street, unfortunately is more typical of the slums than men like Alfred E. Smith. Eddie could not break away from his environment, even when he tried to leave. "It calls me back, man, it calls me back. There is no other place for me but 100th Street," were his plaintive words.

The owners of 311 East 100th Street and all slums like it know that the majority of their tenants become what the tenements make them. It is not their own fault in many instances, but people who are born in the slums and who spend their formative years following the habits and customs of the adults around them often become lazy, careless, shiftless, dirty, and ignorant. Many are completely unaware of their own rights as tenants. They lack dignity and self-respect. Most tenants of number 311 lack education and skills and are therefore unemployed. Their interests are prosaic; their intellects are undeveloped. They have freedom like anyone else in New York, but not freedom from want.

Above all, these people are poor—very poor. Their average income is $3100 per year. Some of them have become members of a group which has been called the permanently poor—second- and third-generation welfare recipients who are so psychologically scarred and frustrated by their attempts to climb over the walls of the ghetto of poverty that they have stopped trying.

As youngsters from these families grow up, some of them become the school dropouts, the juvenile delinquents, the murdering and thieving gang members, the leather-jacketed hoods who set fires, smash car windows, and brutally attack people on the street at night for no apparent reason. Others refrain from violence, but they too are part of a resentful generation which refuses help from all quarters.

Depressed by the world in which they live, angered by feelings of inadequacy and inferiority, and driven to despair by lack of money, the tenants of number 311 have often wrecked their own house; they have broken windows, torn out pipes, smashed holes in the walls and floors and ceilings of their dingy flats. They have broken boilers, thrown garbage out of windows, and excreted in the hallways. There is no doubt that they have helped make the house at 311 East 100th Street what it is in 1964.

So hostile have many of the tenants of number 311 become to outsiders, and to those of different backgrounds, that landlords and officials are frequently unable to establish any working relationship with them. Mayor Wagner characterized what has happened inside some apartments of number 311 this way in a speech in 1963 to a group of social workers:

The spirit of the jungle, rather than of civilized society, has entered into the central core of the city. Different population groups regard each other often suspiciously, sometimes even fearfully across the wasteland of noncommunication and misunderstanding of each other's problems and capacities.[8]

The Case Against the Soul-Makers

Commenting on the age-old saying that "one half of the world does not know how the other half lives," Riis observed in 1892 that when the half at the top became aware of the crowding and discomfort of the half below, the upper half began to inquire into what was the matter. "Information on the subject has been accumulating rapidly since and the whole world has had its hands full answering for its old ignorance," he said.[9]

The inquiry has been going on for six decades in the twentieth century, but little has been learned about how to cope with the damage that has been done. Social workers, clergymen, teachers, lawyers, doctors, and scores of other professional and lay persons devote themselves to the study of the man-made disease known as the slum. Society has created the settlement house and the neighborhood health clinic, the church parish and the government rehabilitation program, but all to no avail. The people in the slums, at times, seem beyond cure. Or perhaps the proper medicine for their social diseases has not yet been discovered.

The challenge Soul-Makers face is indeed more difficult than simply correcting housing violations or refurbishing the apartments in a worn-out building. The rehabilitation of such a tenement as 311 East 100th Street is difficult enough, but the renewal of the people within is sometimes impossible, at least with the present tools available to man. Once the environment of the slums has taken its toll, the road back is long and arduous for the badly damaged tenant. "The tenement," Riis once said, "is the destroyer of individuality and character everywhere."[10]

The frustration that Soul-Makers have felt in their battle with the slum at number 311 is shown in the words of the public-health nurse: "Very often," she said, "we run up against problems which are beyond ourselves." The Rev. Elmendorf turned some of the burden of guilt on his own church which, he testified, "has tended to evacuate the city [and] neglected its social mission."

Part of the failure of the Soul-Makers comes from their inability or unwillingness to penetrate deeply into the back rooms of the tenements. The tenants of number 311 testified that they had seen a few inspectors from city agencies, but none reported that a social worker or minister had been to the house. The reason for this, according to Herschell Ross, the youth worker whose intimate knowledge of the youngsters and their families on the block helped ease tensions there, was that the people on the outside had not made themselves known to those within. Ross testified: "The people in East 100th Street . . . don't know that there are services available for them."

Still another reason for the generally poor record of the private professionals striving to help the slum-dwellers is lack of compassion. This is one of the blind spots which has caused many Soul-Makers to fail. They view their work as helping people who are not only less fortunate than themselves, but less worthy.

The testimony of Preston Wilcox, a veteran East Harlem social worker, makes this point. "People have an attitude toward this area," he declared. "They give us second-class service. They don't believe the people here have any potential or capacity. The area is a product of second-class treatment. What's needed are services which are not merely handed down to the people but which help them to get on their own feet."

The Soul-Makers have tried to find out how the "other half" lives and do something about it. They should not be faulted for trying to treat a disease which is as old as man. They must be blamed, however, for permitting the disease to spread right under their noses, for sometimes working at their tasks half-heartedly or on a part-time basis, and for frequently failing to relate to those whom they are assisting.

The people in the slums cannot be "saved" in a day or a week or a year. The work to replace old values with new ones cannot be done by applying classroom theory and text-book knowledge. It must be done on an around-the-clock basis by people whose hearts and minds are deeply dedicated to such type of reform. It must be done by people who are experts in human behavior as well as theology or medicine or language. The majority of the specialists who fit into the category of Soul-Makers mean well, but few have fought the battle of the slum as it must be fought: by working with and for people rather than with social theories alone. For their failure to comprehend and properly treat all the psychological, spiritual, and physical ills of the poor, the Soul-Makers are also guilty—though not nearly as much as others on trial—for the existence of 311 East 100th Street.

These are the guilty. They have been placed on trial, called to testify, and found guilty, to a greater or lesser degree. Their interests have been different, but their paths have crossed many times and they have all shared a hand in the tragic growth of the slum at number 311.

Beyond all of these people, however, there remains another suspect who has never been brought to trial. For generations he has escaped notice; he has never been inside the house at 311 East 100th Street. He probably does not even know that East 100th Street and hundreds of thousands of streets like it in America exist.

He is unaware of the personal hardships which men,

women, and children in families like his own must endure. He believes that slums are none of his concern because he had no hand in making them and he wants no hand in clearing them. He feels he has enough to do just caring for his own family. He sees no reason why he should become involved in the lives of poor people whom he has never met. He sometimes contributes money. That is enough.

This suspect is the majority of people in New York or Chicago or Los Angeles or Dallas. He is all men who have never been plagued by poverty. He turns his back on the slum because he feels that government or real estate leaders or private community leaders or even the slum tenants themselves will solve the problem.

But no matter how he tries to forget that slums are part of the American horizon, no matter how far away he moves from the house at 311 East 100th Street, from the blighted part of his own city, he can not escape his responsibility. He also must be found guilty of creating and corrupting 311 East 100th Street.

He is the Silent Partner.

The Silent Partner believes that the poor who live in slums like number 311 do so out of their own choice. Because the tenants do not revolt or go on a rampage as a result of the conditions in which they live, they are viewed by him as contented with their surroundings. He believes that a person would not live in the slum if he had the moral fortitude to rise out of it.

He believes that if a man really wants a job or a decent home or education he can go out and get them in the United States if he only tries. It is often said that the unemployed are loafers and that people make the slums, not slums the people. Armed with these beliefs, the Silent Partner fails to see how the slum, even the one on his own block, has anything to do with him.

The slum has been with him so long he has taken it for granted. He sees no connection between poor housing, crime, and disease and inferior educational facilities and rising taxes he pays each year. He fails to establish any link between public-welfare programs skyrocketing in cost and the decline of property values dangerously close to his home.

Economically, the Silent Partner has a share in the city in which he lives and therefore he has a share in the high cost of the slums. In many cities in America, municipal governments spend as much as ten times what they get back in taxes from land and property to service slum neighborhoods. Slums are a luxury which not even the wealthiest businessmen can afford.

Beyond the financial factor there is the cost in moral terms. Every time a slum building such as 311 East 100th Street is ignored by the Silent Partner, the fiber of democracy is weakened. What is the value of boasting that the United States is great and strong if our weakest are not cared for? What is the purpose of erecting glistening glass towers with penthouses and restaurants perched among the clouds if at their feet remain the lowly tenements?

There should be no need to preach to the Silent Partner, for deep down, under the well-protected layer of indifference and self-satisfaction he knows the danger of his hands-off attitude. As Nathan Straus once said, "It is no more necessary to argue the case against the slum than to argue the case against cancer."[11]

Unfortunately, it is still necessary to argue the case, however. It is necessary to impress on the Silent Partner the appalling fact that the slum, like cancer, knows no bounds and can strike at the very heart of the safest and most secure neighborhoods in our nation.

If good housing is good politics, then "the millennium of politics," according to Riis, "when there shall be no slums to fight, will come when every citizen does his whole duty as a citizen, not before."[12]

There was great hope at the beginning of this century that New York, the youngest of the world's great cities, would emerge as the most praiseworthy. "It may be that our century will see it as the greatest of them all," Riis wrote in 1902. "The task that is set it, the problem it has to solve and which it may not shirk, is the problem of civilization, of human progress, of a people's fitness for self-government, that is on trial among us. We shall solve it by the world-old formula of human sympathy, of humane touch."[13]

LET IN THE SUN

*We shape our buildings and afterwards our
buildings shape us.*

—*Winston Churchill, 1943*

IN THIS 64TH YEAR of the twentieth century most of America's leaders are casting their eyes toward the moon in the fanciful hope that by opening another horizon to man this nation's problems on earth will somehow be eased.

With all that such a marvelous scientific feat would mean, however, I doubt seriously if landing a man or even a fleet of rocket ships on the moon would make much difference to the majority of 38 million Americans who do not even have enough money to propel themselves into a better neighborhood.

The national enthusiasm engendered by such a historic event would undoubtedly reach into every United States home. But the salutary effect would soon wear off and the families in the slums would sink back into their vacuum of poverty.

The need to give this nation's domestic problems priority over almost any other national goal was recently summarized by Senator J. William Fulbright, Arkansas Democrat and chairman of the Senate Foreign Relations Committee. Fulbright said it was strange to him that the best minds of both the Western and Communist worlds should want to land a man on the moon "where no solution to our problem awaits us."[1]

Instead, he called for solving the problems of a world which bears the intolerable burden of hunger, disease, poverty, and animosity among people. He would put more stress on the development of the human and physical resources of the United States in order to clean up the slums and raise the standards of education than he would on rocket research.

There is no doubt that America's national prestige would suffer if the Soviet Union should be the first nation to land a man on another planet. However, the question should be not whether the United States will come in first or second in this competition. It should be whether the democratic society and form of government will survive longer than the Communist form of government. This is a far more important race for America to win.

The only way this country can be first on earth, regardless of whether we are first or second in space, is to win the admiration of the rest of the nations of the world by eliminating prejudice and poverty—by wiping out our slums. In the long run, this would be an accomplishment which would dwarf anything man can achieve in outer space.

Dismal slums like 311 East 100th Street which plague the great cities of the United States must surely raise some doubt in the minds of most Americans as to whether our system of government and free enterprise is anywhere as refined and developed as it could be. Instead of looking outward for glory and prestige and power, should not the United States look inward for the solution to our national problems?

Housing was one of the major concerns of President John F. Kennedy when he took office early in 1961. It was the subject of his first major message to Congress. An important housing bill was passed during his administration. And in this election year of 1964, President Lyndon B. Johnson is pledged to carry out the Kennedy-inspired war on poverty and slums.

Critics of federal spending programs are quick to point out that housing, welfare, or health programs have failed to eliminate poverty and slums. They would slash budgets for such expenditures on the theory that the money was being wasted because this nation still has 38 million people living in substandard housing.

To this I would reply: We have not found the solution to cancer either, but do we cut back on medical research and experimentation? It is unfortunate that we are so attuned to the dramatic and the sensational in this country that we often overlook some of the more common—but just as fatal—killers.

When one hundred people die in a flaming airplane crash or ten people are killed in an automobile pile-up, the news is reported widely on the front pages of our newspapers. There is a public clamor for more laws, more protection. But when thousands of people die every year from disease and fires in the slums, little mention of it is made in the press.

The reason for such public apathy is this: We do not see the slum or the diseases it houses. We do not see a neighborhood growing sicker with the passing of each day because it happens so gradually and in so many subtle ways. The popular view about slums is that it took a long time to make them and it will take even longer to eliminate them—if we ever can.

There may be a growing awareness of the social problems in this country, but there is not yet the desire or political motivation to do something drastic about them. However, tugging at the consciences of millions of Americans is the

daily reminder in every town and city of buildings like 311
East 100th Street which tell us that our nation is in ill health.
In every city we try to hide our sickness by covering it over
with huge skyscrapers or futuristic highways or sleek modern
shopping centers. But it is still with us and, beneath our
posture of affluence and well-being, we all know it.

The story of 311 East 100th Street is an example of how
bad planning, bad housing, bad management, and bad government infect an entire community, poison the individual,
the family, the neighborhood, and corrupt the social and
civic life of a whole city.

After listening to the testimony in the trial of all those
persons involved in the creation of the slum on East 100th
Street in New York, there can be little doubt remaining that
housing must become a social responsibility in the same
sense as education and health.

Housing is not simply an economic or real estate or
architectural problem. Housing is people, human beings
whose destinies are directed and shaped by the nature of
the homes in which they are born and in which they grow.

The United States' failure to provide decent housing for
one fifth of its citizens is the weakest link in our domestic
machinery. We have met the fundamental test of providing
enough food and clothing for the masses, but we have not
met the nation's housing needs.

The past sixty years of failure in New York have been
paralleled in every major city in the nation. A staggering
social and economic debt has piled up which threatens to
overcome all of us. The late President Franklin Delano
Roosevelt warned this nation in his second inaugural in 1937
that one third of the people were still inadequately fed,
housed, and clothed. It took a world war to bring full employment and prosperity.

What will it take in the 1960s to raise one fifth of our nation out of the depths of poverty?

There must be a fundamental change in our attitude toward slums in the United States. The 1964 housing legislation in Congress did not provide nearly enough money to build decent shelter for America's 38 million slum dwellers.

Housing must be a major part of the war on poverty if we expect to attain any kind of victory. It will do little good to train, find jobs for, or educate the poor of this nation, especially the young, if they remain confined to slums.

A great upsurge of public opinion is necessary if we are once and for all to renew our cities. To implement further the national antipoverty program, the White House should call upon the Congress to approve a federally aided program of slum clearance which would tie together under a new Cabinet-rank department all the uncoordinated municipal, state, and federal antislum programs.

President Johnson's message on housing, as part of his Better Deal, should carry with it the same sense of urgency and dedication which inspired the Marshall Plan for Europe in 1947.

Former President Harry S Truman launched that epoch-making program with a historic appeal to Congress for aid to Greece and Turkey. The creation and execution of the Marshall Plan speeded the reconstruction of postwar Europe and was one of the finest examples of American democracy in action. Bipartisan cooperation between the executive and legislative branches of government, coupled with the active support of the American people, catapulted the United States into a new role. This country emerged as the leader of the Free World and has since spent more than $4 billion a year on foreign aid to the so-called underdeveloped countries.

The United States now has an opportunity to turn the

skills, resources, and immense national energy it has demonstrated abroad toward the rebuilding of our own "underdeveloped" areas.

The President's call for better housing should begin with every major city in the nation submitting to the federal housing department a report on the money and manpower required to remove its slums. From these reports, a federal housing coordinator should make a long-range estimate of the over-all cost for all the nation. Funds to carry out the program should then be appropriated by Congress over a specified period of time, let us say ten years.

The Better Deal for housing should include some of the following measures:

1. Appoint or elect in each major municipality a deputy mayor or assistant city manager for housing.

2. Create a central inspections department in each municipality and properly staff it to enforce strictly local building and health laws.

3. Review and amend all municipal, state, and federal laws applicable to urban renewal so that the federal housing coordinator can make funds and technical services available on a uniform basis. Take the profit out of slums by legislative amendments to the federal income tax laws.

4. Expand community neighborhood conservation and rehabilitation programs; require municipalities to erect housing on vacant land wherever possible, and to retain the "character" of communities undergoing renewal as much as possible.

5. Create a national social-service organization to employ the energies and talents of millions of young Americans, including those living in the slums who are capable of kindling a spirit of self-help among the slum-dwellers; undertake a work-projects program for able-bodied persons on welfare.

6. Relocate families on welfare from privately owned slums to rehabilitated municipally operated dwellings.

7. Consult with private civic groups in the formulation and carrying out of all housing plans.

8. Adopt a comprehensive and greatly expanded public-housing program which would include construction of many more units than presently planned; combining low- and middle-income families in the same projects, and providing complete community facilities such as stores, garages, schools, churches.

9. Require all private sponsors of government-supported housing to pursue actively a policy of racial integration.

10. Encourage labor and business to finance and construct housing for its own membership or employees.

It is time the United States government launched the biggest and most effective attack on slums the world has ever known. The dark shadow of the house at 311 East 100th Street has loomed over this nation for generations. We must now remove it forever and let in the sun.

APPENDIX

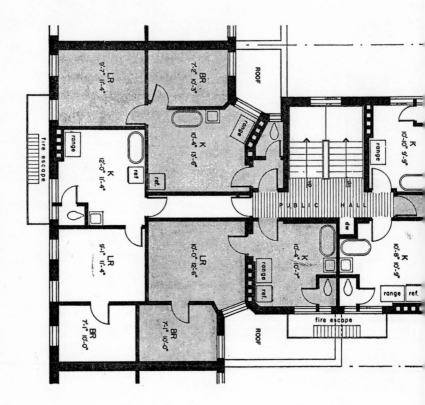

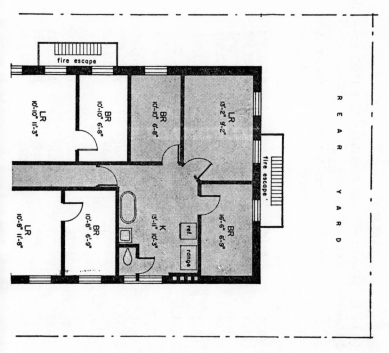

Typical Floor Plan for 311 East 100th Street

TABLE 1

Population and Housing Characteristics for the Manhattan Blocks Containing East 100th Street Between First and Second Avenues, New York City and Manhattan as of April 1, 1960

Item	Block A[1]	Block B[2]	Block A & B Combined	New York City	Manhattan
Population Characteristics					
Total Population	2632	2417	5049	7,781,984	1,698,281
White[3]	1946	1415	3361	6,640,662	1,271,822
Negro[3]	676	982	1658	1,087,931	397,101
Other races	10	20	30	53,391	29,358
Population in Households	2632	2406	5038	7,631,739	1,640,947
Population per Household[4]	3.74	3.37	3.56	2.88	2.36
Age					
0–17	1207	991	2198	2,164,527	385,711
18–64	1336	1280	2616	4,803,630	1,104,870
65 and over	89	146	235	813,827	207,700
Marital Status, Persons 14 and Over	1648	1571	3219	6,024,308	1,380,763
Single	482	428	910	1,518,721	433,660
Married	1013	933	1946	3,817,261	741,702
Separated	144	127	271	184,189	71,615

Item	Block A[1]	Block B[2]	Block A & B Combined	New York City	Manhattan
Widowed	132	166	298	576,124	156,471
Divorced	21	44	65	112,202	48,930
1.51 or More Persons per Room	149	102	251	104,470	45,766
Housing Characteristics					
Condition and Plumbing					
All housing units[5]	721	719	1440	2,758,419	727,401
Sound	396	20	416	2,330,847	536,162
With all plumbing facilities	391	20	411	2,204,892	468,323
Lacking some or all facilities	5	—	5	125,955	67,839
Deteriorating	33	542	575	343,324	150,436
With all plumbing facilities	33	530	563	277,498	110,881
Lacking some or all facilities	—	12	12	65,826	39,555
Dilapidated	292	157	449	84,248	40,803
Occupancy Status					
All occupied units	704	713	1417	2,654,817	695,772
Owner occupied units	4	12	16	578,085	26,405
Renter occupied units	700	701	1401	2,076,732	669,367

TABLE 1 (concluded)

Item	Block A[1]	Block B[2]	Block A & B Combined	New York City	Manhattan
Renter Occupied Units					
Average monthly contract rent	$35	$37	$36	$76	$85
Average number of rooms	3.5	3.5	3.5	3.5	3.2
Measure of Overcrowding					
1.51 or more persons per room	149	102	251	104,470	45,766
% of all occupied units	21.2%	14.3%	17.7%	3.9%	6.6%

SOURCE: U.S. Bureau of the Census, 1960 Census of Population and Housing, Block Statistics and Unpublished Data.

[1] Block A: Block bounded by north side of East 100th Street and south side of East 101st Street between First and Second avenues in Manhattan.

[2] Block B: Block bounded by south side of East 100th Street and north side of East 99th Street Between First and Second avenues in Manhattan.

[3] Includes Puerto Ricans.

[4] Average number of persons per occupied housing unit. Since this figure includes single person households and unrelated individuals and families living in 2 or more person households, it does not represent average family size.

[5] Housing Units: A house, an apartment, or other group of rooms, or a single room is regarded as a housing unit when it is occupied or intended for occupancy as separate living quarters; that is when the occupants do not live and eat with other persons in the structure and where there is either (1) direct access from the outside or through a common hall or (2) a kitchen or cooking equipment for the exclusive use of the occupants.

TABLE 2

311 East 100th Street
ANNUAL ESTIMATED INCOME AND EXPENSES*

RENTAL INCOME	$12,000.00
Less vacancies (7½%)	900.00
TOTAL INCOME:	$11,100.00
EXPENSES (FIXED)	
Taxes ($40,000 AV @ $4.50)	$1800.00
Water and Sewer	505.00
Insurance	
Liability	650.00
Compensation	60.00
Fire and extended coverage	175.50
Misc.	60.00
TOTAL FIXED EXPENSES:	$3250.50
EXPENSES (MAINTENANCE)	
Fuel	$3600.00
Gas and Electric	360.00
Labor and payroll taxes	1500.00
Plumbing	1400.00
Steam and boiler repairs	300.00
Painting	
Apartments	700.00
Public halls $600 (5-yr. period)	120.00
Exterior $728 (5-yr. period)	145.00
Glass	200.00
Carpentry	250.00
Ironwork	50.00
Electrical	150.00
Tile masonry	100.00
Roofing	120.00
Exterminating	100.00
Misc.	150.00
Hardware and supplies	350.00

TABLE 2 (Continued)

Accounting	150.00
Legal	400.00
Management (7½% fee)	832.50
Misc.	150.00

TOTAL MAINTENANCE EXPENSES:	$11,127.50
TOTAL EXPENSES:	$14,378.00
TOTAL INCOME:	11,100.00
ANNUAL LOSS FROM OPERATION:	$ 3,278.00

* Estimates by Howard M. Sonn, of Sonn-Saalberg Co., 4060 Broadway, New York City.

TABLE 3

311 East 100th Street
Roof to Cellar Inspection Report
List of Violations
Health Inspector Samuel Gartner
1963

Roof

    1) Filled with dog feces.
    2) Skylight glass broken.
    3) Door to roof not properly fitted.
    4) Dog feces at inside of door to roof.
    5) Peeling paint on bulkhead (hallway from top floor to roof).

Public hallway, top floor

    6) One windowpane missing.

Apt. 33 Pacheco, 2 bedrooms, 3 adults and 3 children, $18.62 per month.

Apt. 32 Matos, 3 rooms, 5 persons, $22.50 per month.

    7) Peeling paint in kitchen ceiling.
    8) Peeling paint in living-room ceiling.

Apt. 31 Walcott, 2 adults, 3 rooms, no violations, $31.89 per month.

Apt. 30 Herd, 7 in family (one on way), 3 rooms, $27.44 per month.

    9) Peeling paint in living room.

Apt. 29 Dummit, 2 in family, 4 rooms, $38.34 per month, no violations.

Apt. 28 Rios, 3 in family, $22.69 per month.

    10) Cracked wall in bathroom.
    11) Peeling paint in kitchen.
    12) Cracked wall below ceiling in living room.

TABLE 3 (Continued)

Apt. 27 Stern, 3 rooms, 4 in family, $27.16 per month.

    13) Leaky overhead bathroom tank.
    14) Leaks around window.
    15) Loose toilet bowl.

Apt. 26 Williams, 3 rooms, 4 in family, $28.15 per month.

Apt. 25 Green, 3 rooms, 8 in family, $21.93 per month.

    16) Broken window in bathroom.
    17) Loose toilet bowl.
    18) Leaks from hot water faucet in kitchen.
    19) Faulty wiring.
    20) Broken window in living room.

Apt. 24 William Reynolds, 3 rooms, $25.85 per month.

    21) Defective gas stove (overflame).
    22) Peeling paint in last room.

Apt. 23 Johnson, 4 rooms, 7 in family, $23.92 per month.

    23) Loose toilet bowl.
    24) Defective kitchen floor.

Apt. 22 Wilson, 3 rooms, $21.20 per month.

    25) Hole around riser in bathroom.
    26) Hole around riser in living-room and leaks from ceiling around riser.
    27) Broken floor near living-room riser.

Public hallway, fourth floor.

    28) Bx Cable exposed.
    29) Broken window in public hallway.

Apt. 21 José Maldonado, 4 in family, 4 rooms, $22.29 per month.

    30) Hole in floor in front of toilet bowl.
    31) Defective ceiling around water riser in bathroom.
    32) Defective plumbing fittings in bathtub.

Apt. 20 Mitchell, 3 rooms, 6 in family, $24.78 per month.

    33) Leaks from ceiling in living room.
    34) Leaks from ceiling around bedroom riser.

Apt. 19 Vacant, no access.

Apt. 18 Gutierez, 3 rooms, 1 person, $29.03 per month, no violations.

Apt. 17 Rodriguez, no access.

Apt. 16 Torres, 3 rooms, 5 in family, $21.92 per month.
  35) Leaks from faulty water lines in bathroom.
  36) Leaks from overhead toilet tank.

Apt. 15 Roman, 3 rooms, 2 in family, $26.09 per month.
  37) Leaks in bathroom.

Apt. 14 Anna Maria Vargas, 3 rooms, 2 in family, $32.19 per month.
  38) Large hole in floor around water riser in bathroom.
  39) Hole in wall at right of gas stove.
  40) Defective gas stove.

Apt. 13 Hendrix, 3 rooms, 1 person, $24.20 per month.
  41) Potbelly stove (for wood burning).
     Very poor housekeeping.

Apt. 12 Rodriguez (see Apt. 11).*

Apt. 11 Rodriguez, 11 rooms,* 10 in family, $60.27 per month, no violations.

Apt. 10 Rodriguez, Jr., 3 rooms, 2 in family, $30.30 per month.
  42) Defective kitchen plumbing.
     Very poor housekeeping.

Apt. 9 Davies, superintendent, no rent.

Apt. 8 Troche, Magdalena, 3 rooms, 7 in family, $26.07 per month (overcrowded).
  43) Hole in ceiling in kitchen cabinet.
  44) Hole in wall under kitchen sink.
  45) Leaks under kitchen sink.
  46) Cracked kitchen ceiling.
  47) Broken windowpane in kitchen.
  48) Defective ceiling in bathroom.
  49) Hole in bathroom floor. Mice excreta in evidence.

TABLE 3 (Continued)

50) Defective and broken north wall in bedroom.
51) Defective ceiling light in bedroom.

Apt. 7 Rios, 3 rooms, 6 in family (one on way), $31.00 per month (overcrowded).

Apt. 6 Rios, 3 rooms, 7 in family, $26.06 per month (overcrowded).

Apt. 5 Felix Ortez, 4 rooms, welfare case, $33.61 per month.

52) Leaks around kitchen risers.
53) Hole in wall at left of sink.

Apt. 4 Cruz, 3 in family, $36.37 per month.

54) Leaks from ceiling around riser in living room.

Public hallway, ground floor:

55) Front door glass panels missing.
56) Defective electric fixture in front hallway.
57) Garbage cans and loose garbage on floor in rear of hallway.
58) Stairway loose.

Cellar:

59) Large rathole in sewer pit near exit door (electric meter hallway).
60) Exit door not rodent proof.
61) Rathole in back of hallway (electric meter hallway).
62) Open sewer line in back of electric meter hallway (small compartment).
63) Side door of that compartment (62) not rodent proof.
64) Heavy rat infestation (fresh rat excreta).
65) Left cellar compartment at entrance to cellar filled with disused mattresses, furniture, and rubbish.
66) Rathole in ceiling around steam riser in that compartment (65).

* Two apartments combined.

TABLE 4

A Summary of the Most Important Changes Effected in New Tenement Houses by the Tenement House Act (1901)

Old-law tenement	New-law tenement
1. Dark rooms—10 out of 14.	1. All rooms light.
2. Unventilated rooms—10 out 14.	2. All rooms well ventilated.
3. Public halls dark and narrow.	3. Public halls light and ventilated.
4. 75 percent of lot occupied.	4. 70 percent of lot occupied.
5. No limit to height of buildings on narrow streets.	5. Height limited to 1½ times the width of the street.
6. Yards of interior lots 10 feet deep.	6. Yards of interior lots (6-story buildings) 13 feet deep, and 1 foot more for each additional story.
7. Yards of corner lots 5 feet.	7. Yards of corner lots 10 feet.
8. Air shafts 28 inches wide.	8. Large courts 12 feet wide.
9. Air shafts with no means of ventilation at bottom.	9. Courts with an intake or tunnel at the bottom, renewing the air constantly.
10. Air shafts in center of building 28 inches wide.	10. Inner courts in center of building 24 feet wide.
11. Windows of rooms opening within 28 inches of windows in adjoining house.	11. No windows within 6½ feet of another window, generally 12½ feet apart, often 25 feet.
12. Rooms with only 60 square feet of floor.	12. No room less than 70 square feet.
13. No requirement for size of living rooms.	13. One room of 120 square feet in each apartment.
14. Access to other rooms and water closets through bedrooms.	14. Sole access through bedrooms prohibited.

279

TABLE 4 (Continued)

Old-law tenement	New-law tenement
15. Water closets used in common by two families located in public halls.	15. Private water closet for each family entirely within its own apartment.
16. Cellar rooms permitted with ceilings only 2 feet above ground level.	16. Ceilings of cellar living rooms to be 4½ feet above ground level.
17. Cellar walls and floor not protected against dampness.	17. Cellar walls and floors to be damp proof.
18. Nonfireproof tenements 8 stories high permitted.	18. Nonfireproof tenements limited to 6 stories.
19. Fire escapes with vertical ladders permitted.	19. Substantial stairs required for fire escapes.
20. Fire escape balconies 30 inches wide permitted.	20. Balconies required to be 3 feet wide.
21. Fire escapes located in air shafts.	21. Fire escapes forbidden in shafts.
22. Iron gratings permitted in shafts without ladders or stairs.	22. Gratings forbidden, stairs required.
23. Public halls narrow.	23. No public halls less than 3 feet wide, wider with more families.
24. Stairs narrow	24. No stairs less than 3 feet wide.
25. Stairs so steep as to injure the health of women.	25. No stairs with a rise of more than 8 inches.
26. Wooden stairs and nonfireproof halls permitted in 5-story buildings.	26. Stairs and halls to be completely fireproof.
27. Public halls not shut off from nonfireproof parts of the building.	27. Public halls shut off from nonfireproof parts of the building.
28. Wooden tenement houses for 6 familes permitted outside of fire limits.	28. No wooden tenement houses to be occupied by more than 4 families.

NOTES

PART ONE: THE CRIME

CHAPTER 1

[1] This conversation is an excerpt from a tape-recorded interview made by the author with the addict in the spring of 1963.

CHAPTER 2

[1] On a city-wide basis, 44 per cent of the nonwhite housing is considered "substandard or deteriorating," while only 18 per cent of the white rental apartments fall into either of these two categories, according to the 1960 special census study, *Potential Housing Demands of Non-White Population in Selected Metropolitan Areas,* December, 1962, Office of the Administrator, Housing and Home Finance Agency, Table C.

[2] *Community Profile,* East Harlem: Area Served by Union Settlement and James Weldon Johnson Community Center, United Neighborhood Houses Pre-Teen Delinquency Prevention Project, 1962.

[3] Televised Nov. 22, 1961, and July 25, 1962.

CHAPTER 3

[1] According to police records of the 23rd Precinct.

[2] Effective July 1, 1961; City of New York, Department of Welfare, Home Economics Program.

[3] The reduction actually was only 25 per cent, ordered on July 28, 1961, by the State Rent Commission.

[4] Opinion of Judge Irwin D. Davidson, Court of General Sessions, *New York Law Journal*, June 19, 1962, p. 12.

[5] According to records of Field Surveys, Inc., 28 Cliff Street, New York City, Dec. 24, 1963.

CHAPTER 4

[1] According to *The New York Times*, April 20, 1906.

[2] Jacob A. Riis, *How the Other Half Lives* (New York: Charles Scribner's Sons, 1892), p. 282.

[3] Lawrence Veiller, *Reminiscences* (Columbia University Oral History Project, No. 5, Part I, 1949), p. 20.

[4] The tenement-house law superseded all previous laws, including the Building Code of 1899. Almost ten years after the law was passed, however, an attempt was made to draw a legal distinction between a new-law tenement and an apartment house. The Court of Appeals held in a Feb. 13, 1912, opinion that an apartment house, even though built for three families or more, was in fact something different from a tenement house, and that an apartment house was governed only by the Building Code of 1899 and therefore was outside the scope of the tenement-house law. Before too many property owners could take advantage of this ruling, however, the state legislature responded to the court's decision by amending the tenement-house law on March 5, 1912, to bring the apartment house within its coverage. Not until 1929, when the state multiple-dwelling law was passed, were all multifamily buildings commonly referred to as "apartment houses."

[5] Veiller, *op. cit.*, p. 36.

[6] Robert W. de Forest, *First Report*, Tenement House Department, City of New York (Martin B. Brown Press, 1904), Vol. I, p. 5.

[7] *Ibid.*, pp. 139–40:

[8] Edmond J. Butler, Tenement House Commissioner, "Recent Tenement Construction," *Standard Real Estate Annual* (New York, 1908), pp. 306–12.

[9] James Ford, *Slums and Housing* (Cambridge, Mass.: Harvard University Press, 1936), Vol. I, p. 205.

[10] Veiller, *op. cit.*, p. 58.

[11] John William Leonard, "History of the City of New York, 1609–1909," *Journal of Commerce and Commercial Bulletin* (New York, 1910), pp. 414–16.

[12] Edmond J. Butler, *Third Report*, Tenement House Department (New York, 1906), p. 36.

[13] Mary Louise Mark, "The Upper East Side: A Study in Living Conditions and Migration," *American Statistical Association Journal* (Boston), Vol. X (September, 1907), p. 40.

[14] *Ibid.*, p. 42.

CHAPTER 5

[1] Jacob A. Riis, *How the Other Half Lives* (New York: Charles Scribner's Sons, 1892), p. 25.

[2] E. Idell Zeisloft, ed., *The New Metropolis, 1600–1900* (New York, D. Appleton and Co., 1899), p. 635.

[3] According to memo from the Charity Organization Society to the Tenement House Commission, April 24, 1911.

[4] Emily Wayland Dinwiddie, "The Work of New York's Tenement House Department," *Charities*, Vol. XVII (1906), pp. 11–12.

[5] *Forty Years of Housing*, The Story of the Tenement House Committee of the Charity Organization Society of the City of New York (New York, 1938), p. 9.

[6] Edmond J. Butler, Tenement House Commissioner, "Recent Tenement Construction," *Standard Real Estate Annual* (New York, 1908), pp. 306–12.

[7] James Ford, *Slums and Housing* (Cambridge, Mass.: Harvard University Press, 1936), Vol. I, p. 223.

[8] *Forty Years of Housing, op. cit.*, pp. 15–16.

[9] Ford, *op. cit.*, p. 226.

[10] *Housing Betterment* (New York: National Housing Association), Vol. II, No. 1 (March, 1913), pp. 7–8.

[11] *Forty Years of Housing, op. cit.*, p. 18.

[12] From speech of Mayor John Purroy Mitchel, May 2, 1916, *Mayors' Speeches, Mitchel, 1914–1916* (Municipal Reference Library, New York), p. 29.

[13] It was sold twice in 1909, once in 1910, twice in 1911, and three times in 1913.

[14] *Housing Betterment*, Vol. V, No. 2 (May, 1916), p. 18.

[15] *Ibid.*, Vol. VI, No. 1 (January, 1917), p. 1.

[16] *Ibid.*, Vol. VIII, No. 2 (June, 1919), p. 7.

[17] *Ibid.*, Vol. VII, No. 2 (May, 1918), pp. 35–36.

[18] *Ibid.*, Vol. X, No. 4 (December, 1921), p. 372.

[19] *Forty Years of Housing, op. cit.*, p. 22.

[20] Paul Blanshard and Norman Thomas, *What's the Matter with New York?* (New York: Macmillan, 1932), p. 250.

[21] *Ibid.*, pp. 255–257.

[22] William F. Deegan, *Tenth Report*, Tenement House Department, City of New York (Report for the Years 1918–1929), p. 12.

[23] *Housing News*, Citizens' Housing Council, New York (May–June 1945), p. 3.

[24] From an address to members of the New York Board of Trade.

[25] The block was in an official health area which included 18,314 persons, of whom 15,500 were Italian, 250 German, 250 Irish, 250 Jewish, and 167 Negro, according to the U.S. Census of 1930. For all of East Harlem, the population of 170,000 persons included 29,500 Negro, 28,000 Jewish, 19,000 Irish, 11,000 German, 4000 Slavic, 5000 British, 4000 Scandinavian, and 1500 Greek.

[26] From an interview with Mrs. Stern by the author in the spring of 1963.

[27] From Social Base Map, Local Neighborhoods (New York University, Department of Sociology, prepared under direction of Frederic M. Thrasher, 1932).

[28] *A Decade of District Health Center Pioneering*, A Report of Ten Years' Work of the East Harlem Health Center and the New York Chapter of the American Red Cross, prepared under the direction of Kenneth D. Widdemer, executive officer (New York, 1932), p. 17.

[29] *Ibid.*, p. 18.

[30] *The New York Times* (Dec. 30, 1933), 15:6.

[31] *Ibid.* (March 4, 1934), 1:4.

[32] *Ibid.* (March 17, 1934), 1:2.

[33] *Ibid.* (April 9, 1934), 1:6.

[34] *Ibid.*

[35] *Ibid.*

[36] From an interview with Mr. Prince by the author in the winter of 1963.

[37] *Harlem 1934: A Study of Real Property and Negro Population*, Real Property Inventory of New York and Land Utilization Committee, New York Building Congress, for New York City Housing Authority, 1934, pp. 5–7.

[38] Morris L. Ernst, *Preliminary Report*, The Mayor's Commission on Conditions in Harlem (New York, April 8, 1935), pp. 2–3.

[39] *The New York Times* (April 22, 1935), 1:6.

[40] From a transcript of a radio talk by Langdon W. Post, station

WNYC, June 11, 1935, contained in press release by New York City Housing Authority, p. 3.

[41] *Ibid.*, pp. 5–6.

[42] From an interview with Mr. Prince by the author in the winter of 1963.

[43] Langdon W. Post, *Sixteenth and Final Report*, Tenement House Department (New York: Burland Printing Co., 1937), pp. 17–18.

[44] Mayor's Committee on City Planning, *Report on Project No. 165–97–6037*, East Harlem Community Study, conducted under the auspices of the Works Progress Administration (New York, 1937), pp. 12, 19.

[45] Howard H. Spellman, *Report to Housing Committee of the New York City Council* (New York: The Court Press, Inc., 1938), p. 2.

[46] *Housing the Metropolis*, Report of the Citizens' Housing and Planning Council (New York, June 1938), p. 1.

[47] *Harlem Housing*, Report of the Citizens' Housing and Planning Council (New York, August 1939), p. 1.

[48] *Ibid.*

[49] *Citizens' Housing and Planning Council News* (New York, March 1940), p. 1.

[50] *Association News Bulletin* (Savings Bank Assn., State of New York, Feb. 9, 1940), pp. 1, 2.

[51] *Citizens' Housing and Planning Council News* (February 23, 1940), p. 1.

[52] *Citizens' Housing and Planning Council News* (November, 1944), p. 4.

[53] The Manhattan Development Committee, *A Realistic Approach to Private Investment in Urban Redevelopment Applied to East Harlem as a Blighted Area* (New York: *The Architectural Forum*, 1945), Ch. 1, p. 5.

[54] Robert Moses, "Slums and City Planning," *Atlantic Monthly* (Jan., 1945), p. 66.

[55] *Ibid.*, p. 67.

[56] *The New York Times*, May 18, 1946, p. 21.

[57] Robert F. Wagner, "We Are Responsible for Eight Million Lives," comments as Commissioner of Department of Housing and Buildings, *Rockaway (N.Y.) Review* (June, 1947), pp. 29–30.

[58] Robert F. Wagner, (as chairman of the City Planning Commission), *Report on Housing Conditions in New York City* (to Mayor William O'Dwyer), 1948, p. 21.

[59] Edwin Friedman, *East Harlem Community Study: 1940–1950*, (January 15, 1953), p. 94.

[60] *Citizens' Housing and Planning Council News*, New York (July, 1950), p. 1.

[61] *Ibid.*, p. 4.

[62] *The New York Times* (October 1, 1950), Section 8, p. R7:4.

[63] From an interview with Mr. Sulzberger by the author in the winter of 1963.

[64] Robert F. Wagner, in a statement issued on October 18, 1951, as borough president of Manhattan, at meeting of Citizens' Housing and Planning Council, p. 5.

[65] *Ibid.*, p. 6.

[66] *Ibid.*, p. 5.

[67] *Ibid.*, p. 4.

[68] Letter from Ira S. Robbins, executive vice-president of the Citizens' Housing and Planning Council, to Mayor Vincent R. Impellitteri, November 15, 1951.

[69] Letter from Mayor Vincent R. Impellitteri to Ira S. Robbins, executive vice-president, Citizens' Housing and Planning Council, January 22, 1952.

[70] Under the city's 1938 charter, the City Planning Commission was directed to prepare master plans embracing every type of municipal improvement.

[71] *New York World-Telegram and Sun* (January 26, 1954), p. 1.

[72] *A Housing Program for New York City*, Report by the City Club of New York (March, 1954), p. 10.

[73] Mayor Robert F. Wagner, *Workable Program*, An Official Plan for Dealing with Slums and Blight for the City of New York (New York: Charles Francis Press, March 13, 1955), p. 2.

[74] *New York City's Slum Clearance Committee: A Critical Study*, City-wide Council for Better Housing (New York, October 31, 1957), p. 1.

[75] Mayor Wagner made this comment to the author in his office following a meeting between the Mayor and the Rev. James A. Gusweller, a crusading Episcopal priest from Manhattan's West Side, on December 15, 1958.

[76] Charles Abrams, "U.S. Housing, A New Program" (pamphlet) (New York: The Tamiment Institute, 1958), p. 17.

[77] From a statement by Gov. Rockefeller on April 8, 1959.

[78] From an interview with Mr. Panuch by the author on September 10, 1959.

[79] Named after State Sen. MacNeil Mitchell (R., Man.) and State Assemblyman Alfred A. Lama (D., Bklyn.), who co-sponsored the 1955 law which gave the city authority to use the power of condemnation, to give tax concessions, and to make low-interest loans to private builders of middle-income housing.

[80] *Report of Mayor's Committee on Harlem Affairs*, New York, Dec. 11, 1959, p. 4.

[81] From Mayor Robert F. Wagner's speech on WRCA–TV (Dec. 27, 1959), p. 1.

[82] J. Anthony Panuch, *Building a Better New York*, Final Report to Mayor Robert F. Wagner (March 1, 1960), p. 17.

[83] *Ibid.*, pp. 35–36.

[84] *Ibid.*, pp. 38–39.

[85] From a statement by Mayor Robert F. Wagner on December 3, 1960, at rededication of First Houses, New York.

[86] John V. Lindsay, "Our City's Need: Middle Income Housing," *Congressional Record* (February 2, 1961), p. 1685.

[87] "Memo to the Members of the Legislature" from Mayor Robert F. Wagner, March 23, 1961, which included copy of letter from Leona Baumgartner, M.D., Commissioner of Health and Peter J. Reidy, Commissioner of Buildings, dated March 22, 1961.

[88] In a letter from Mr. Lindsay to the House Subcommittee on Housing, made public July 31, 1961.

[89] Statement by Mr. Fino, released in Washington August 18, 1961, p. 1.

[90] Statement by Mayor Robert F. Wagner, released by Citizens for Wagner, Beame and Screvane, August 29, 1961.

[91] From "The New Action Program for Better New York Housing," A Statement by Mayor Robert F. Wagner (August 29, 1961), p. 1.

[92] From a speech prepared for delivery by Mayor Robert F. Wagner during the first week in September 1961.

[93] Statement by Mayor Robert F. Wagner, released by Citizens for Wagner, Beame and Screvane (October 27, 1961), p. 2.

[94] *The New York Times* (October 10, 1961), 29:3.

[95] Statement by Mayor Robert F. Wagner at "victory dinner," Citizens for Wagner, Beame and Screvane, Waldorf Astoria Hotel (January 29, 1962), pp. 1–4.

[96] From an interview with Mr. Felt by the author on June 21, 1962.

[97] From an interview with Mayor Wagner by Norton Mockridge, city editor; Robert H. Prall, assistant city editor; and Walter Mac-

Donald, Albany correspondent, *New York World-Telegram and Sun*, August 22, 1962.

[98] *East Harlem, Planning Area No. 308*, City Planning Commission, Department of City Planning, Community Renewal Program, Raymond and May Associates, Report by Dorothy Senerchia (Sept. 4, 1962), p. 47.

[99] John V. Lindsay, "The Housing Crisis in New York City," *Congressional Record* (October 3, 1962), pp. 21939–21941.

[100] Robert F. Wagner, *The New York Times Magazine* (October 7, 1962), pp. 47–48.

[101] Letter from Harold Birns, Commissioner of Buildings, to William F. Shea, Director of the Budget, New York (December 19, 1962), pp. 1–2.

[102] Statement by Mayor Robert F. Wagner, New York (January 18, 1963), p. 3.

[103] Speech by James W. Gaynor, New York State Commissioner of Housing and Community Renewal, Fourth Annual Luncheon of Citizens' Housing and Planning Council, New York (May 14, 1963), p. 6.

[104] Statement by Mayor Robert F. Wagner, New York (June 7, 1963), p. 1.

[105] Speech by Milton Mollen, chairman of the New York City Housing and Redevelopment Board, at the regional meeting of the New York State Welfare Conference, New York (September 23, 1963), p. 3.

[106] From an interview with Mr. Ballard by the author and other newsmen over WABC-TV's *Page One* show, November 10, 1963.

[107] Robert F. Wagner, *Testimony on Proposed Housing Legislation* (Housing and Community Development Act of 1964) before the Committee on Banking and Currency, Washington, D.C. (Feb. 20, 1964), pp. 2–4.

[108] Statement by the Rev. Norman Eddy, of the East Harlem Protestant Parish, who led the march sponsored by the Metro North Citizens' Committee, according to *The New York Times*, April 26, 1964, 53:1–2.

[109] Speech by William F. R. Ballard, chairman, New York City Planning Commission, at the Community Service Society meeting, New York, May 19, 1964, p. 10.

[110] From a column by Whitney M. Young, Jr., executive director, National Urban League, in *The N.Y. Amsterdam News*, May 16, 1964, 10:7–8.

PART TWO: THE SUSPECTS

CHAPTER 6

[1] According to records of conveyances and mortgages in the Hall of Records, New York City.

[2] Bankruptcy petition No. 62B–243, filed in United States Court for the Southern District of New York, Foley Square, N.Y.

CHAPTER 7

[1] Rents remain fixed in rent-controlled apartments until a tenant moves out. The landlord is then entitled to a 15 per cent increase in the vacated apartment, according to the city rent laws.

CHAPTER 8

[1] The author accompanied Inspector Gartner on his tour of the building on March 16, 1963.

[2] Robert Moses, "Slums and City Planning," *Atlantic Monthly* (January, 1945), p. 63.

[3] *Ibid.*, pp. 63–64.

[4] *The New York Times* (October 10, 1961), 29:3.

[5] Mayor Robert F. Wagner, in a report to the people delivered on WCBS-TV, February 21, 1962, p. 3.

[6] Statement by Mayor Robert F. Wagner, December 8, 1961, p. 2.

[7] *The New York Times* (December 28, 1959), 29:4–7.

[8] Statement by Attorney General Louis J. Lefkowitz prepared for delivery at a meeting of Baptist ministers in Harlem, October 23, 1961, p. 2.

[9] From an interview with Governor Rockefeller by the author over Radio Station WMCA, New York, March 25, 1963.

[10] In a letter to the author from Governor Mark O. Hatfield dated February 25, 1963.

[11] From a statement by Dr. Weaver in a letter to the author on March 18, 1963.

[12] Attorney General Kennedy visited East 100th Street in March, 1961. His remarks were made in an interview with the author on August 6, 1963.

CHAPTER 9

[1] Testimony by the Rev. Norman Eddy at a hearing before the subcommittee to investigate juvenile delinquency of the Committee on the Judiciary of the United States Senate, 87th Congress, Second

Session; in New York City, September 20, 1962; from pamphlet "Juvenile Delinquency" (Washington, D.C.: U.S. Government Printing Office, 1963), pp. 3150–51.

² Report of *The East Harlem Project in 1963* (East Harlem Project, 1963), p. 1.

³ *Ibid.*, p. 1.

⁴ *Ibid.*, p. 12.

⁵ *Ibid.*, p. 13.

⁶ Report and recommendations of the Committee on Housing Management (Abraham Goldfeld, chairman), Citizens' Housing and Planning Council, New York, June, 1938, p. 1.

PART THREE: THE VERDICT

CHAPTER 10

¹ Jacob A. Riis, *The Battle with the Slum* (New York: Macmillan, 1902), p. 65.

² *Ibid.*, p. 427.

³ *Ibid.*, p. 51.

⁴ Jacob A. Riis, *How the Other Half Lives* (New York: Charles Scribner's Sons, 1892), p. 148.

⁵ Charles Abrams, from speech entitled "Planning for Racial Equality," delivered before 46th annual conference of the American Institute of Planners, Milwaukee, October 30, 1963, p. 6.

⁶ Jacob A. Riis, *The Peril and the Preservation of the Home* (Philadelphia: George W. Jacobs & Co., 1903), pp. 141–42.

⁷ Riis, *How the Other Half Lives*, p. 273.

⁸ Robert F. Wagner, remarks at annual meeting of Federation of Protestant Welfare Agencies, New York, Feb. 26, 1963, p. 5.

⁹ Riis, *How the Other Half Lives*, p. 1.

¹⁰ *Ibid.*, p. 246.

¹¹ Nathan Straus, *Two Thirds of a Nation* (New York: Alfred A. Knopf, 1952), p. 10.

¹² Riis, *The Battle with the Slum*, p. 414.

¹³ *Ibid.*, p. 438.

CHAPTER 11

¹ From a speech by Senator J. William Fulbright at a banquet session of the American Council for Judaism, New York, May 9, 1963.

INDEX

ABOUT THE AUTHOR

Born in 1929, Woody Klein was graduated from Dartmouth College in 1951, with honors in his major, sociology. The following year he received an M.S. from the Graduate School of Journalism at Columbia University. After serving in the Army during the Korean War, Mr. Klein worked in Washington as a reporter for the *Washington Post and Times-Herald*. In 1956 he joined the reporting staff of the *New York World-Telegram and Sun*, where he now specializes in housing, civil rights, politics, and social welfare.

During the summer of 1959, Mr. Klein was assigned to live in New York's slums as an undercover reporter. The series of articles he wrote, entitled "I Lived in a Slum," won him a Page One Award for feature writing in 1960 from the Newspaper Guild of New York. He was also the recipient of the Sigma Delta Chi professional journalistic society award in 1960 for outstanding journalistic achievement in the New York metropolitan area, the Newspaper Reporters Association award in 1961 for a series on Puerto Rican migration to New York, and a 1962 Alumni Award from Columbia University for distinguished service to journalism.

Mr. Klein has been an instructor and lecturer in journalism at New York University. He is a housing consultant to radio and television stations and frequently serves as moderator and guest reporter on programs about housing and municipal affairs. A native New Yorker, he lives with his wife, Audrey, and his daughter, Wendy, in Manhattan.